Binary Analysis Research Workshop 2021 (BAR 2021)

Online
21 February 2021

ISBN: 978-1-7138-3762-6

Printed from e-media with permission by:

Curran Associates, Inc.
57 Morehouse Lane
Red Hook, NY 12571

Some format issues inherent in the e-media version may also appear in this print version.

The Internet Society
11710 Plaza America Drive, Suite 400
Reston, VA 20190
U.S.A.

Phone: (703) 439-2120
Fax: (703) 326-9881

www.internetsociety.org

Additional copies of this publication are available from:

Curran Associates, Inc.
57 Morehouse Lane
Red Hook, NY 12571 USA
Phone: 845-758-0400
Fax: 845-758-2633
Email: curran@proceedings.com
Web: www.proceedings.com

Table of Contents

Organizing Committee

Binary Analysis

1 SN4KE: Practical Mutation Testing at Binary Level
Mohsen Ahmadi, Pantea Kiaei, Navid Emamdoost

10 Short Paper: Declarative Demand-Driven Reverse Engineering
Yihao Sun, Jeffrey Ching, Kristopher Micinski

17 PyPANDA: Taming the PANDAmonium of Whole System Dynamic Analysis
Luke Craig, Andrew Fasano, Tiemoko Ballo, Tim Leek, Brendan Dolan-Gavitt, William Robertson

31 Effects of Precise and Imprecise Value-Set Analysis (VSA) Information on Manual Code Analysis
Laura Matzen, Michelle A Leger, Geoffrey Reedy

Binary Fuzzing

43 JMPscare: Introspection for Binary-Only Fuzzing
Dominik Maier, Lukas Seidel

51 icLibFuzzer: Isolated-context libFuzzer for Improving Fuzzer Comparability
Yu-Chuan Liang, Hsu-Chun Hsiao

Embedded Systems

62 Is Your Firmware Real or Re-Hosted? A case study in re-hosting VxWorks control system firmware
Abraham A. Clements, Logan Carpenter, William A. Moeglein, Christopher Wright

74 Dinosaur Resurrection: PowerPC Binary Patching for Base Station Analysis
Uwe Müller, Eicke Hauck, Timm Welz, Jiska Classen, Matthias Hollick

85 Polypyus – The Firmware Historian
Jan Friebertshäuser, Florian Kosterhon, Jiska Classen, Matthias Hollick

Proceedings

BAR 2021

Workshop on Binary Analysis Research

February 21, 2021
Virtual

Published by the

Internet Society

Internet Society
11710 Plaza America Drive
Suite 400
Reston, VA 20190

Address your correspondence to: NDSS Program Manager, Internet Society, 11710 Plaza America Drive, Suite 400, Reston, VA 20190 USA, tel. +1 703 439 2120, fax +1 703 326 9881, ndss@elists.isoc.org.

The papers included here comprise the proceedings of the meeting mentioned on the cover and title page. They reflect the authors' opinions and, in the interest of timely dissemination, are published as presented and without change. Their inclusion in this publication does not necessarily constitute endorsement by the editors or the Internet Society.

Internet Society
11710 Plaza America Drive
Suite 400
Reston, VA 20190
tel +1 703.439.2120
fax +1 703.326.9881
http://www.internetsociety.org

Organizing Committee

Program Chair

Brendan Dolan-Gavitt, *New York University*

Program Committee

Yan Shoshitaishvili, *Arizona State University*
Xinyu Xing, *Penn State University*
Andrea Lanzi, *University of Milan*
Lorenzo Cavallaro, *King's College London*
Sophia d'Antoine, *Margin Research*
Tim Bryant, *Vector 35*
Taegyu Kim, *Purdue University*
Sébastien Bardin, *CEA LIST*
Zhiqiang Lin, *Ohio State University*
Antonio Bianchi, *Purdue University*
Maverick Woo, *Carnegie Mellon University*
Daniele Cono D'Elia, *Sapienza University of Rome*
Sarah Zennou, *Airbus*
Konrad Rieck, *TU Braunschweig*
Ruoyu "Fish" Wang, *Arizona State University*
Edward J. Schwartz, *Carnegie Mellon University*
Martina Lindorfer, *TU Wien*
Mariano Graziano, *Cisco Talos*
Christophe Hauser, *Information Sciences institute, University of Southern California*
Juan Caballero, *IMDEA Software Institute*
Aurélien Francillon, *EURECOM*
Grant Hernandez, *Qualcomm*
Alexei Bulazel, *Independent Security Researcher*

SN4KE: Practical Mutation Testing at Binary Level

Mohsen Ahmadi
Arizona State University
pwnslinger@asu.edu

Pantea Kiaei
Worcester Polytechnic Institute
pkiaei@wpi.edu

Navid Emamdoost
University of Minnesota
navid@cs.umn.edu

Abstract—**Mutation analysis is an effective technique to evaluate a test suite adequacy in terms of revealing unforeseen bugs in software. Traditional source- or IR-level mutation analysis is not applicable to the software only available in binary format. This paper proposes a practical binary mutation analysis via binary rewriting, along with a rich set of mutation operators to represent more realistic bugs. We implemented our approach using two state-of-the-art binary rewriting tools and evaluated its effectiveness and scalability by applying them to SPEC CPU benchmarks. Our analysis revealed that the richer mutation operators contribute to generating more diverse mutants, which, compared to previous works leads to a higher mutation score for the test harness. We also conclude that the reassembleable disassembly rewriting yields better scalability in comparison to lifting to an intermediate representation and performing a full translation.**

I. INTRODUCTION

In many contexts software is accompanied with test suites when delivered to the customer. In such cases, the test suite is the primary and mostly the only leverage to assure correctness of the software. This demonstrates the importance of test suite adequacy. Evaluating such adequacy requires a separate analysis which is known as mutation analysis. Such analysis generates *mutants* of the original program via making small changes either at source or IR level. Such mutants then are ran through the test suite. If the test suite successfully differentiates a mutant from the original program based on its observed output, it is said that it has *killed* that mutant. The ratio of killed mutants to all tried mutants is called *mutation score* which is the metric to describe the adequacy of the test suite.

In order to create mutants, many researches proposed various mutation operators which are the rules for changing statements or instructions in the original program to get a new mutant. A good mutation operator is representative of a real world bug that may be introduced as a result of errors either in development or the building process. For example, consider a bug-fixing patch which is accompanied with a test. A mutation operator to evaluate the test's adequacy would be undoing the effect of the patch, e.g if the patch introduces a bounds check, the mutation operator causes skipping the check.

In many scenarios the program source code is not available like in proprietary software or shared libraries. In these cases the mutation tool should still be able to generate mutants from the original binary. Binary level mutation has been explored previously [16], [4]. The major challenge on binary mutation tools is practical and scalable binary rewriting which in turn imposes limitation on the binary mutation operators. In order to generate mutants from the original binary, the mutation tool needs to restore a higher level code representation like assembly and then apply the mutation operator which may change the instructions address layout. Binary rewriting has found many applications in program analysis, security and etc. Mutation analysis is another application of binary rewriting which requires generation working mutants by making changes at instruction level.

Binary rewriting techniques have been extensively incorporated in security enforcement tools like [25], [37], [38], [15] where the instructions are aligned, inserted or replaced to enforce measurements like control flow integrity or fault isolation and etc. In recent years reliable binary rewriting techniques (like Ddisasm [17] or Ramblr [33]) have been proposed which expand the domain of such measurements applications to the programs available only in binary format. Previously researchers have demonstrated the applicability of reassembleable disassembly for binary mutation [16]. They used Uroboros [34] and were able to mutate binaries from SPEC CPU. Limitations imposed by Uroboros obstructs the practicality of such application, more specifically authors reported fragility of the tool in a way that it worked for specific compilation options. Their implemented mutation operators are limited to only conditional jump and move instructions.

In this paper, we revisit the notion of binary mutation in light of recent advancements in binary rewriting to implement a practical binary mutation tool that can support real-world binaries. Additionally, we employ a richer set of mutation operators that span over conditional, logical, and arithmetic instructions in order to have a more rigorous evaluation of the test harness. Our binary mutation tool named SN4KE is accessible at https://github.com/pwnslinger/sn4ke/.

The rest of the paper is as follows: in section II we discuss the related work on the subject of binary mutation analysis of tests. section III presents our approach and design of SN4KE, specifically the set of mutation operators and the binary rewriting engine. section IV describes our evaluation of SN4KE on SPEC CPU benchmarks and the comparison of performance of the two binary rewriting tools we used. section V discusses some of interesting challenges we had in adapting rev.ng for our purpose. Finally, section VII concludes the paper.

Workshop on Binary Analysis Research (BAR) 2021
21 February 2021, Virtual

https://dx.doi.org/10.14722/bar.2021.23017
www.ndss-symposium.org

TABLE I: Mutation Operator Classes

<table>
<tr><th>Mutation Class</th><th>Description</th></tr>
<tr><td>Arithmetic</td><td>Replace arithmetic assignment operators from the set of {+=, -+, *=, /=}
Replace with an operator from the set of {+, -, *, /, %}</td></tr>
<tr><td>Logical</td><td>Substitute with another bit-wise logical operator from {^, |, &}
replace with a logical assignment from {^=, |=, &=}
Substitute the connector with another logical operator from {&&, ||}</td></tr>
<tr><td>Conditional</td><td>Substitute any conditional jump with an unconditional branch to force taking the branch
taking the fall-through (instruction following the branch) edge of branch by NOPing the condition</td></tr>
<tr><td>Constants</td><td>Replace any immediate value c with one another constant from set {-1, 0, 1, -c, c+1, c-1}</td></tr>
<tr><td>Skip</td><td>Replace instructions from set Arithmetic, Logical, and Conditional with a NOP operator to skip the execution of that operator</td></tr>
</table>

II. Related Work

Generating variants of a program has been employed in the context of security: fuzzing tools like T-Fuzz [28] negate the conditions to pass the blocking conditions and explore new paths; additionally, tools like EvilCoder [29] LAVA [14] insert exploitable bugs in the program to provide testing corpus for vulnerability detection tools. In a broader context, mutation analysis tends to generate variations of the software and use it as a data set to evaluate the adequacy of tests to catch such variants. Authors in [16] employed Uroboros [34], a reassembleable disassembly binary rewriting tool to recover the assembly representation of a binary and apply the mutation at the assembly level. They applied a limited set of mutation operators mainly focusing on flag-use instructions and used the generated mutants to evaluate the adequacy of tests for SPEC CPU benchmarks. Their findings demonstrates that the tests designed for performance benchmarking catch fewer mutants compared to tests designed for code coverage.

As we are focused on mutation analysis at binary level, therefore we describe works related to mutation analysis and binary rewriting in the following subsections.

A. Mutation Analysis

Since its introduction [8], [10], mutation testing has been studied extensively. Numerous mutation tools have also been proposed for different programming languages like C [20], Java [24], C# [12], Fortran [36], SQL [31]. Mutation on intermediate representation (IR) has been studied as well [11]. In [19] authors compared source-level and IR-level mutation testing and observed closely correlated mutation scores.

Mutation testing relies on two fundamental hypotheses: Competent Programmer Hypothesis [1], and Coupling Effect hypothesis [26]. The former hypothesis states that the programmer tends to develop the program with minimal faults and close to the correct. Therefore, a mutation analysis with simple mutation operators still can simulate actual faults that are introduced by programmer. The latter hypothesis states that complex program faults can be de-coupled into simpler ones. Therefore a test that catches simple faults can catch a high percentage of complex ones, where complex faults are associated to making more than one change into the original program. The mutation operators that we used in this paper are based on the ones in [18] which target four main categories: conditional instructions, logical instruction, arithmetic instructions, and constant values. We explain these mutation operators in more details in subsection III-A.

Offutt et al [27] formulated the conditions that a test suite can kill a mutant. First of all, the mutated instruction should be *reachable* by at least one test input in the test suite. Second, the reached mutated instruction should enter the execution to an incorrect state. Third, the incorrect state should propagate and reach the program output.

Depending on the mutation operators and level of mutation application, the number of generated mutants varies. Hariri et al [19] reported that source-level mutation produced fewer mutants compared to IR-level mutation. Our experience is in alignment with this finding where binary level mutation may create numerous mutants. Not all the generated mutants have same quality in evaluating test adequacy. In this paper we filter out the *trivial* mutants which are the ones that fail to execute on any input data. Such mutants has no contribution in evaluating the effectiveness of the test suite.

B. Binary Rewriting

In this section, we will go through the publicly available binary rewriting solutions and compare their approach with regard to structural recovery, data type extraction, and limitations on supported architectures. Binary rewriting is the process of modifying a compiled program in such a way that it remains executable and functional without accessing the source-code. Binary Mutation is the process of purposefully introducing faults into a program without having the source-code. While in the definition of that there is not any criteria on soundness of the resulting binary, for the purpose of test suite evaluation we require the injected fault passes some trivial tests.

There are two methods of modifying the binary, one statically and the other over the span of a program execution which is called dynamic. In static approach, we keep a copy of modifications on a separate file on disk. However, dynamic rewriting which is denoted as instrumentation applies the modifications at the runtime.

Dynamic rewriters like PIN [23] and DynamoRio [6] apply instrumentation at defined locations in memory. Compared to static rewriter, at runtime there is only one code block to translate and deal with. However, depending on the implementation, frequent control flow changes or context switches between rewriter built-in virtual machine (VM) and operating system adds up overhead. Another kind of dynamic rewriting

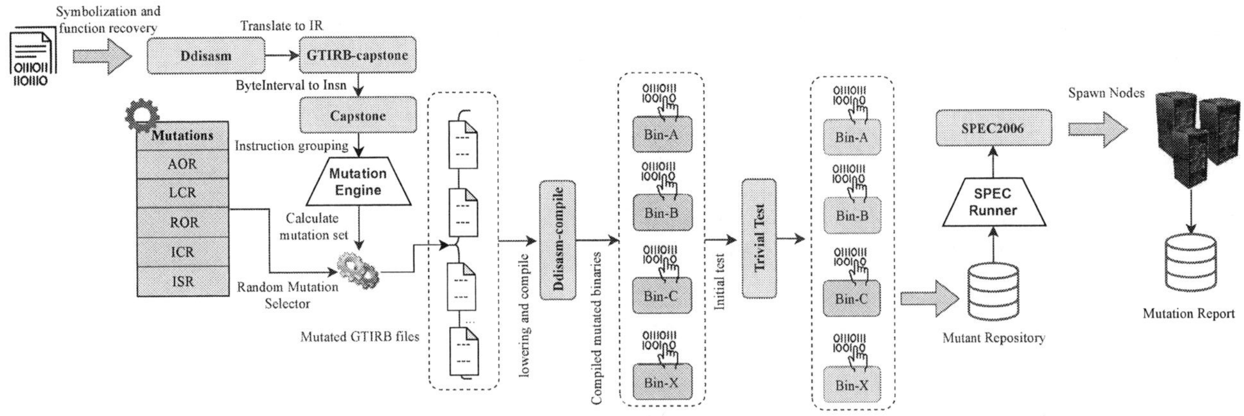

Fig. 1: Workflow of SN4KE: First, we pass the binary under test to Ddisasm for reconstructing the relocation table by identifying the instruction boundaries using backward and forward traversal techniques described in their paper [8]. As a result, we can retrieve the lifted binary in GTIRB representation which contains symbolized addresses for references and variables. Gtrib-capstone is the built-in rewriter, and we modified the code to fix some bugs related to shifting the symbolic expression of blocks following the insertion point. Gtirb represents binary as a module contains sections, and each section is a byte-interval. Blocks point to ranges into the byte interval to represent their bytes that either is DataBlock or *CodeBlock* objects. Hence, a byte-interval encapsulates all of the blocks for that section. Next, the mutation engine finds the matching operators and calculates all possible mutations that fall under mutation class categories. Then by applying each mutation resulting Gtirb file passed to Ddisasm-compiler to re-compile the disassembly. The resulting binaries should pass initial tests before passing them out to the SPEC Runner.

has been introduced by dynamic translating of program to an IR [5]. Tools like Valgrind or QEMU can lift the binary to an IR and perform code mutations on top of the generated IR. Then, they can translate it back to apply those modifications during execution. While this approach seems to be effective, it suffers from runtime overhead.

Our focus is on static rewriting schemes and hence we dedicate the rest of this section to it. There are three known static rewriting schemes. The oldest one is based on *detouring* at assembly level. *Detouring* works by hooking out the underlying instruction. There are two flavors of detouring technique, *patch-based instrumentation* and *replica-based instrumentation* [35]. *Patch-based instrumentation* replaces the instruction with an unconditional branch into a new section containing instrumentation, replaced instruction, and a control flow transfer back to the patch point. Detouring is a direct rewriting and is ISA dependent which makes the approach inconvenient. This approach introduces a high performance degradation given the two control transfers at patch points.

Replica-based instrumentation method places jump instructions at control flow changing destinations to a replicated code section containing both a copy of the original code and instrumentation. All memory references in this section are modified to maintain less control flow transfers between original and replicated section. While the performance of this approach is better compared to the *patch-based*, the size of the resulting binary is noticeably increased. [2] incorporated replica-based instrumentation in the malware domain by hooking APIs often used by malware authors to detect analysis environment.

Reassembleable disassembly is another static rewriting technique which works by recovering relocatable assembly code. Hence, instrumentation could be inlined and reassembled back to a working binary. This approach first introduced by UROBOROS [34] and then expanded and improved by Ramblr [33]. This approach enhances the performance since inlined assembly avoids inserting control flow changing instructions at instrumentation points. As a result, performance penalty caused by jump instructions is alleviated. Ddisasm [17] is the state-of-the-art tool for reassembling disassembly developed in Datalog and combines novel heuristics in function recovery and data access pattern.

Among the three options, we chose Ddisasm as our candidate for reconstructing disassembly because of the following reasons: 1) Compared to Ramblr, Ddisasm is about five times faster. 2) UROBOROS scans the data section linearly and considers any machine word-sized buffer whose integer representation falling in a memory region as a memory reference. This assumption under the compiler optimization introduces False-positive and False-negatives [33]. 3) Ramblr improved the *content classification* by applying strong heuristics like *localized value-set analysis* and *Intra-function data dependence analysis*. To achieve a higher accuracy in Control Flow Graph (CFG) recovery Ramblr heavily relies on using symbolic execution which slows down the rewriting process. Apart from Ramblr heuristics, ddisasm incorporated register value analysis (RVA) as an alternative over traditional Value Set Analysis (VSA). In addition, they introduced Data Access Pattern (DAP) analysis which uses the results of def-use analysis combined with the results of register value analysis for a refined register value inference at any given data access point.

Full-translation approach works by translating a low-level machine code to a high-level intermediate representation (IR) using a compiler-based front-end for architecture independent binary rewriting. The process of translating the binary to the IR is called *lifting*, while assembling the IR back to a working executable is denoted as *lowering*. Advantages of lifting the binary to a high-level IR are two folds. First, relying on IR makes the rewriting framework ISA-agnostic, as a result leading to support more architectures. Second, providing the ability to apply program analysis techniques like Value Set Analysis (VSA) [3] and optimization passes like Simple Expression Tracker (SET) and Offset Shifted Register Analysis (OSRA) conveniently [13]. On the other hand, complete translation suffers from changing the structural integrity such as cache locality and CFG.

rev.ng [13] relies on full binary translation by lifting the binary to TCG (the IR used in QEMU) and translating TCG to LLVM IR to benefit from more advanced transformation and analysis passes for CFG and function boundary recovery. Frameworks like angr [32] use lifting to apply more advanced binary analysis on top of the intermediate-level representation. While rev.ng has shown to be useful for modifying the binary file [21], tools like angr do not have the functionality of lowering the resulting transformations back to the binary. Moreover, rev.ng heavily relies on code pointers for identifying function entry points and leverages value-set analysis for a more precise value boundary tracking.

III. Approach

Mutation analysis has been widely studied to evaluate the effectiveness and quality of test suites concerning code coverage and semantic integrity of program. Mutation testing works by replacing operators or operands with a list of candidates inheriting similar behavior. These studies apply mutations directly on source-code or by lifting the code to an intermediate representation (IR) [19]. In the previous research [16], authors applied Uroboros [34], a static binary rewriter for the purpose of mutation generation. Uroboros recovers program structures from stripped binaries and provide an API for recovering the Control Flow Graph (CFG) and call graphs of a binary. Since Uroboros is capable of recovering the lost relocation information, it is possible to inline assembly in the middle of the binary. While Uroboros provides a relocatable disassembly, we discussed in Section II-B that it is not scalable to real-world examples and lacks correctness and soundness in symbolization process.

In this paper, we introduce SN4KE, a light-weight scalable binary mutation framework backed with a rich set of mutation operators analogous to source-level mutation engines like SRCIROR [19]. Relying on binary rewriters which does not work on top of an IR or does not provide any API to work with the intermediate representation, decreases the portability of mutation engine over architectures. SN4KE is a conglomerate of two powerful binary rewriting frameworks, rev.ng [13] and Ddisasm [17]. Ddisasm works on top of the Grammatech Intermediate Representation for Binaries (GTIRB) [30], which lifts the binary to an IR and maps it to an assembly representation. Hence, this mapping facilitates the re-assembling of binary. To incorporate the power of LLVM IR passes for applying more powerful mutations, we integrated rev.ng with SRCIROR. rev.ng lifts the binary to Tiny Code Generator (TCG), QEMU's IR, and para-lifts the result to LLVM IR. In Section IV, we evaluate the benefit and challenges of applying these two engines in program mutation domain. In the following, we describe the mutation operators used over the course of our experiments.

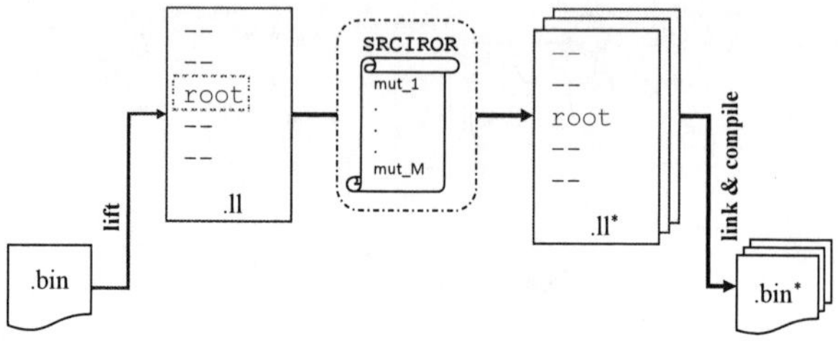

Fig. 2: Integration of rev.ng and SRCIROR to generate mutant binaries

A. Mutation Operators

Numerous mutation generation engines introduced on source-code and to provide the same level of confidence in binary mutation, having an engine close to those is needed. Emamdoost et. al. [16] manifested a mutation engine based on Uroboros which only covers conditional branch mutations. To make the assumption close and realistic to errors might occur during development and software patches, they created mutations for either fall-through or taken branch. While control flow modifiers constitute a large amount of effective instructions, we see that there are lots of faults might happen because of Off-by-One (OBO) or integer wrap-around errors which are related to arithmetic operations.

Hence, In our mutant generation, we consider five classes of mutation operators: replacing one arithmetic operator with another different arithmetic operator (AOR), replacing a logic operator with another different logic operator (LCR), replacing the constant operand in an operation with another different constant value (ICR), and replacing the predicate of a comparison with another different predicate (ROR), and skipping instruction by replacing with NOP operator (ISR). We apply only first order mutations, i.e., for each mutated binary only one mutation operator is applied.

As Table I shows, in arithmetic replacements, we substitute every occurrence of an arithmetic operations with an operator from the set of {+, /, *, %}. For logical connectors, we divide them into three sub-categories of logical assignments, logical operators, and bitwise operators of set {and, or, xor, not}. For constant replacement we look at the operands passed to an operator and check the immediate values. Then we select a random constant *c* and generate mutants for any combination of {c+1, c-1, 0, 1, -1, -c}. For conditional operators, on the assembly level, we either take the next instruction coming after the branch by NOPing the instruction or changing the predicate to take the branch using an unconditional branch.

To apply the above mentioned mutations, we transfer the target binary to another domain with different abstraction. As discussed in the following sections, we use two different binary rewriters using which we can apply the mutations either at the level of assembly code or at the level of LLVM IR. Even though our mutation operators are similar in the two tools, the difference in the level of application of mutations leads into different results. More specifically, the mutations applied by Ddisasm have a one-to-one relationship with the mutations in the binary whereas the mutations applied by rev.ng at the level of LLVM IR go through the compiling process and therefore may result in modifications to multiple instructions in the binary. Given the optimizations performed on the IR level for rev.ng size and structure of the resulting binaries are different compared to the original binary.

B. Rewriting Strategies

1) Ddisasm: Ddisasm is the main module used for recovering the lost structures and symbolization of unresolved memory addresses. For compatibility with other binary analysis tools, Ddisasm incorporates Google's Protobuf protocol to serialize recovered data and analysis results in GITRB. One distinction between GTIRB and other IRs like VEX, LLVM IR [22], and BAP's BIL [7] is that mainly IRs used to represent the semantics of assembly instruction with more verbosity level to include architecture modifications to registers and CPU flags. While, the main idea behind GTIRB is to represent the binary structure from a high-level while preserving the assembly content. Simply, GTIRB acts like a container of binary analysis in conjunction with assembly content.

We show our framework pipeline in Figure 1. In the beginning, framework takes a binary as input and passes it over to Ddisasm to generate a relocatable disassembly in GTIRB representation. GTIRB contains different abstraction for storing information of *Module*, *Symbols*, *SymbolicExpressions*, *Sections*, *ByteIntervals*. As part of our contribution, we modified the default rewriter in Gtirb-capstone to fix the symbolic expressions for the Code and Data blocks following the insertion points and any reference to shifted symbols in the Auxiliary Data.

Capstone is an ultimate disassembly engine designed for binary analysis and security research. Unfortunately, for the purpose of our research Capstone had a limited set of instruction grouping which was not sufficient for mutation analysis. We added new set of groups to better cover our analysis. At the moment of writing the paper, Capstone only supported JUMP, CALL, RET, and INTERRUPT groups. We added Arithmatic, Logical, and Bitwise grouping. Next, decoded instructions from *ByteInterval* passed to the Mutation Engine to calculate all the possible first-level mutations based on the instruction category.

For the purpose of our experiments, we randomly sampled 1000 mutations and passed the resulting mutated GTIRB file to Ddisasm-compiler. During this process, some of the mutations failed the compilation step due to either missing *.eh_frame* section or conflicting *.ctor* and *.dtor* sections. In the latter case, further investigation proved that default linker put elements from *.ctor* and *.dtor* into *.init_array* and *.fini_array* sections lead to misalignment in sections. Finally, to make sure the mutated binary will not crash because of Segmentation Fault or corrupted heap bins, we pass the mutated binaries to a trivial test. This test basically executes the binary with inputs like *-h* or *-v* to assert the healthy state.

2) rev.ng: To apply our mutations at the level of LLVM IR, we chose rev.ng. rev.ng's ability to lift the binary to LLVM IR provides a few advantages. First, manipulating LLVM IR is simple and comes with a vast set of open-source tools. Second, applying changes to the IR language of a compiler will not allow generating code that is not compilable hence filters out the unsuitable mutations.

In Figure 2, we show our methodology. We first lift the binary using rev.ng's lifter. We then apply our mutations from the aforementioned set of mutation operators to the lifted binary. This is implemented in the form of LLVM's compiler optimization passes. We used the SRCIROR's IR mutation setup [19] for this purpose. Once we have the mutated LLVM IR of the binary, we run LLVM's linker and compiler to generate the mutated binary.

From the rev.ng setup, the `translate` tool is the main rewriter. `translate` is able to translate a binary from one target architecture to another. It works by lifting the binary to LLVM IR using its own lifter and compiling for another architecture. As a result of lifting, rev.ng adds extra functions (QEMU helper functions) to the lifted LLVM IR while keeping the code of the original binary inside a function called `root`. To integrate SRCIROR and rev.ng, we adjusted the SRCIROR setup for LLVM version 10.0.1 to be consistent with Clang's version used in rev.ng tools. We also modified it to mutate only the parts from the original binary file, i.e. only the root function. We then separated the lifting from the link and compile processes in `translate`. After lifting, we use SRCIROR to enumerate all the possible points and types of mutation with our set of mutation operators. Next, we apply each of the possible mutations one at a time, generating mutated IRs. Finally, we run the linker and compiler processes in `translate` to generate the mutant binaries.

IV. Evaluation

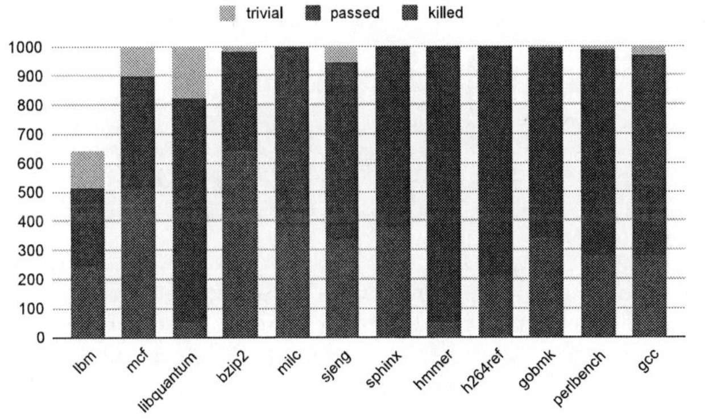

Fig. 3: Mutation results for SPEC 2006 benchmark with test input set

To demonstrate the SN4KE's scalability and practicality, we used it to generate binary mutants of SPEC CPU 2006 benchmarks compiled for x64 architecture. SPEC CPU is a collection of programs along with three different data sets to evaluate performance of compiler, processor, and or memory. The provided input sets are designed for performance evaluation rather than fault detection or code coverage. That said, the benchmarks are carefully observed to match the expected output. Three different input sets mainly differ in size and purposes: the `test` input is used for checking the benchmark's functionality, `train` input is used at build time

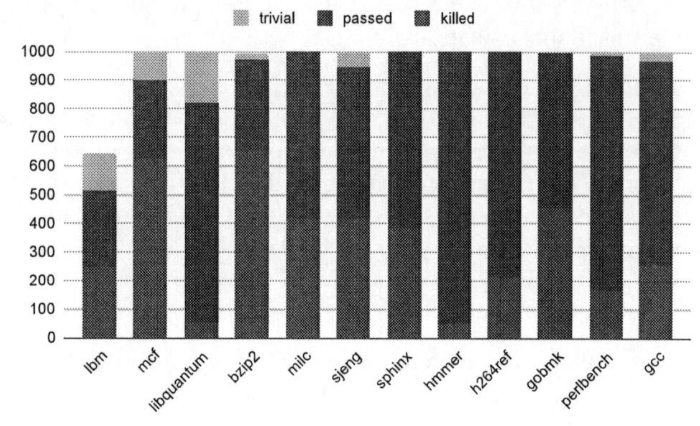

Fig. 4: Mutation results for SPEC 2006 benchmark with train input set

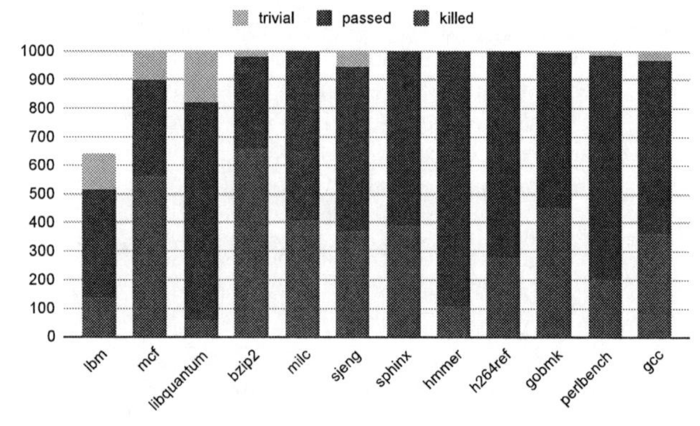

Fig. 5: Mutation results for SPEC 2006 benchmark with ref input set

of the benchmark for feedback directed optimizations, and `ref` input is the largest and actual input data used for performance evaluation.

Based on the approaches described in section III we generate as many as possible mutants, but for the purpose of mutation analysis, we randomly select a subset of 1000 mutants and calculate mutation score per each input data set. Figure 3 shows the ddisasm mutation engine results on the `test` input set. The experimental results on the `train` set is presented in Figure 4 and Figure 5 includes the results of `ref` set. The proportion of killed mutants for the `test` input set is relatively lower than for the `train` and `ref` input sets. That is mainly because the `test` input is smaller in size and more simple in a way that does not cover most portions of the code. `perbench` is an outlier here, as the `test` input set has kill more mutants compared to other two input sets. That is because based on SPEC CPU documentations, the `test` input set is derived from the actual test harness shipped with Perl 5.8.7.

The number of mutants generated for each benchmark directly correlates with the code size. However, the mutants' diversity in terms of applied mutation operator follows a common pattern among all the benchmarks. Compared to the previous work by Emamdoost et al., we were able to generate more mutants due to our richer mutation operator set. Except for `lbm`, we could generate more mutants than the sampling rate threshold. While `lbm` code base only consists of 1500 instructions, we can generate 641 mutants, which means 42% of instructions fall under at least one mutation category.

TABLE II: Mutation score of `test`, `train`, and `ref` sets. Mutations score denoted as the number of killed mutants over the total number of mutants. This measure used in assessing the quality of test suite.

Binaries	**Mutation score**		
	test	**train**	**ref**
lbm	37.8%	38.8%	21.8%
mcf	51.4%	60.0%	56.4%
libquantum	5.2%	5.7%	6.0%
bzip2	64.4%	65.7%	66.1%
milc	37.7%	41.6%	40.9%
sjeng	33.3%	42.0%	37.0%
sphinx	37.7%	38.4%	38.8%
hmmer	5.1%	5.0%	10.8%
h264ref	20.9%	21.6%	28.0%
gobmk	34.0%	45.5%	45.5%
perlbench	27.8%	16.9%	20.4%
gcc	28.2%	25.5%	36.4%

We classify mutants in three categories: passed, killed, and trivial based on the initial health-check tests and expected functionality test results. Passed mutants are the ones that generate outputs consistent with original benchmark binaries. Killed mutants are defined as those that fail to generate the same output as the baseline binary because of either calculation errors or falling into an infinite loop. The set of mutants which fail the initial health-check tests or never make the execution due to a segmentation fault or pipe error are classified as trivial. Initial health-check test is a short light-weight input for each binary. For example, in case of `gcc` is an empty file.

Infinite loops happen when we apply a control-flow related mutation or changing the logical operator following a comparison. Unbounded loops put the program in a non-returning state. Hence, to cover these edge cases, we applied a timeout chosen twice of the original runtime.

Figure 6a provides the mutant's breakdown based on the operator used in each mutant generated by `ddisasm` rewriter. The three most common classes of mutants are arithmetic switching, constant switching, and instruction skip (NOP). This observation constitutes to our initial thought on the diversity of new mutants beyond control flow changing instructions. Dominance of branch mutations in `gcc` comes from the supremacy of control-flow instructions compared to other binaries which comprises the 22% of the whole instructions.

Breakdown of killed mutants on the `ref` test at Figure 6b follows a constant pattern complies with Figure 6a. Table II manifest the mutation score which is the percentage of mutants killed over the total number of mutants. Compared to [16] results, generally we observed higher mutation scores. For example, in `gcc` they reported a score of less than 15% for a large code base while ours is 36.4%. Based on their results, mutation score and binary size has inverse relation. The greater the size of the binary is, the lower mutation score they reported. Since they only relied on conditional branches for mutation,

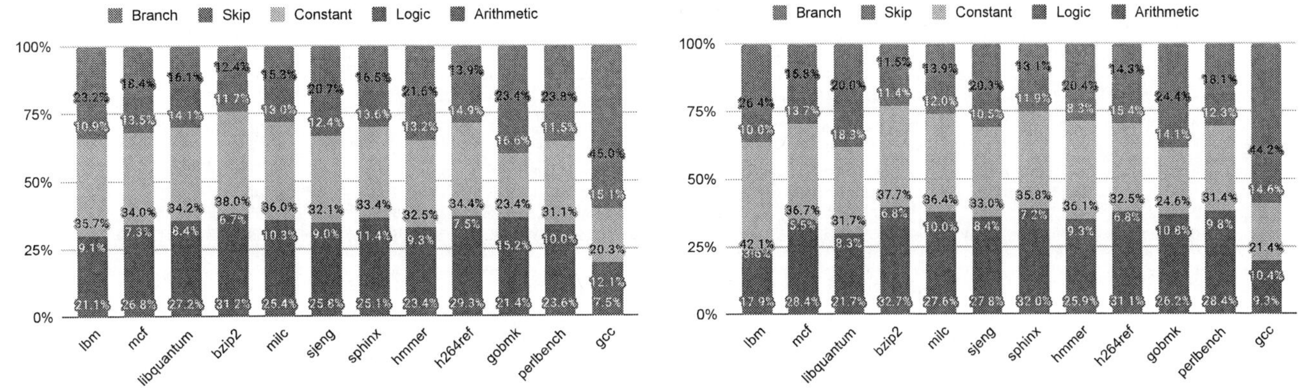

(a) Selected set mutation breakdown.

(b) Killed mutants of `ref` set breakdown.

Fig. 6: Mutation Breakdown of 1000 randomly selected mutants over five mutation categories resulting by `ddisasm` engine. In all of the cases, Arithmetic, NOP (Skip), and Constant operations have greater share compared to others. Greater the size of the binary is the more mutants we are going to expect.

TABLE III: Size and number of possible mutations on the lifted LLVM-IR by Revng

benchmark	IR size	possible mutations
lbm	14MB	53215
mcf	14MB	47390
libquantum	24MB	177310
bzip2	30MB	270217
milc	46MB	476663
sjeng	53MB	496435
sphinx	63MB	699322
hmmer	103MB	1228840
h264ref	177MB	2110590
perlbench	367MB	4759791
gcc	986MB	13117690
gobmk	283MB	3507198

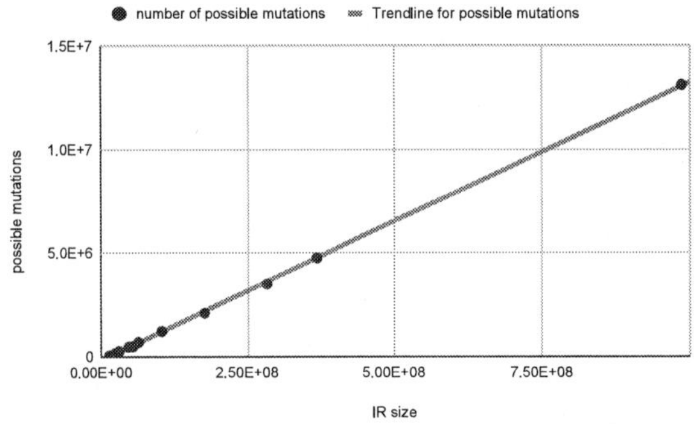

Fig. 7: Number of possible mutations by SRCIROR vs. size of the lifted IR by rev.ng

their score for smaller binaries are larger which shows the effectiveness of branch mutation in relatively small binaries.

Based on [16], they reported problems with compilation flags of `gcc` and `gobmk` binaries and their rewriter was limited to a specific version of GCC compiler. In both of our approach, because of powerful binary structure recovery provided by both `Rev.ng` and `ddisasm`, we never had such an issue. This shows the portability of our approach compared to their in stable binary mutation of real-world binaries.

V. Discussion

Mutant generation using the rev.ng tool had scalability issues that prohibited us from thoroughly analyzing the mutants generated from SPEC CPU 2006.

Mutant binary size increase becomes a serious issue, specifically when the original binary has a moderate code size. Table IV shows the size of the rewritten binaries in SPEC 2006 test suite using rev.ng and Ddisasm. The rewritten binaries from rev.ng had a size of from 10× to 70× the original binary, while the Ddisasm rewriter kept the rewritten binaries stable in size. We tracked down the reason behind size expulsion and found that during the lifting process to the TCG IR, rev.ng imports a large portion of helper function calls in the resulting binary. rev.ng authors suggested applying the function isolation pass to reduce the binary size by dropping the root function. CRISPR [9] is a tool that allows static binary patching using rev.ng with minimized binary size overhead. While we didn't test either of these approaches, they believe even after applying this method, we still should expect a binary greater than the original one.

Mutant generation time was another factor that rendered rev.ng a less appealing rewriting tool for binary mutation. As mentioned before, the number of possible mutants goes beyond millions for binaries with moderate code size like `gcc`. In such cases the generation time per mutant becomes a decisive factor on practicality and scalability of the binary mutation tool. Generation of the IR from binaries by rev.ng took less than a minute for small binaries such as `lbm` and `mcf` but about 20 minutes for `perlbench` and 30 minutes for lifting `gcc`. Furthermore, the generated IR itself is of significant size as pointed out in Table III. The bulky size of the lifted IR made the total number of applicable mutations very large. As

TABLE IV: Overhead in code size resulted from Revng and Ddisasm binary rewriters for SPEC 2006 binaries

benchmark	original size	Revng		Ddisasm	
		rewritten size	rewrite overhead	rewritten size	rewrite overhead
lbm	22kB	1.2MB	54.5×	22kB	1×
mcf	23kB	1.2MB	52.2×	22kB	0.96×
libquantum	51kB	3.5MB	68.6×	46kB	0.9×
bzip2	69kB	4,1MB	59.4×	68kB	0.99×
milc	142kB	5.7MB	40.1×	134kB	0.94×
sjeng	154kB	8.1MB	52.6×	149kB	0.97×
sphinx	198kB	7.5MB	37.9×	196kB	0.99×
hmmer	314kB	13MB	41.4×	308kB	0.98×
h264ref	566kB	22MB	38.9×	552kB	0.98×
perlbench	1.2MB	47MB	39.2×	1.5MB	1.25×
gcc	3.6MB	127MB	35.3×	3.5MB	0.97×
gobmk	3.9MB	39MB	10.0×	4.3MB	1.1×

Figure 7 shows, number of possible mutations by SRCIROR is linearly related to the size of its IR input with the trendline of $0.0134x - 172510$ and coefficient of determination of $R^2 = 1$.

VI. Future Work

In this research, we addressed the limitations of binary mutation by employing more robust binary rewriting approaches and also, adopting a richer set of mutation operators inspired by source-level mutation. However, we did not explore the possible vulnerabilities that could be introduced by each of those mutations that resemble a real-bug in a program. Such observations can be helpful for example to further investigate which mutation works better for proof-testing patches in a binary. For example to generate mutants resembling double fetch vulnerabilities by performing a light-weight def-use chain analysis on the operators working on same memory locations. One possible mistake causing this issue is the incorrect replacement of lines of code during a patch. While a manual test-case might fall short to test the patch comprehensively, a good binary mutation engine can test for these corner cases.

VII. Conclusion

In this paper, we proposed SN4KE, a new binary mutation tool. SN4KE's modular design allowed us to adapt and compare the two latest binary rewriting tools: Ddisasm and rev.ng. Based on our implementation and evaluation, Ddisasm proved to be more practical and scalable in terms of both resulting mutant binary size and mutant generation time. SN4KE is able to mutate any binary independent of the original compilation configuration in use. Compared to the previous works on binary mutation, SN4KE enjoys a richer set of mutation operators. These operators are better representative of real world faults, and thanks to the scalable underlying binary rewriting technique, are easily applicable to any binary program paving the way to generate many mutants. Applying SN4KE to SPEC CPU 2006 benchmarks, we demonstrated its applicability and effectiveness in terms of generating diverse set of mutants. Such diverse mutants evaluated the adequacy of tests for SPEC CPU binaries.

References

[1] A. T. Acree, T. A. Budd, R. A. DeMillo, R. J. Lipton, and F. G. Sayward, "Mutation analysis." Georgia Institute of Technology School of Information and Computer Science, Tech. Rep., 1979.

[2] M. Ahmadi, K. Leach, R. Dougherty, S. Forrest, and W. Weimer, "Mimosa: Reducing malware analysis overhead with coverings," 2021.

[3] G. Balakrishnan and T. Reps, "Analyzing memory accesses in x86 executables," in *International conference on compiler construction*. Springer, 2004, pp. 5–23.

[4] M. Becker, C. Kuznik, M. M. Joy, T. Xie, and W. Mueller, "Binary mutation testing through dynamic translation," in *IEEE/IFIP International Conference on Dependable Systems and Networks (DSN 2012)*, June 2012, pp. 1–12.

[5] ——, "Binary mutation testing through dynamic translation," in *IEEE/IFIP International Conference on Dependable Systems and Networks (DSN 2012)*. IEEE, 2012, pp. 1–12.

[6] D. Bruening, Q. Zhao, and S. Amarasinghe, "Transparent dynamic instrumentation," in *Proceedings of the 8th ACM SIGPLAN/SIGOPS conference on Virtual Execution Environments*, 2012, pp. 133–144.

[7] D. Brumley, I. Jager, T. Avgerinos, and E. J. Schwartz, "Bap: A binary analysis platform," in *International Conference on Computer Aided Verification*. Springer, 2011, pp. 463–469.

[8] T. A. Budd, R. A. DeMillo, R. J. Lipton, and F. G. Sayward, "The design of a prototype mutation system for program testing," in *Proceedings of the AFIPS National Computer Conference*, vol. 74, 1978, pp. 623–627.

[9] F. Cremonese, "CRISPR: Binary Editing with High Level Languages," Nov. 2020. [Online]. Available: https://github.com/revng/crispr

[10] R. A. DeMillo, R. J. Lipton, and F. G. Sayward, "Hints on test data selection: Help for the practicing programmer," *Computer*, vol. 11, no. 4, pp. 34–41, April 1978.

[11] A. Denisov and S. Pankevich, "Mull it over: Mutation testing based on llvm," in *2018 IEEE International Conference on Software Testing, Verification and Validation Workshops (ICSTW)*, April 2018, pp. 25–31.

[12] A. Derezińska, "Advanced mutation operators applicable in c# programs," in *Software Engineering Techniques: Design for Quality*, K. Sacha, Ed. Boston, MA: Springer US, 2007, pp. 283–288.

[13] A. Di Federico, M. Payer, and G. Agosta, "rev.ng: a unified binary analysis framework to recover CFGs and function boundaries," in *Proceedings of the 26th International Conference on Compiler Construction*, 2017, pp. 131–141.

[14] B. Dolan-Gavitt, P. Hulin, E. Kirda, T. Leek, A. Mambretti, W. Robertson, F. Ulrich, and R. Whelan, "Lava: Large-scale automated vulnerability addition," in *2016 IEEE Symposium on Security and Privacy (SP)*. IEEE, 2016, pp. 110–121.

[15] N. Emamdoost and S. McCamant, "The effect of instruction padding on SFI overhead," in *Binary Analysis Research (BAR)*. Internet Society, 2018.

[16] N. Emamdoost, V. Sharma, T. Byun, and S. McCamant, "Binary mutation analysis of tests using reassembleable disassembly," in *Binary Analysis Research (BAR)*. Internet Society, 2019.

[17] A. Flores-Montoya and E. Schulte, "Datalog disassembly," in *29th USENIX Security Symposium (USENIX Security 20)*, 2020.

[18] F. Hariri and A. Shi, "Srciror: A toolset for mutation testing of c source code and llvm intermediate representation," in *Proceedings of the 33rd ACM/IEEE International Conference on Automated Software Engineering*, 2018, pp. 860–863.

[19] F. Hariri, A. Shi, V. Fernando, S. Mahmood, and D. Marinov, "Comparing mutation testing at the levels of source code and compiler

intermediate representation," in *2019 12th IEEE Conference on Software Testing, Validation and Verification (ICST)*. IEEE, 2019, pp. 114–124.

[20] Y. Jia and M. Harman, "Milu: A customizable, runtime-optimized higher order mutation testing tool for the full c language," in *Testing: Academic Industrial Conference - Practice and Research Techniques (taic part 2008)*, Aug 2008, pp. 94–98.

[21] P. Kiaei, C.-B. Breunesse, M. Ahmadi, P. Schaumont, and J. van Woudenberg, "Rewrite to reinforce: Rewriting the binary to apply countermeasures against fault injection," *arXiv preprint arXiv:2011.14067*, 2020.

[22] C. Lattner and V. Adve, "Llvm: A compilation framework for lifelong program analysis & transformation," in *International Symposium on Code Generation and Optimization, 2004. CGO 2004.* IEEE, 2004, pp. 75–86.

[23] C.-K. Luk, R. Cohn, R. Muth, H. Patil, A. Klauser, G. Lowney, S. Wallace, V. J. Reddi, and K. Hazelwood, "Pin: building customized program analysis tools with dynamic instrumentation," *Acm sigplan notices*, vol. 40, no. 6, pp. 190–200, 2005.

[24] Y.-S. Ma, J. Offutt, and Y.-R. Kwon, "Mujava: A mutation system for java," in *Proceedings of the 28th International Conference on Software Engineering*, ser. ICSE '06. New York, NY, USA: ACM, 2006, pp. 827–830. [Online]. Available: http://doi.acm.org/10.1145/1134285.1134425

[25] S. McCamant and G. Morrisett, "Evaluating SFI for a CISC architecture." in *15th USENIX Security Symposium.* USENIX Association, 2006.

[26] A. Offutt, "The coupling effect: Fact or fiction," in *Proceedings of the ACM SIGSOFT '89 Third Symposium on Software Testing, Analysis, and Verification*, ser. TAV3. New York, NY, USA: ACM, 1989, pp. 131–140. [Online]. Available: http://doi.acm.org/10.1145/75308.75324

[27] A. J. Offutt and J. Pan, "Automatically detecting equivalent mutants and infeasible paths," *Software Testing, Verification and Reliability*, vol. 7, no. 3, pp. 165–192, 9 1997. [Online]. Available: https://doi.org/10.1002/(SICI)1099-1689(199709)7:3⟨165::AID-STVR143⟩3.0.CO;2-U

[28] H. Peng, Y. Shoshitaishvili, and M. Payer, "T-fuzz: fuzzing by program transformation," in *2018 IEEE Symposium on Security and Privacy (SP).* IEEE, 2018, pp. 697–710.

[29] J. Pewny and T. Holz, "Evilcoder: automated bug insertion," in *Proceedings of the 32nd Annual Conference on Computer Security Applications.* ACM, 2016, pp. 214–225.

[30] E. Schulte, J. Dorn, A. Flores-Montoya, A. Ballman, and T. Johnson, "Gtirb: intermediate representation for binaries," *arXiv preprint arXiv:1907.02859*, 2019.

[31] J. Tuya, M. J. Suarez-Cabal, and C. de la Riva, "Sqlmutation: A tool to generate mutants of sql database queries," in *Second Workshop on Mutation Analysis (Mutation 2006 - ISSRE Workshops 2006)*, Nov 2006, pp. 1–1.

[32] F. Wang and Y. Shoshitaishvili, "Angr-the next generation of binary analysis," in *2017 IEEE Cybersecurity Development (SecDev).* IEEE, 2017, pp. 8–9.

[33] R. Wang, Y. Shoshitaishvili, A. Bianchi, A. Machiry, J. Grosen, P. Grosen, C. Kruegel, and G. Vigna, "Ramblr: Making reassembly great again." in *NDSS*, 2017.

[34] S. Wang, P. Wang, and D. Wu, "Uroboros: Instrumenting stripped binaries with static reassembling," in *2016 IEEE 23rd International Conference on Software Analysis, Evolution, and Reengineering (SANER)*, vol. 1. IEEE, 2016, pp. 236–247.

[35] M. Wenzl, G. Merzdovnik, J. Ullrich, and E. Weippl, "From hack to elaborate technique—a survey on binary rewriting," *ACM Computing Surveys (CSUR)*, vol. 52, no. 3, pp. 1–37, 2019.

[36] W. E. Wong and A. P. Mathur, "Reducing the cost of mutation testing: An empirical study," *Journal of Systems and Software*, vol. 31, no. 3, pp. 185–196, 1995.

[37] B. Yee, D. Sehr, G. Dardyk, J. B. Chen, R. Muth, T. Ormandy, S. Okasaka, N. Narula, and N. Fullagar, "Native client: A sandbox for portable, untrusted x86 native code," in *2009 30th IEEE Symposium on Security and Privacy.* IEEE, 2009, pp. 79–93.

[38] M. Zhang and R. Sekar, "Control flow integrity for COTS binaries," in *22nd USENIX Security Symposium (USENIX Security 13)*, 2013, pp. 337–352.

Declarative Demand-Driven Reverse Engineering

Yihao Sun*, Jeffrey Ching†, and Kristopher Micinski‡
Department of Electical Engineering and Computer Science, Syracuse University
Email: *ysun67@syr.edu, †cching01@syr.edu, ‡kkmicins@syr.edu

Abstract—**Binary reverse engineering is a challenging task because it often necessitates reasoning using both domain-specific knowledge (e.g., understanding entrypoint idioms common to an ABI) and logical inference (e.g., reconstructing interprocedural control flow). To help perform these tasks, reverse engineers often use toolkits (such as IDA Pro or Ghidra) that allow them to interactively explicate properties of binaries. We argue that deductive databases serve as a natural abstraction for interfacing between visualization-based binary analysis tools and high-performance logical inference engines that compute facts about binaries. In this paper, we present a vision for the future in which reverse engineers use a visualization-based tool to understand binaries while simultaneously querying a logical-inference engine to perform arbitrarily-complex deductive inference tasks. We call our vision declarative demand-driven reverse engineering (D^3RE for short), and sketch a formal semantics whose goal is to mediate interaction between a logical-inference engine (such Soufflé) and a reverse engineering tool. We describe a prototype tool, d3re, which are using to explore the D^3RE vision. While still a prototype, we have used d3re to reimplement several common querying tasks on binaries. Our evaluation demonstrates that d3re enables both better performance and more succinct implementation of these common RE tasks.**

I. Introduction

Binary reverse engineering (henceforth RE) is the process by which we start with some input binary (sequence of bytes) and employ various reasoning principles to explicate its behavior when executed as code. While RE tasks are often partially automated (e.g., via decompilation), full automation is often impossible: the extreme semantic expressivity afforded to binaries (including encrypted code, stripped symbol tables, etc..) often necessitates open-ended exploration and case-specific reasoning. Recent literature suggests that many practicioners follow an iterative approach involving several rounds of hypothesis formation and validation/falsification, often assisated via a combination of static and dynamic analysis [1]–[3].

To rapidly interact with a binary, RE practicioners often use reverse engineering tools such as Ghidra [4], IDA Pro [5], or Radare2 [6]. The goal of these tools is to allow an RE[1] to quickly explore the binary and visualize it (typically interactively, via a GUI or CLI) in a variety of ways. For example, a reverse engineer looking for a time bomb may first search for calls to the system's time function, and then walk backwards to understand whether each call is associated with legitimate or malicious behavior. In doing so, the RE may need to reason about, e.g., indirect control flow, or even identify the time function (in a stripped binary). Because REs are expert users, and often skilled programmers, RE tools provide programmatic interfaces that enable REs to systematize reasoning tasks via extensions. A broad range of popular extensions exist for several tools which perform such tasks as loading the results of static analyses [7], [8], interacting with debuggers [9], and identifying common cryptographic-relevant code [10].

In this paper, we argue that *deductive databases* (e.g., Datalog) serve as a natural abstraction boundary between RE tools and logical inference tasks over binaries. We envision a future in which a reverse engineer interactively explores a binary using an RE tool while simultaneously querying arbitrarily-complex logical properties written in a terse declarative style. We call this Declarative Demand-Driven Reverse Engineering (henceforth D^3RE). In D^3RE, an RE interacts with a deductive database by giving inputs (e.g., the currently highlighted address) to a rule-based deductive inference system written in a declarative language such as Datalog. Rules inductively compute *relations* over facts about the binary. As an example, consider a relation direct_call $\in Addr \times Addr$ which relates callsite addresses (offsets within the binary) to procedure invocation target addresses. In our vision, D^3RE allows REs to interactively compute with and visualize the results of queries over these deductive rules.

We see D^3RE as a natural extension of several observations about the state of the start. First, many existing RE tools assemble databases to index various properties (e.g., addresses, symbols, etc...) of binaries for quick exploration. Deductive databases further allow REs to write arbitrary logical queries which are computed maximally efficiently via, e.g., compilation to relational algebra kernels as done in Soufflé. Deductive databases have also enabled several recent advances in binary analysis demonstrating both efficiency and robustness over conventional techniques. For example, the Datalog-based disassembler ddisasm achieves both faster and more-precise disassembly than other state-of-the-art disassemblers, and OOAnalyzer uses Prolog to enable declarative recovery of classes from compiled C++ code.

In this short paper we describe our progress in implementing a prototype tool, d3re, which we are building to realize the

[1]When unambiguous, we will use the term RE both to mean the process of reverse engineering and a reverse engineering practicioner

Network and Distributed Systems Security (NDSS) Symposium 2021
21 February 2021, Virtual

https://dx.doi.org/10.14722/bar.2021.23011
www.ndss-symposium.org

D^{3}RE vision. d3re allows REs to interactively define and calculate queries of arbitrary complexity over large production binaries and then visualize their results using Ghidra. To implement d3re we have designed an interface, which we call the *mediator*, that sits between a traditional Datalog solver and an RE tool. We briefly formalize this interaction between the RE tool and logic solver in Section III, and go on to describe our prototype Ghidra extension that enables visualizing the results of binary analyses in our tool. Using this formalism, we describe how d3re readily enables a broad range of binary analyses and sketch a vision for how we believe D^{3}RE will prove to be a natural ergonomic for reverse engineering.

We have measured the robustness of d3re in several ways. First, we wanted to know whether d3re could truly live up to our vision of being a natural replacement for the kinds of scripts REs already use in their day-to-day work. To evaluate this, we reimplemented a set of currently-existing Ghidra scripts. We happily observed that d3re was not only an ergonomic advantage (allowing us to write succinct but obviously-correct queries) but also a performance advantage. For example, many Ghidra scripts play tricks to avoid unnecessarily complexity that would arise in a straightforward implementation, e.g., iterating over a set of functions in a loop to check a property resulting in super-linear complexity. In d3re, the Datalog solver was naturally able to compile and organize work in an optimal way. We discuss this and other results in Section IV. We conclude with a brief overview of related work and our outlook on future directions in Section V

Specifically, we claim the following three contributions:

- A formalization of our metadatabase as a database of databases used to optimize subsequent invocations of the Datalog solver (Section III).
- A prototype tool, d3re, consisting of a server which wraps ddisasm with logic to enable chaining multiple subsequent calls via the metadatabase. Also included in d3re is an extension to the Ghidra RE toolkit to enable visualizing results computed using d3re.
- An evaluation of d3re on a set of benchmarks demonstrating positive initial results indicating that d3re could replace present-day binary analysis infrastructure (e.g., Ghidra scripts) and directly enable more efficient and succinct implementation.

II. Overview

In this section, we demonstrate the vision and application of D^{3}RE by illustrating how a reverse engineer might explicate a vulnerability due to an uninitialized global variable. We consider a particular binary, CROMU_00038, from DARPA's Cyber Grand Challenge which contains a function pointer which is uninitialized when an invalid flag is set in the metadata portion of an input file [11], [12]. We demonstrate how our prototype tool, d3re, can be used to build a declarative query to find uninitialized function entry points and visualize them within Ghidra. We do not claim that d3re can immediately or automatically discover vulnerabilities—in this section we try to focus on how its declarative reasoning instead enables rapidly exploring a binary to uncover some property.

```
1  // swap_short and swap_word only initialized
       within if
2  if (tiff_hdr->Byte_Order == 0x4949) {
3    printf("Intel formatted integers\n");
4    swap_word = intel_swap_word;
5  }
6  else if (tiff_hdr->Byte_Order == 0x4d4d) {
7    printf("Motorola formatted integers\n");
8    swap_word = motorola_swap_word;
9  }
10 #ifdef PATCHED
11 else {
12   printf("Invalid header values\n");
13   _terminate(-1);
14 }
15 #endif
16 // might cause an uninitialized variable bug here
17 offset = swap_word(tiff_hdr->Offset_to_IFD);
```

Fig. 1: Uninitialized variable vulnerability in CROMU0038 source code

```
>>> load dl/use_def_global.dl
>>> run dl/use_def_global.dl
>>> load dl/uninitialized.dl
>>> run dl/uninitialized.dl
>>> highlight
>>> comment
>>> query use_before_def_global
00004feb 0000a180 swap_short
00005017 0000a188 swap_word
...
0000515e 0000a180 swap_short
```

Fig. 2: d3re REPL session used in this overview.

The vulnerable segment of code is a use-before-definition bug shown in Figure 1. The swap_word function is initialized inside of the main function based on a value parsed in a TIFF header—if the flag does not match 0x4949 or 0x4d4d the function is left uninitialized and the call on line 17 crashes.

Loading the binary: To begin an analysis of a binary, an RE will load the binary into a reverse engineering tool. In our current implementation of d3re, a user opens two processes silmultaneously: a GUI-based instance of Ghidra, and a terminal running d3re's REPL. The user can explore the binary using all of the normal features of Ghidra and use all of its conventional analyses (e.g., to recover entrypoints). However, d3re's REPL communicates with Ghidra so that when d3re's analysis finishes Ghidra's views update as appropriate.

Initial processing: It is conventional that reverse engineering tools will apply a set of analyses to a binary to disassemble it and index various items such as entrypoints and callsites In d3re, the user builds queries in Datalog starting from a large initial set of Datalog rules that build on top of ddisasm, a Datalog-based disassembly engine [13]. Analogously to the indexing and analysis operations provided by Ghidra (and other RE tools), d3re invokes ddisasm once

```
def_global(EA,dest) :-
  code(EA), instruction_get_dest_op(EA,Index,_),
  pc_relative_operand(EA,Index,dest),
  defined_symbol(dest,_,"OBJECT","GLOBAL",_,_).

used_global(EA,dest,Index) :-
  code(EA), instruction_get_src_op(EA,Index,_),
  pc_relative_operand(EA,Index,dest),
  defined_symbol(dest,_,"OBJECT","GLOBAL",_,_).

def_used_global(EA_def,GA,EA_used,Index) :-
  used_global(EA_used,GA,Index),
  block_last_def_global(EA_used,EA_def,GA).

def_used_global(EA_def,GA, EA_used, Index) :-
  last_def_global(Block,EA_def,GA),
  code_in_block(EA_used, Block),
  used_global(EA_used, GA, Index),
  !block_last_def_global(EA_used,_,GA),.
```

Fig. 3: Global Var Use-Def analysis

to build an initial database.

Building on top of ddisasm was initially a strategic choice—ddisasm already includes facilities to parse object files and transform them into input databases in the style required by Soufflé. Initially, we extended ddisasm's set of rules with additional user-specific queries—a slow process, as ddisasm can take several minutes to run on large binaries. This was at odds with our goal of enabling rapid real-time feedback to users of d3re.

D^3RE builds upon a key observation that we have found crucial to enable efficient interactive binary analyses in practice: because Datalog is monotonic, we can evaluate an extended program (i.e., a program extended with a set of additional rules or queries) by using the database resulting from the calculation of the previous program. Thus, running ddisasm *once* allows pre-populating a large set of inferred relations for a wide range of interesting facts about binaries, including intraprocedural reachability and calling conventions.

When a binary is loaded, d3re invokes ddisasm with one slight modification: every Datalog relation in ddisasm's rule database (used by ddisasm to build a disassembly) is modified to be an output relation. In ddisasm, only dissassembly-relevant relations are output, rather than internal relations (e.g., those that relate to intraprocedural reachability). By marking all ddisasm's relations as output relations, d3re provides them to the user as primitives with which to build queries over binaries[2]. After the binary is loaded, all rules declared in ddisasm will be available for querying. Additionally, ddisasm will be run only once, even if the user uploads the same binary several times. All facts generated in this step will be stored in a temporary folder on disk managed by the metadatabase (described in Section III).

Designing a query to explicate use-before-define: In the D^3RE approach, REs interactively build queries to highlight various portions of the program that match certain properties.

[2]A relevant analogy might be that ddisasm is the standard library of d3re

```
use_before_def_global(EA_used,GA,Name) :-
  used_global(EA_used,GA,Index),
  !def_used_global(_,GA,EA_used,_),
  defined_symbol(GA,_,"OBJECT","GLOBAL",_,Name).

use_before_def_global(EA_used,GA,Name) :-
  used_global(EA_used,GA,Index),
  def_used_global(EA_def,GA,EA_used,_),
  !def_null_global(EA_def,GA),
  defined_symbol(GA,_,"OBJECT","GLOBAL",_,Name).
```

Fig. 4: uninitialized variables

They then manually inspect the results of their queries and use their intuition to build subsequent queries. Along the way, the RE may choose to add comments to various instructions, functions, or other forms and browse those instructions in Ghidra. In d3re, the communication between the logical rules and the state of the RE tool is reconciled by input and output tables—RE users can write queries that consume the state of the RE tool (such as currentAddress, the currently-selected address) as input relations, perform logical inference, and leave their output in relations such as comment(addr,"vuln").

Like ddisasm, d3re uses the Soufflé Datalog engine to perform logical inference over binaries. Users of d3re can incrementally build up more rules in the interactive REPL (shown in Figure 2). Currently, our REPL allows loading rules by loading new files—we plan on adding direct support for new rules, along with error-reporting feedback soon.

Knowing there was an uninitialized global function pointer being used, a user of d3re might first define a set of relations to build up def-use-chains of global variables. Datalog code to implement these queries is illustrated in Figure 3. The last two rules build up a relation def_used_global(EA_def,GA,EA_used,Index), which infers that at address EA_def, the global variable (at address GA) is defined and used at address EA_used at operand index Index. While this is a relatively coarse query, we envision the user could run the query on the binary to visualize a large answer set. In our setting, this can be done using the highlight or comment commands, which display the data marked to be highlighted by the most recent result computation.

Based on our definitions in Figure 3, we can define a relation for variables which are possibly used before they are defined. We demonstrate this in Figure 4. In the first rule, we say that if there is some usage of a global variable at some address, but in that address, we can't find any definition related to it, then we will consider variable there as an uninitialized variable; The second clause says that for some usage of a global variable even if it has some definition associated with it, if that definition is nullptr, we will still consider that there is a use-before-def vulnerability here.

Refining the query: In d3re, users can easily access the result of the rule and all facts generated by ddisasm through the GUI by writing into output tables using d3re rules. Unfortunately, our above query produces over 50 possible results—checking each occurrence would still be a timely endeavor. Next, we narrow down the query space to the range of just the main function. We use an auxiliary predicate, code_in_range, which we seed with constants for the beginning and end of the main function we gain from inspecting the binary in Ghidra.

```
code_in_range(19490,21704).
use_before_def_global(EA_used, GA, Name) :-
  code_in_range(from, to), EA_used >= from,
      EA_used < to,
  used_global(EA_used,GA,Index),
  !def_used_global(_,GA,EA_used,_),
  defined_symbol(GA,_,"OBJECT","GLOBAL",_,Name).
```

After new rules are applied, the output of the program becomes empty: however, this does not specify the program is free from the vulnerability. First, because of our constraint, only the main function is searched, bugs may still hide in other functions. Secondly, if all usage of a variable is before it's definition, null pointer error can still appear: programmers may initialize a variable to NULL and use several non-total branches to initialize the pointer, leaving the pointer uninitialized at the join point when no switch fires. We modify our rules to account for this:

```
def_null_global(EA,GA) :-
  def_global(EA,GA), instruction_get_src_op(EA,_,
      Op),
  op_immediate(Op,offset), offset=0.

use_before_def_global(EA_used, GA, Name) :-
  code_in_range(from,to),
  EA_used >= from, EA_used < to,
  used_global(EA_used,GA,Index),
  def_used_global(EA_def,GA,EA_used,_),
  !def_null_global(EA_def,GA),
  defined_symbol(GA,_,"OBJECT","GLOBAL",_,Name).
```

This change results in 19 addresses to search, and combining these results with use-def information in the previous step and intra-procedural control-flow graph in Ghidra, we can fairly easily infer that the global variable swap_word is initialized to 0 at address 0x4c2a, that both conditional jumps 0x4f80 and 0x4fb8 fail, and observe a subsequent usage of swap_word at 0x5017 which will trigger a crash. At any stage in our process, we can sync Ghidra's UI with the current database using several REPL commands (an example is shown in Figure 5). In a fully-fledged implementation of d3re, we hope to have UI gadgets (or templates) to help users interactively build queries. For example, we may allow the user to select a region of the binary and build a rule that applies only to that region, or right-click on a function and build a rule specific to callers of that function. We believe this will need to be informed by a combination of interviews with expert users, participatory design, and (perhaps) user studies. This is work we plan to undertake now that we have proven initial success to ourselves with d3re.

We conclude this section by remarking upon the nature of our analyses. Our analyses would be considered naïve by the standards of industrial static analyses. Indeed, our reasoning is not even sound—we can restrict ourselves to looking at results for only one function or ignore complex behavior. Still, we believe that this iterative ad-hoc reasoning is a technique many reverse engineers already employ—the vision of D^{3}RE is to harmoniously leverage state-of-the-art deductive reasoning engines while performing human-guided RE tasks.

III. Design and Implementation

In this section, we present both a formal semantics for D^{3}RE and describe our implementation of d3re. The high-level architecture of d3re is outlined in Figure 6. Conceptually, the key idea of our semantics is to maintain a *metadatabase* to allow efficient incremental reuse of previously-computed databases. In d3re, this metadatabase takes the form of a server which accepts Datalog programs to run to a fixed-point.

The metadatabase (server) interacts with both the REPL process and Ghidra to render output databases into view annotations (e.g., highlights or comments) in the Ghidra UI based on REPL commands. Our visualization is currently limited to printing to Ghidra's console, highlighting a set of lines (typically some output relation), or annotating a line with a comment (whose contents may be dynamically determined via a Datalog query). We plan to investigate adding comments to other Ghidra UI elements (such as inferred classes) and other visual integration as future work.

A. *Formal semantics of* D^{3}RE

Due to space restrictions, we present only a sketch of a formal semantics for D^{3}RE. Semantics of Datalog programs are typically phrased in terms of an extensional database (EDB), an extensionally-enumerated set of ground facts, and intensional database (IDB), the set of rules defining the program [14]. Datalog's semantics is given by a least-fixed-point of an "immediate consequence" operator over the rules for the program. Because Datalog programs have a finite Herbrand

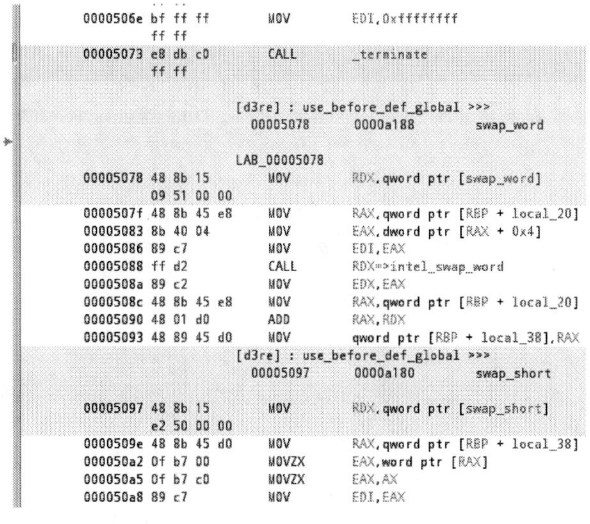

Fig. 5: Ghidra with highlights and comments declaratively specified to output results inferred via d3re for our example.

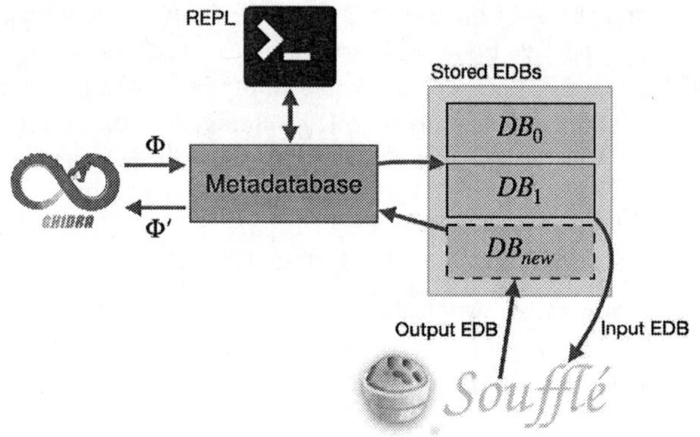

Fig. 6: High-level components and their interactions in d3re.

base (sets of atoms), this fixed-point necessarily exists (though in practice Datalog engines allow extra-logical behavior such as arithmetic). Datalog's conventional semantics is *monotonic*, in the sense that strictly more facts are accumulated as the fixed-point computation evolves—negation is allowed only when it may be stratified.

We define an *EDB metadatabase* as a graph of EDBs with labeled edges, $(\Delta, \xrightarrow{P})$, where Δ is a set of EDBs, each EDB enumerating tuples for a given set of relations, and $\xrightarrow{P}$ is a relation in $\Delta \times \mathit{Rules} \times \Delta$. When we process a program, P, using an input EDB, we traverse the graph $(\Delta, \xrightarrow{P})$ to find the most optimal, *compatible* EDB to start execution of P. Aided by Datalog's monotonicity, we define an EDB as compatible if it was produced by a subset of rules (or facts) from the input program / EDB. We conclude our formalism sketch by remarking that $(\Delta, \xrightarrow{P})$, given our usage, also forms a lattice.

B. Implementation of d3re

d3re is implemented in two parts: a REPL that communicates with Ghidra's GUI and a background service to manage the metadatabase and run the Datalog engine. The REPL currently communicates with Ghidra via a third-party extension named ghidra_bridge [15], which we plan to replace imminently with an extension using protocol buffers.

To execute a Datalog program P, d3re analyzes the file using the logic sketched in the above section to determine an optimal compatible EDB to use. In the common case, a user will gradually accumulate a stream of programs P, P', P''' consisting of a mix of rules and assumptions. In the future, we envision that certain assumptions (e.g., about calling conventions) may be implemented as GUI extensions rather than, e.g., manually-enumerated facts. After each run, the metadatabase will index the output facts and associate them with the program P, establishing an edge in the aforementioned graph. In our experiments, we refer to this as "caching."

IV. Evaluation

We evaluated d3re both qualitatively, by implementing several queries, and quantitatively by measuring its performance in benchmarks. While d3re is still a work in progress, we had several hypotheses we aimed to test as we designed and conducted these experiments. First, we wanted to understand whether d3re provided the necessary building blocks to enable replacing currently-existing Ghidra scripts. Second, we wanted to understand whether d3re could offer performance competitive with the kinds of Ghidra scripts that reverse engineers typically use. Last, we wanted to understand the performance of Ghidra for performing several repeated queries that might mirror a realistic end-to-end workload using d3re.

Ghidra Script Replication Study: we wanted to determine whether d3re could realistically be used to accomplish the kinds of tasks that reverse engineers face on a day-to-day basis. This is an admittedly challenging question, which we plan to eventually evaluate in several ways including user studies. However, as initial work in this direction we arbitrarily selected four Ghidra scripts listed in the `awesome-ghidra` GitHub repository [16]. The scripts we chose are listed in Table I, along with their corresponding lines of code in Python / Datalog. While Ghidra scripts may consist of a mix of Python and Java, our experience is that most scripts use a small subset of the Python API. The first three are relatively small and find instructions that match a specific template, e.g., non-xor finds xor instructions that aren't zeroing registers, and overflow heuristically searches for potential overflows in calls to common functions such as strcpy. Our largest was findcrypto, which looks for common cryptographic constants.

Qualitative Results of our Replication Study: Our experience using d3re to replace Ghidra scripts must be understood in the context that we are expert users and the developers of d3re. However, we are pleasantly surprised that d3re enabled us to succinctly write equivalent implementations of each Ghidra script: we rewrote each script in substantially less Datalog code. This is because the declarative nature of Datalog

TABLE I: Script size (lines of code) of Ghidra script (Python) vs. d3re Datalog

	Ghidra Python	d3re Datalog
non-xor	33	8
basicblk	37	4
overflow	60	18
findcrypto	166	45

TABLE II: Running time of Ghidra scripts vs. equivalent implementation in d3re (all numbers in seconds).

	bison	souffle	gzip	re2c	redis	rsync
non-xor Ghidra	3.569	107.5	2.205	3.903	10.52	3.050
non-xor d3re	0.518	6.515	0.097	0.756	1.306	0.486
overflow Ghidra	0.370	0.247	0.600	0.240	0.760	0.180
overflow d3re	0.617	0.319	0.051	0.094	0.095	0.044
basicblk Ghidra	340.6	–	4.664	472.1	1806	107.4
basicblk d3re	0.539	7.13	0.094	0.812	1.433	0.571
findcrypt Ghidra	0.207	1.033	0.224	0.214	0.475	0.289
findcrypt d3re	1.287	14.53	0.224	1.701	2.938	1.186

TABLE III: Runtime of successive invocations to d3re with (C) and without (S) rule caching.

	ddisasm	stack_var	heap_var	static_var	unl_static
souffle C	170	11.88	58.35	5.008	0.039
souffle S	170	11.79	66.02	67.00	66.52
bison C	7	0.932	1.409	0.545	0.022
bison S	7	0.934	1.916	2.122	2.075
re2c C	9	1.457	4.417	0.704	0.025
re2c S	9	1.494	5.257	5.449	5.458
redis C	11	1.918	2.544	1.302	0.025
redis S	11	1.919	3.525	3.712	3.726
rsync C	8	0.766	0.908	0.481	0.028
rsync S	8	0.783	1.325	1.423	1.384

eliminates the need for much of the conventional ceremony around, e.g., looping over instructions and checking against a type that we found in our evaluation scripts. Key to D^{3}RE's success, we believe, is its ability to directly use relations from ddisasm: we found that much of the necessary work of, e.g., filtering instructions by their type or operand was very useful at achieving succinct Datalog in practice. We are in the initial planning stages of developing a reverse engineering tutorial (or mini-course) around d3re, and are hoping to use this to recruit developers to get more realistic assessment of d3re's usability by professional REs.

Quantitative Results of our Replication Study: We hoped that d3re, being based on a high-performance Datalog solver, would offer performance competitive with Ghidra's current scripts. Each of our evaluation scripts processed the entire binary and would highlight or label certain instructions. To test the Ghidra scripts, we used Python's standard time function before and after the script's work finished. We evaluated the corresponding Datalog program by using Soufflé's internal performance timers. We then benchmark Ghidra vs. d3re on a corpus of six binaries (all sized less than 10MB), five from ddisasm's test suite and Soufflé, shown at the top of Table II. We used the latest versions of each pre-built in the latest Arch Linux, but we used a pre-built version of Soufflé. For each script, we waited for all of Ghidra's typical analyses to finish, and similarly we ran ddisasm to build up the initial input database for d3re.

The body of Table II compares the runtime of each Ghidra script versus its corresponding implementation in d3re. The single occurrence of – indicates that Ghidra did not finish within an hour. Broadly, we found that d3re outperformed Ghidra for each of the scripts in our replication study. As we had hoped, d3re's design allowed us to leverage useful relations from ddisasm. We found that many scripts do things like naive loops over sets of functions or symbols to locate some property. By contrast, the declarative style of d3re allowed us to write these not only more succinctly (e.g., Datalog naturally aggregates results) but also more efficiently—Soufflé optimally compiles input programs to efficient relational algebra kernels that loop only when necessary. We did observe various ways in which d3re's limitations could cause performance issues. For example, the findcrypto script scans the binary for 256-segments of code. d3re is built on Soufflé, which supports 64-bit primitive ints, but not 256-byte sequences. Thus, we had to build up sequences via a set of Datalog rules, causing inefficient memory representation due to the necessary duplication due to representing subsequences as Datalog facts.

Evaluating End-to-End Behavior in Subsequent Invocations: To understand the effect of caching via repeated calls to d3re, we ran four subsequent analysis queries in a row using both our caching-based approach and without caching (wherein we started only with the results of ddisasm). Our results are shown in Table III: the time of the cached run (C) is shown above the time for the correspond sequential run (S). As each query builds on the previous, we expect caching to reduce the amount of work and commensurately reduce the runtime. stack_var finds stack-allocated variables, while heap_var calculates stack variables holding pointers to heap values based on stack_var. static_var and unl_static attempt to find uninitialized global variables. Overall, we found rule caching was especially important on larger binaries versus sequential runs, justifying our choice to structure the metadatabase as a graph.

V. Related Work and Conclusion

We conclude with a brief discussion of proximately-related work that lies at the synthesis of reverse engineering and static / dynamic analysis, and contextualize this work in terms of our aspirations for the future of D^{3}RE. There has been extensive work using logic programming, and in particular Datalog, for static analysis of higher-level langauges such as Java [17]–[19]. The success of the Soufflé Datalog engine has inspired recent adoption of logic programming within the binary analysis community. For example, Datalog Disassembly uses Soufflé to achieve both faster and more-precise disassembly than the state-of-the-art disassembler Ramblr [13]. Similarly, OOAnalyzer uses XSB-Prolog, a version of Prolog implemented as a library [20]. We are currently reimplementing OOAnalyzer in d3re targeting C++ Linux binaries. We feel particularly excited about this direction because we believe Soufflé will be immediately more scalable than XSB-Prolog.

While there are a broad range of plugins for Ghidra and IDA Pro to load the *results* of static analyses, we believe d3re is the first to focus on the combination of open-ended deductive logical inference and rapid interactivity (enabled by our metadatabase). We believe the most closely related work is Ponce [21], which enables GUI-based symbolic execution. We plan to integrate symbolic execution into d3re as a long-term goal, inspired by the recent work of Formulog [22].

Our goal in this work was to introduce a new vision for reverse engineering, D^{3}RE, wherein expert users rapidly query high-performance logical inference engines to help them accomplish their day-to-day work in RE, vulnerability construction, and penetration testing. Visualization-based tools such as Ghidra are of immense value in understanding a binary, but have fundamentally different design considerations than high-performance logical inference engines (such as Soufflé).

Recent work in compiling Datalog to parallel relational algebra (e.g., Gilray et al. [23]) has enabled a new frontier in scale of Datalog-based analyses. We hope that developments such as these will someday enable realizing fully the vision of D^3RE to help reverse engineers perform powerful static binary analyses at unprecedented scale.

References

[1] D. Votipka, S. Rabin, K. Micinski, J. S. Foster, and M. L. Mazurek, "An observational investigation of reverse engineers' processes," in *USENIX Security 2020*, pp. 1875–1892, 2020.

[2] J. Smith, B. Johnson, E. Murphy-Hill, B. Chu, and H. Richter Lipford, "Questions developers ask while diagnosing potential security vulnerabilities with static analysis," pp. 248–259, 08 2015.

[3] B. Johnson, Y. Song, E. Murphy-Hill, and R. Bowdidge, "Why don't software developers use static analysis tools to find bugs?," pp. 672–681, 05 2013.

[4] "Ghidra released by national security agency." https://ghidra-sre.org/.

[5] Hexray, *Hex-rays:The IDA Pro disassembler and debugger.*

[6] "Radare2." https://github.com/radareorg/radare2.

[7] E. Schulte, J. Dorn, A. Flores-Montoya, A. Ballman, and T. Johnson, "Gtirb: Intermediate representation for binaries," 07 2019.

[8] Grammatech, "Gtirb." https://github.com/GrammaTech/gtirb-ghidra-plugin.

[9] "ret-sync." https://github.com/bootleg/ret-sync.

[10] "py-findcrypt-ghidra." https://github.com/AllsafeCyberSecurity/py-findcrypt-ghidra.

[11] "Grammatech's cyber grand challenge program repository." https://github.com/GrammaTech/cgc-cbs. Accessed: 2020-01-10.

[12] "Qualifier challenge - cromu_00038." https://github.com/GrammaTech/cgc-cbs/tree/master/cqe-challenges/CROMU_00038. Accessed: 2020-01-10.

[13] A. Flores-Montoya and E. Schulte, "Datalog disassembly," in *29th USENIX Security Symposium (USENIX Security 20)*, 2020.

[14] S. Ceri, G. Gottlob, and L. Tanca, "What you always wanted to know about datalog (and never dared to ask)," *IEEE Transactions on Knowledge and Data Engineering*, vol. 1, no. 1, pp. 146–166, 1989.

[15] "Ghidra bridge." https://github.com/justfoxing/ghidra_bridge. Accessed: 2020-01-10.

[16] "Awesome ghidra." https://github.com/AllsafeCyberSecurity/awesome-ghidra.

[17] Y. Smaragdakis, G. Kastrinis, and G. Balatsouras, "Introspective analysis: context-sensitivity, across the board," in *Proceedings of the 35th ACM SIGPLAN Conference on Programming Language Design and Implementation*, pp. 485–495, 2014.

[18] H. Jordan, B. Scholz, and P. Subotić, "Soufflé: On synthesis of program analyzers," in *International Conference on Computer Aided Verification*, pp. 422–430, Springer, 2016.

[19] B. Scholz, H. Jordan, P. Subotić, and T. Westmann, "On fast large-scale program analysis in datalog," in *Proceedings of the 25th International Conference on Compiler Construction*, CC 2016, (New York, NY, USA), pp. 196–206, Association for Computing Machinery, 2016.

[20] E. J. Schwartz, C. F. Cohen, M. Duggan, J. Gennari, J. S. Havrilla, and C. Hines, "Using logic programming to recover c++ classes and methods from compiled executables," in *Proceedings of the 2018 ACM SIGSAC Conference on Computer and Communications Security*, CCS '18, (New York, NY, USA), pp. 426–441, Association for Computing Machinery, 2018.

[21] "Ponce (ida pro plugin)." https://github.com/illera88/Ponce. Accessed: 2020-01-10.

[22] A. Bembenek, M. Greenberg, and S. Chong, "Formulog: Datalog for smt-based static analysis," *Proc. ACM Program. Lang.*, vol. 4, Nov. 2020.

[23] T. Gilray and S. Kumar, "Distributed relational algebra at scale," in *2019 IEEE 26th International Conference on High Performance Computing, Data, and Analytics (HiPC)*, pp. 12–22, 2019.

PyPANDA: Taming the PANDAmonium of Whole System Dynamic Analysis

Luke Craig*, Andrew Fasano*†, Tiemoko Ballo*, Tim Leek* Brendan Dolan-Gavitt‡ William Robertson†
*MIT Lincoln Laboratory {Luke.Craig,Andrew.Fasano,Tleek,Tiemoko.Ballo}@ll.mit.edu
†Northeastern University fasano.a@northeastern.edu, w.robertson@northeastern.edu
‡New York University brendandg@nyu.edu

Abstract—When working with real world programs, dynamic analyses often must be run on a whole-system instead of just a single binary. Existing whole-system dynamic analysis platforms generally require analyses to be written in compiled languages, a suboptimal choice for many iterative analysis tasks. Furthermore, these platforms leave analysts with a split view between the behavior of the system under analysis and the analysis itself—in particular the system being analyzed must commonly be controlled manually while analysis scripts are run. To improve this process, we designed and implemented PyPANDA, a Python interface to the PANDA dynamic analysis platform. PyPANDA unifies the gap between guest virtual machines behavior and analysis tasks; enables painless integrations with other program analysis tools; and greatly lowers the barrier of entry to whole-system dynamic analysis. The capabilities of PyPANDA are demonstrated by using it to dynamically evaluate the accuracy of three binary analysis frameworks, track heap allocations across multiple processes, and synchronize state between PANDA and a binary analysis platform. Significant challenges were overcome to integrate a scripting language into PANDA with minimal performance impact.

I. Introduction

Although program analyses commonly focus on individual programs, real-world computing environments are generally complex, multi-process systems running with various privilege levels (i.e., kernel and userspace) where data flow between processes through porous interfaces. Program analysis frameworks capable of supporting such environments are able to conduct whole-system instrumentation [5], slicing [11], and multi-process taint tracking [15], all of which can be used in reverse engineering, vulnerability discovery, and root cause analysis. These whole-system analyses are largely conducted dynamically (through emulation), as statically reasoning about whole-system interactions requires understanding OS internals (e.g., scheduling, IPC) as well as reasoning about an exponentially growing set of feasible states.

While single-application static and dynamic analysis frameworks such as angr [47], Manticore [25], Triton [39], IDA Pro[1], and Ghidra[2] all support conducting analyses from scripting languages, such functionality is rarely present in whole-system dynamic analysis platforms leading to cumbersome workflows. For example, consider the task of conducting a whole-system dynamic taint analysis on data sent to a custom kernel module that ultimately flow into a user space application. An analyst must approach this task through two distinct, but complementary, processes. First, they must drive the guest system's behavior: boot the system, log in, obtain the relevant source code and toolchains, compile the code (or copy in a prebuilt binary), and load the kernel module. Then, once the system under test is properly configured, the actual analysis can begin by further driving the guest system's behavior to send data into the kernel module and, at the same time, asking the analysis platform to apply taint labels to the data in the guest's memory. After some indeterminate amount of time, the analyst would then need to query the analysis platform to identify where and how tainted data reached the userspace application.

This workflow highlights a number of significant challenges largely related to user experience, as well as an active research problem. The research challenge lies in bridging the semantic gap [18] to extract meaning from the emulator's view of guest memory (e.g., how the results from the taint analysis can be tied back to process names and non-randomized program counters). The user experience challenges are easier to tackle, but no less important from an end-user's perspective. These include copying files into the guest, driving guest behavior, and synchronizing guest behavior with analysis tasks.

To address these challenges, we designed and implemented PyPANDA: a Python 3 interface to the PANDA [10] whole system analysis platform. PyPANDA allows for driving a guest execution, running Python code at any PANDA callback (capable of reading or writing guest state), and interacting with PANDA plugins. Since Python has a large ecosystem of libraries, PyPANDA also enables novel combinations of existing libraries with a whole system dynamic analysis framework.

The remainder of this paper is structured as follows. §II

Workshop on Binary Analysis Research (BAR) 2021
21 February 2021, Virtual

https://dx.doi.org/10.14722/bar.2021.23001
www.ndss-symposium.org

[1]https://hex-rays.com/products/ida
[2]https://ghidra-sre.org

covers necessary background information on the PANDA framework. The overall design goals for the project are presented in §III, and the implementation details are discussed in §IV. In §V, we detail PyPANDA's key features. §VI examines three program analysis tasks conducted with PyPANDA: comparing binary analysis frameworks on-the-fly, dynamically monitoring user and kernel-space heap allocations, and an entropy analysis of packed binaries linked with a web interface which transfers program state to Ghidra. We discuss our implementation of PyPANDA in §VII. Finally, we examine related work and conclude in §VIII and §IX.

II. PANDA

As PyPANDA builds atop PANDA, we provide background information on the PANDA dynamic analysis platform in this section. PANDA forks the QEMU emulator [1] to add callbacks before significant events in the emulation workflow, a record and replay system to enable offline analyses of guest behavior, and APIs for reading and writing guest state [10]. Together, these features enable dynamic analyses of "guest" systems (virtual machines) running under PANDA. PANDA's plugin system allows analysts to create tailored dynamic analyses by combining reusable, core plugins (e.g., a taint system) with custom, analysis-specific logic. PANDA has been used for reverse engineering, malware analysis, crash analysis, and trace collection [40, 42, 43, 27].

PANDA provides 48 callbacks at which plugins can register custom code to run. Each callback represents a low-level, architecture-agnostic operation such as before a basic block of code is executed, after a virtual memory address is read, or before the address space identifier (ASID) changes.

PANDA's record and replay system enables analysts to efficiently record guest behavior with little overhead and later replay its behavior under analysis. This allow for running slow analyses without the risk of analysis overhead affecting guest behavior.

PANDA has a small API for plugins to query and alter guest state but these interactions largely occur by plugins directly modifying emulator internal state.

PANDA provides a set of reusable plugins to enable common dynamic analysis tasks. Three notable plugins are PANDA's dynamic taint system taint2, a syscall tracking system syscalls2, and OS-introspection for both Linux and Windows OSI[3]. Plugins interact with one another through PANDA's plugin-to-plugin interface (PPP) which allows for plugins to provide custom callbacks which other plugins can request to be notified of. Plugins can also expose custom APIs which can be consumed by other plugins. The PPP interface allows for composition of plugin logic. For example, the file_taint plugin which applies taint labels to data read from a specified file, builds off syscalls2 and OSI to identify when data is read from the specified file and then uses taint2 to apply taint labels to those bytes.

[3]PANDA's OS-introspection requires using OSI profiles for the guest which describe sizes and offsets of key kernel data structures. These profiles can be generated from inside the guest or by analyzing a kernel's DWARF information when such information is available.

The workflow for a custom PANDA analysis typically begins by capturing a recording of an analyst interactively driving a guest system to exhibit some behavior of interest. With this recording in hand, the analyst begins the process of creating a new PANDA plugin in C or C++. That plugin can use the PPP interface to interact with other plugins and query the guest memory or registers at any point in time.

In our experience developing dozens of such plugins, we have found this task to be an iterative process. In their presentation of PANDA, Dolan-Gavitt et al. describe this clearly:

> "Plugins are typically written quickly and iteratively, running the replay over and over to construct more and better and deeper understanding of the important aspects of system execution, given the RE task." [10]

Although this task is quick and iterative, more akin to prototyping than production development, PANDA only supports plugin development in C and C++.

III. Design Goals

We begin our discussion of PyPANDA by identifying five design goals for the project.

1) High Performance Scripting: It is well known that Python programs typically execute slower than equivalent programs written in compiled languages such as C and C++ [13]. However, scripting languages such as Python are often better for rapid prototyping and gluing components together [29]. With this in mind, we determined that adding a new scripting interface to PANDA could greatly improve the project if the performance impact was acceptable.

2) Unified Analysis: The traditional PANDA workflow involves writing a plugin and either creating a recording manually or by using a script to control the serial console and PANDA monitor. This leads to scenarios in which key code is disparate: the process necessary to reproduce results may be scattered across different scripts or require manual effort.

We wish to replace this fragmented view of analysis and implementation and unify interaction outside the machine and analysis at the callback level. Beyond enabling a standardized reproducible method to generating recordings, this also allows for the entirety of the analysis to be done in a single script.

3) Facilitation of Integration: Integrations with publicly available libraries and frameworks enable developers to rapidly develop analyses without rebuilding common components. By expanding PANDA's interfaces to work

with a new language, we will allow PANDA developers to easily integrate with many additional libraries.

4) Ease of Use: Whole-system dynamic analysis can be difficult to learn due to the complexity of the systems being analyzed and unpolished user interfaces. We wish to lower the barrier of entry to this class of analyses by simplifying the PANDA interface without limiting experienced users.

5) Access to Core Emulator Data Structures: The API provided by PANDA enables analysts to complete common tasks such as reading or writing memory, but developing new dynamic analyses often requires interacting with a guest system in novel ways. To avoid limiting users to just features directly exposed by the PANDA API, users of our tool should be able to access and modify internal emulator data structures representing the guest system's state.

IV. System Design

To implement PyPANDA, we modified PANDA to build as a shared object and automatically generate headers parsable by CFFI. We then created a Python module to provide clean interfaces to PANDA's APIs, new features, unit tests, and examples. PyPANDA was implemented in 7,791 lines of Python code (after excluding autogenerated files) as measured by SLOCCount [48].

A. PANDA as a Library

PANDA is traditionally built as a series of binaries, one per supported architectures (panda-system-x86_64, panda-system-arm, etc.) and plugins are built for each architecture as shared objects. PANDA currently supports x86, AMD64, ARM, AArch64, PowerPC, and MIPS, but can be extended to support additional architectures. To enable PyPANDA we elected to build PANDA itself as a shared object. This allows us to intentionally invert the control the traditional PANDA model. In doing so we can provide unify the disparate components of whole-system dynamic analysis into a single script. Additionally, analyses will have full access to the emulator's internal data structures by means of shared library exported variables.

We chose not to simply embed a Python interpreter within the emulator, as done by PyREBox [7]. Although that approach would have simplified the development process, it cannot support our desired inversion of control model.

Constructing the libpanda objects required significant modifications to PANDA's Makefile and its codebase. In particular, PANDA's main function had to be split onto multiple stages such that control could transfer between PANDA and PyPANDA during initialization. Additionally, we expanded the PANDA API, a foreign-language agnostic interface for controlling PANDA and utilizing its functionality, in order to allow for library

Fig. 1. PyPANDA's architecture.

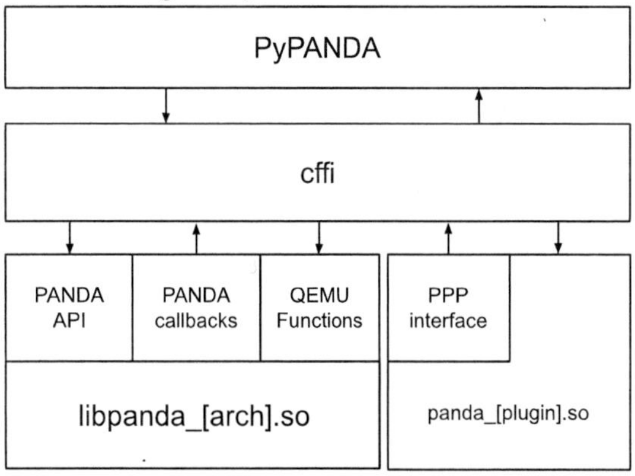

consumers to interact with the core of PANDA as well as its shared object plugins.

PyPANDA's overall architecture is shown in Figure 1. The libpanda objects and PANDA API are designed to allow clients to control PANDA (e.g., begin running a guest) as well as registering callbacks, interacting with C/C++ plugins, and altering guest state by exposing PANDA's APIs and internal objects. Together, these APIs and object allow for efficient control of and communication with PANDA from any language with a C foreign function interface[4].

B. Header Files

CFFI[5] enables interaction between C shared libraries and Python; it uses pycparser[6] to parse C header files that define structures along with function declarations and represents objects as if they were members of a traditional Python class. Unfortunately, pycparser, a pure Python parser for C, can only operate on preprocessed C headers—it cannot support preprocessor declarations such as ifdef and define. This presents a difficult problem when working with a project as large as PANDA. Pycparser documentation recommendations using the C Preprocessor to generate a single header file to avoid this problem. This is quite difficult in practice because pycparser is unable to parse C source which contains data format specifiers, such as attributes. An extra layer of complexity is added for the PANDA project because the output of the build process is not a single executable, but multiple executables targeted at various guest architectures. Structures are commonly defined using preprocessor macros to include different fields for different architectures. Attempting to generate preprocessed headers for PANDA with the C preprocessor produced over 50,000 lines of code and still caused parsing

[4]Although this work focuses on PyPANDA, we note that others have begun development of PANDA-rs, a Rust-interface to PANDA building off the architecture changes we introduced.

[5]https://cffi.readthedocs.io

[6]https://github.com/eliben/pycparser

Algorithm 1: Simplified Header Generation Process

```
Input: List of structure names, requiredStructureList to
       recursively pull definitions for
Output: Headers for all reachable types
for structure in requiredStructureList do
    potentialHeader ← pahole(structure)
while True do
    errors ← cffiBuild(potentialHeader) ;
    if errors = ∅ then
        break ;
    else
        missingStruct ← parseError(errors);
        if missingStruct is nested struct then
            potentialHeader ← pahole(missing) ;
        else
            potentialHeader cast missingStruct as void*;
return potentialHeader;
```

Fig. 2. PyPANDA Lifecycle

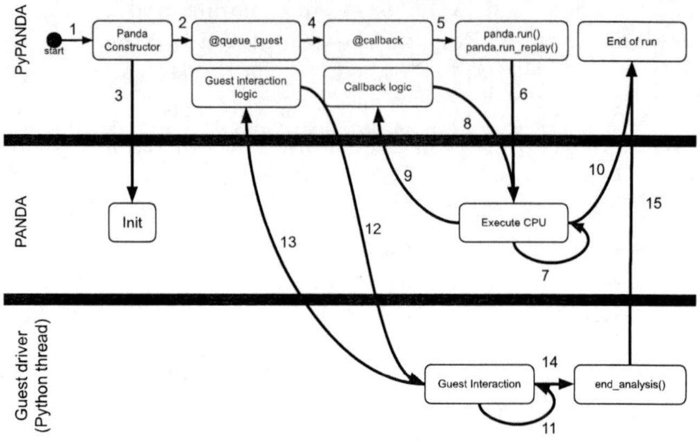

errors for pycparser. Even if the errors could be rectified, this approach is inefficient.

Instead of parsing the source code of PANDA, we use debug information from our compiled shared objects. We use Poke-a-Hole (or pahole) [38], a utility to parse DWARF debug information, to gather information about each structure. Poke-a-Hole was selected because it allows interpretation of classes as structures, suppression of aligned attributes, and suppression of force paddings.

We present a simple solution to this problem in Algorithm 1. For each architecture we support we begin by identifying a list of necessary structures manually. Using Poke-a-Hole, the definitions of these structures are added to a header file. This file and the corresponding shared object is provided into CFFI which may generate errors. These errors will identify the structures referenced, but not defined. When we identify a reference, but not defined structure we add it when necessary. Nested structures must be incorporated into the header file to capture the structure size and relative offsets of its members. On the contrary, referenced structures are merely pointers with an assigned type. We do not need to understand their structure layout to understand the previous type because a pointer is a constant size on a given architecture. To remove unnecessary structure reference we simply represent pointers to structures which are unnecessary as void pointers. Since these structures were not in the initial list of required structures, skipping their definition is acceptable. Our process continues adding structures until CFFI parses the header file without any errors. This solution produces a header file containing a minimal number of structures required (about 60) to operate PyPANDA, which in turn allows it to function with minimal overhead while maintaining in-depth knowledge of all necessary structures. Once generated, CFFI can consume this core header file along with other PANDA headers when running the relevant architecture.

V. Key Features

PyPANDA was created to enable rapid development of whole-system dynamic analysis through a simple, yet powerful Python interface. In this section, we walk through the sample code presented in Listing 1, its position in the lifecycle flow with Figure 2, and discuss the key features of PyPANDA.

```
1  from pandare import Panda
2  panda = Panda(generic='i386') # or x86_64, arm, etc.
3
4  @panda.queue_blocking
5  def drive_guest():
6    panda.revert_sync('root')
7    panda.copy_to_guest('host_directory')
8    print(panda.run_serial_cmd('host_directory/a_binary'))
9    panda.end_analysis()
10
11 @panda.cb_before_block_exec
12 def demo_before_block_exec(cpu, translation_block):
13   # Called before PANDA executes a basic block of code
14   print(f'About to run block at 0x{translation_block.pc:x}')
15   if translation_block.pc == 0x1234:
16     panda.disable_callback('demo_before_block_exec')
17
18 @panda.ppp('callstack_instr', 'on_call')
19 def calling(cpu, dest_addr):
20   #Called by callstack_isntr plugin on function call
21   print(f'Call to 0x{dest_addr:x}')
22
23 @panda.ppp('callstack_instr', 'on_ret')
24 def returning(cpu, dest_addr):
25   # Called by callstack_isntr plugin on function return
26   print(f'Return to 0x{dest_addr:x}')
27
28 panda.load_plugin('asidstory', {'width': 80})
29 panda.run() # Run emulation until call to end_analysis
```

Listing 1: Example PyPANDA script.

A. PANDA Constructor

As shown in Listing 1 on Lines 1 – 2, a script interacts with PANDA by importing the pandare package and constructing a Panda object. The constructor may specify an architecture, the guest memory size, a QCOW file (the QEMU virtual machine disk format which is used by PANDA), and other configurable properties. For convenience, a user may alternatively request a generic image from a list of nine images covering each architecture PyPANDA supports. For each generic image, we provide a QCOW file of a Linux system complete with a snapshot taken post-login and an OSI profile. The provided QCOW will be downloaded to disk prior to use.

B. Guest Interaction

Once a PANDA object has been created, the guest can be controlled through numerous functions as shown on Lines 4 – 9. Instead of waiting for the guest system to boot and then authenticating, an analysis can begin by reverting to a provided snapshot taken after log in. From there, a script can interact with the guest by sending commands over the serial console.

PyPANDA is running both the emulator as well as interacting with the guest. Guest interactions are labeled with @panda.queue_blocking which queues the function to run in a separate thread after the emulation begins. This multithreaded design avoids the risk of deadlocking when the analysis waits for the guest to complete a command. It can be seen visually in Figure 2 through its registration process with @queue_guest and its Guest Interaction loop. Only a function with such a decorator is allowed to call synchronous functions that depend on guest behavior such as revert_sync or run_serial_cmd.

PyPANDA supports copying files into a guest by creating an ISO file, connecting it to the guest system's emulated CD drive, mounting the drive and copying the files to a writable directory. For example, if the host machine has a directory called host_directory containing a binary named binary, the example code would copy that directory into the guest, run the binary, and end the analysis.

C. Starting and Stopping

Once the PANDA object is created and a function is queued up to drive the guest's behavior, a script must start the emulation with a call to panda.run() (Line 29). Once this function is called, the main Python thread will block until the guest powers off or the analysis is ended by another thread such as the call to end_analysis on Line 9 which correspond to Figure 2 edges 10, 14, and 15.

D. PANDA Callbacks

A PyPANDA script can register Python functions to run at any of PANDA's 48 callback functions through a decorator. Lines 10 – 16 show a function running on the before_block_exec callback. This will be called before each basic block of code is executed inside the guest. This callback function is run with two arguments, a CPUState structure which contains details of the virtual CPU and memory as well as a TranslationBlock which describes the block of code to be executed.

The decorator registering a function as a callback can take arguments to give the callback a specific name or to disable it. Figure 2 shows a call to @callback which registers callback logic below it after edge 2. By default the callback is enabled and named the same as the decorated function. A user can enable or disable callbacks by name.

E. PANDA Plugins

PyPANDA may load or unload compiled PANDA plugin and provide arguments as shown on Line 28. PyPANDA may also register callbacks through the PANDA's PPP interface (Lines 18 – 26) which will be triggered by a plugin. Plugins referenced by PPP decorators will be automatically loaded if necessary.

F. Record and Replay

Not shown in Listing 1 is PyPANDA's support for PANDA record and replay. PyPANDA provides a helper function to revert the guest to a snapshot, copy a directory from the host machine into the guest, and record the execution of a command.

```
@panda.queue_blocking
def take_recording(cpu, tb)
  panda.record_cmd('./host_directory/mybin',
          copy_dir='host_directory',
          recording_name='my_recording')
```

A PyPANDA script can register callbacks to introspect guest behavior and then—instead of running a live system—replay a recording using panda.run_replay('replay_name').

VI. Evaluation

In this section we present three case studies using PyPANDA and a comparison of its performance to PANDA. Code and a Docker container to reproduce these examples are available at https://github.com/panda-re/bar2021.

A. Dynamic Oracle IR Testing

1) Motivation: Modern binary analysis tools and techniques are often predicated on the ability to lift raw bytes encoding native processor instructions to a higher-level symbolic form, e.g. an Intermediate Representation (IR). IRs strive to faithfully represent the operational semantics of the underlying code while simultaneously abstracting away architecture-specific details.

Due to the sheer range of static and dynamic analysis tasks a binary analysis IR might support, from static decompiliation to dynamic taint analysis, there is no widely-accepted default criteria for evaluating the efficacy, correctness, or overall design of a given IR. Martignoni et al. [24] utilize differential fuzzing, comparing CPU state between IR-based emulators and physical processors. This technique has drawback of relying on random test case generation, the empirical likelihood of observing meaningful divergence is low. Kim et al. [21] introduce N-version IR Testing, essentially diffing the output of independently developed IRs for a given set of single-instruction inputs. This approach is hampered by a lack of semantic context, it only considers differences between single-instruction IR outputs.

In this PyPANDA case study, we briefly prototype a novel approach for comparing IRs that has practical applications for real-world reverse engineering: Dynamic Oracle IR Testing. QEMU, and, transitively, PANDA use TCG IR to emulate a range of native ISAs. Although this means that neither can be treated as absolute ground truth, both emulators are capable of booting entire operating systems kernels and running complex desktop and sever applications. Thier fidelity is sufficient for real-world tasks like performing malware analysis [22] and collecting code coverage metrics [8].

We assert that this fact makes PANDA a suitable oracle from which to derive practical conclusions about program execution, even if, like prior work in IR evaluation, the derived results do not carry formal guarantees. Our analysis evaluates disparate IRs against dynamic execution events observed for real-world programs under PANDA. Unlike differential fuzzing, we use realistic and non-random inputs. Unlike N-version IR testing, we evaluate against the outcomes of concrete dynamic emulation—not between the static IR lift results.

2) Experiment Design: In our demonstration of Dynamic Oracle IR Testing, we seek to compare the efficacy of leading binary analysis IRs for a real-world reverse engineering task: identifying function call and return semantics in an architecture-neutral fashion. Collecting dynamic call-stack traces is useful for general program understanding—it is a semantically meaningful metric of coverage and shines light on higher-level logic.

Whereas traditional userspace instrumentation utilities can trace system or library calls (e.g. strace and ltrace respectively), they do not have the ability to hook arbitrary internal functions. OS-assisted solutions, like patching bytes to trigger interrupts caught by a debugger, are intrusive. Moreover, static function identification in stripped binaries is, in the general case, an unsolved research problem—knowing where to patch a priori is difficult.

A whole-system emulator, on the other hand, can pause any user or kernel space program at an arbitrary point in execution without patching the target program. Our only remaining problem is function entry and exit identification. Assuming scope is a single concrete execution and not identification of all functions present: how, when analyzing stripped binaries, do we efficiently identify function boundaries and correlate them back to native-ISA program counters? While using a disassembler to check the encoding of every executed instruction might work for a single architecture, the ideal architecture-neutral solution is lifting to an IR to capable of encoding function call semantics.

Thanks to PyPANDA's ecosystem composability, an analyst is able to leverage any binary analysis IR that offers Python bindings. We select three such IRs and evaluate their ability to perform just-in-time call tracing as follows:

- Immediately following the execution of every basic block, filtering by process, we read the bytes encoding that block's instructions out of the guest.
- Each of three different IRs under test lift this basic block "shellcode" to their respective representation.
- We query each representation to find direct (e.g. offset-based) calls, indirect (e.g. register-based) calls, and returns.
- To measure correctness, we evaluate the IR's output when the subsequent basic block is executed—did the IR successfully identify a call and resolve the correct target?

PANDA serves as our dynamic oracle, generating both realistic non-random inputs (instruction byte streams from real-world programs) and expected conclusions (the next basic block executed is the correct destination for any direct call).

This is just one example application of Dynamic Oracle Testing. Our approach, essentially a feedback loop of concrete inputs and concrete results produced by faithful emulation, can be generalized to test any conclusion that can drawn from lifting native instruction streams to an IR.

3) IRs Under Test: We select three IRs based on three criteria:

- Readily available Python bindings: can be rapidly integrated into PyPANDA without the need to compile a library from source.
- Meaningful adoption: forms the basis of tooling used in industry or the by the security research community.
- Multi-architecture: capable of lifting, at minimum, x86, x64, ARM, and MIPS binaries.

VEX, our first selection, was originally introduced in the Valgrind memory profiling and debugging tool [41]. It represents a solution with wide general-purpose adoption, often appearing in industry software development workflows [44]. We test PyVEX v9.0.4663 [32], the modified variant used in the Angr symbolic execution toolkit and countless other open-source security tools.

PCODE [30], our second selection, underpins Ghidra—a reverse engineering application released by the NSA in 2019 and quickly gaining community traction as an alternative to paid, closed-source solutions. PCODE represents a government-generated technology developed in largely in isolation, though its roots trace back to academic work [35]. Despite being relatively new to the public, we have already seen community support for lifting new processors via PCODE's underlying SLEIGH specification format. We test PyPCODE v0.0.2 [31] and use SLEIGH definitions from Ghidra 9.2.

BAP [4], our final selection, powered the winner for DARPA's 2016 Cyber Grand Challenge [9]. BAP represents an academia-generated solution, widely citied in

TABLE I
Userspace Call/Return Semantic Detection Rates by IR

IR	DCall TP	IDCalls	Rets	Fails
VEX (x86)	637	75	342	0
PCODE (x86)	635	85	342	0
BAP (x86)	637	75	342	0
VEX (x64)	474	47	333	0
PCODE (x64)	396	45	333	1323
BAP (x64)	474	47	333	0
VEX (ARM)	532	58	338	0
PCODE (ARM)	529	58	338	0
BAP (ARM)	529	0	338	0
VEX (MIPS)	252	608	526	9
PCODE (MIPS)	244	608	531	0
BAP (MIPS)	DNF	DNF	DNF	DNF

TABLE II
Kernelspace Call/Return Semantic Detection Rates by IR

IR	DCall TP	IDCalls	Rets	Fails
VEX (x86)	3631	0	1922	4
PCODE (x86)	3644	0	1925	0
BAP (x86)	DNF	DNF	DNF	DNF
VEX (x64)	4448	0	2504	9
PCODE (x64)	4172	6	2501	4418
BAP (x64)	DNF	DNF	DNF	DNF
VEX (ARM)	2119	158	1490	0
PCODE (ARM)	2117	158	1484	0
BAP (ARM)	DNF	DNF	DNF	DNF
VEX (MIPS)	2635	212	1581	236
PCODE (MIPS)	2614	238	1590	0
BAP (MIPS)	DNF	DNF	DNF	DNF

relevant research. Though BAP does not enjoy a level of community adoption comparable to our other two IRs, it remains actively developed. We test BAP's 2.2.0 Debian release along with the 1.3.1 pip package — the latter subprocesses the former.

In the interest of reproducibility, we opt not to evaluate closed-source, commercial IRs that we cannot redistribute—notably Binary Ninja's LLIL and MLIL [2].

4) Experiment Results: Testing is performed on a Linux guest executing a sample binary (GNU coreutils program whoami). For all supported architectures, we leverage PyPANDA's record and replay functionality to make all results fully reproducible. For each IR, we measure ability to detect call and return semantics for both userspace and kernelspace code as shown in Tables I, II.

DCall TP is the number of direct call true positives found. IDCalls is the number of indirect calls found (we do not count these against a static IR, which has no way to determine call target). Rets is the number of returns found. Fails is the number of times an IR failed to disassemble a basic block, meaning either an exception occurred or no statements were produced. The first three metrics are for unique basic blocks, meaning we do not count multiple loop iterations—each block is lifted only once and the results are cached. Failure count does not represent unique blocks: it is a raw total that can increase with loop iterations.

These data indicate that VEX is the most accurate and robust IR of the three, particularly for x64 lifting. PCODE performs slightly better in x86 kernel space due to support for privileged instructions missing from the other IRs (e.g. sysexit) and better ability to resolve call encodings with high destination addresses. Where DNF appears for BAP, our analysis run did not finish due to a Python subprocess API, Popen, hanging indefinitely when attempting to run the BAP binary. We checked a random selection of these failures and found that the BAP binary produced correct output when run manually via a terminal. Unfortunately, this means our results for BAP are inconclusive — although it's correctness is comparable to that of VEX in analyses which finish.

In addition to lift accuracy measures, we consider lift performance. VEX is consistently the fastest of the three ($\approx$0.3 ms/block), lifting blocks at approximately 1.25x the speed of PCODE ($\approx$0.4 ms/block) and 20x the speed of BAP ($\approx$7.0 ms/block). BAP's relative sluggishness is the result of Python interoperability, not the IR itself: BAP's Python bindings subprocess an OCaml binary and collect it's output over a pipe. By contrast, VEX and PCODE's Python bindings call into C/C++ libraries via CFFI.

PCODE has a considerable setup cost, taking about 800 ms to parse a SLEIGH specification and initialize the lifter. We chose to exclude this setup time from our measurements because it is a one-time initialization step and does not factor into how long it takes to subsequently lift basic blocks, whereas we are concerned with measuring per-block performance. It is worth noting that this initialization strategy gives PCODE a potential advantage: the core library does not need to be re-compiled to support new architectures, as the lifter is dynamically configured using the SLEIGH specification file.

B. Heap Monitoring

Many dynamic analysis tasks depend on the ability to track function calls, arguments, and return values from specific library or kernel functions. For example, Valgrind [41], Dr. Memory [3], and other systems monitor calls related to heap allocations (e.g., malloc, free, __kmalloc, kfree, etc.) in order to identify memory errors. Such analyses have been traditionally been built by modifying compilers (e.g., Purify [37]), preloading libraries at runtime (e.g., Malt [45]), or through virtual machine introspection (e.g., Undangle [6]).

We implement a heap tracking analysis using PyPANDA in under 200 lines of Python code. The script hooks kernel heap allocation made with __kmalloc and freed with kfree as well as userspace heap allocations made with malloc and freed with free through libc. To simplify this example, we do not attempt to track all possible heap allocations (e.g., those made with calloc).

The key components of PyPANDA that enable this analysis are its ability to drive guest execution, hook specific guest program counters to trigger callback functions, and its ability to extract process-level information using PANDA.

1) Hook Setup: PANDA's hooks plugin allow for registering a function to run before the guest executes an instruction a given program counter. To begin this analysis, the script must first identify the addresses that must be hooked. The address of kfree, ___kmalloc and vmalloc can be extracted from the System.map file using standard Linux utilities controlled by PyPANDA's run_serial_cmd function. These addresses are in the kernel and will not change while data are collected.

To record the necessary information, the requested size must be recorded when ___kmalloc and vmalloc are entered and the return values must be recorded when they returns. This script includes a simple helper function to store this information and then call a user-provided function when the function returns:

```
def hook_ret_with_args(panda, name, entry_addr, func=None,
                                    asid=None, kernel=False):
  hooked_args = []

  @panda.hook(entry_addr, asid=asid, kernel=kernel)
  def __enter(cpu, tb, h):
    # Grab ret_addr off stack and first two args
    sp = panda.arch.get_reg(cpu, 'rsp')
    ret_addr = panda.virtual_memory_read(cpu, sp, 8, fmt='int')
    hooked_args = [panda.arch.get_arg(cpu, i) for i in range(2)]

    # Setup a new hook to run just once at ret_addr
    # and call user-provided func
    @panda.hook(ret_addr, asid=asid, kernel=kernel)
    def __return(cpu, tb, h):
      h.enabled = False
      retval = panda.arch.get_reg(cpu, 'rax')
      func(cpu, hooked_args, retval)
```

The script also needs to hook libc functions for tracking userspace heap behavior. Like with ___kmalloc, the analysis for malloc requires tracking both the size passed into the function as well as the pointer that is returned. The hook_ret_with_args function can be used again to do this.

The script captures the offsets into libc to malloc and free using the run_serial_cmd function again. Since libc can be loaded at different base addresses for each process, the hooked address for each process must be the libc base address plus the offsets of these functions.

2) Process Hooking: Whenever a process may load libc into memory, we must check if it was loaded and, if so, add a new set of hooks for that process. We may discover libc has been loaded after a context switch or after a process uses the mmap or brk syscall to load a library. The script registers PPP-style callbacks for these events with the OSI and syscalls plugins and calls add_hooks_if_necessary after each. At each callback, we check if the current process lacks hooks, and if so use the OSI plugin to determine if a library named libc has been loaded into its memory space. If so, it calculates the address of malloc and free and adds the relevant hooks.

```
def add_hooks_if_necessary(cpu):
  if not analysis_active: return # Don't setup hooks until we're ready

  asid = panda.current_asid(cpu)
  if asid in hooked_asids: return # Already hooked this process

  name = panda.get_process_name(cpu)
  # Find current libc address and update hooks
  for mapping in panda.get_mappings(cpu):
    if mapping.file != panda.ffi.NULL and \
       b'/libc-' in panda.ffi.string(mapping.file):
      hooked_asids.add(asid)
      hook_ret_with_args(panda, f'{name}_malloc', mapping.base +
        malloc_offset, asid=asid,
        func=lambda cpu, in_args, retval: add_alloc(retval, in_args[0],
            asid=panda.current_asid(cpu),
            name=panda.get_process_name(cpu)))

      # Note for free we don't need return val, just the entry args
      @panda.hook(mapping.base+free_offset, asid=asid, kernel=False)
      def process_free(cpu, tb, h):
        buf = panda.arch.get_reg(cpu, 'rax')
        asid = panda.current_asid(cpu)
        rem_alloc(buf, asid=asid)
```

3) Allocation Tracking: With the hooks set up, the implementation of heap allocation tracking is trivial: when objects are allocated, their size, address, and requesting ASID is recorded in a dictionary. Kernel allocations are indicated by storing an ASID of 0. When objects are freed they are deleted from the dictionary using the ASID and address.

4) Guest Control: After all the hooking and allocation tracking logic is configured, a binary is copied into the guest and executed. During its execution, the hooks are enabled and a callback is setup to report the current allocations every 1,000 basic blocks.

5) Visualization: The recorded data are visualized through the Python library matplotlib [17] as shown in Figure 3. The total number of active heap allocations is presented for each ASID running in the guest system.

Fig. 3. Visualizing heap objects allocated over time.

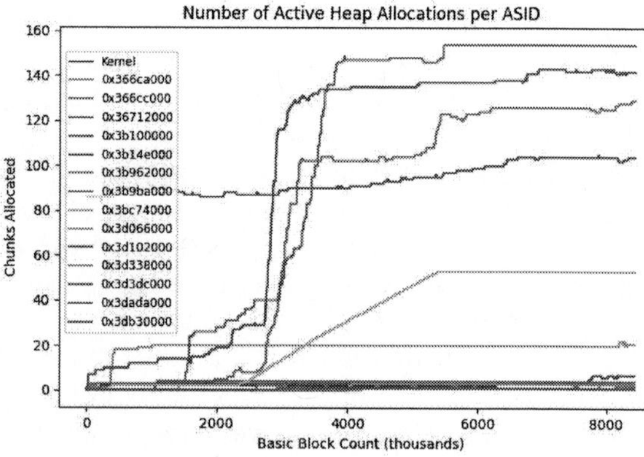

6) Summary: This section describes building a standalone dynamic analysis tool for heap analysis with PyPANDA. The hook_ret_with_args helper function

demonstrates how a complex functions not supported by the PANDA API can easily be implemented in PyPANDA. The entire analysis is built in under 200 lines of Python code and runs with a wall time of 17.24s on average (n=100).

C. Extracting and Transferring Packed Executables to Ghidra with human-in-the-loop Entropy Analysis

A common technique seen in malicious software is runtime packing. In malware, runtime packing is used as a means of obfuscating the binary to make it more difficult to identify it as malicious [19]. This is typically accomplished by providing a binary to a "packer" program. The packer program takes the binary and either compresses or encrypts it and produces a new program with the binary data. When run this program takes the encrypted or compressed binary data from its data section, reverses the operation applied to the data, and then transfers control to the original program. This has the effect of making reverse engineering the program statically very difficult. However, the process of packing leaves a mark: packed regions typically have high entropy [23]. This characteristic can be used to make an educated guess as to whether or not a binary may be packed. PANDA is uniquely suited to analyze malware as its position in the hypervisor makes it more difficult to detect and its record and replay features allow for reproducibility of functionality.

In this section we will discuss a PyPANDA script which records a whole-system running a packed binary. The script is given a process name to consider and computes the entropy of all segments of memory throughout the life of the process. As it performs this analysis, the script spawns a Python Flask[7] web server which serves live-updating graphs the entropy of the process memory. If a user is interested in looking at the program state at some point along the graph they may click on the point. The Flask server will receive their selection and spawn a new process which replays the recording up to the point of interest, extracts all mapped virtual memory in the process, and transfers it to static analysis platform Ghidra through the use of ghidra_bridge[8], It does all of this, including generating the recording, in fewer than 250 lines of Python.

1) Entropy Analysis: Entropy analysis is quite simple in PyPANDA. We begin by identifying the ASID for the process of interest by registering a callback on asid_changed. After each asid change, we check if the name of the current process matches the provided name.

Once the ASID is identified, the entropy analysis can begin. We set a callback on before_block_exec which first cheks that the correct ASID is running and the guest is in userspace. We provide an tunable parameter, granularity, which controls how frequently we compute the process' entropy. When it is time to compute entropy, the script reads all memory in the process by iterating over the mappings provided by the OSI plugin. We then format the data, compute a value for the entropy using the scipy library [46], and record it along with the current instruction count.

2) Flask server: In order to display this data to the analyst we use the Flask Python module. The Flask server runs using multiprocessing with a dedicated thread per connection to enable live-updating of entropy visualization as new data become available. When a point on the graph is clicked, the Flask server starts a new process to transition the program state at that point in time into Ghidra.

Figure 4 shows this graph for a binary packed by UPX [28] running. After unpacking, the binary reaches a steady state and performs normal operations.

Fig. 4. Entropy graph of a packed process unpacking itself and running as seen through Flask.

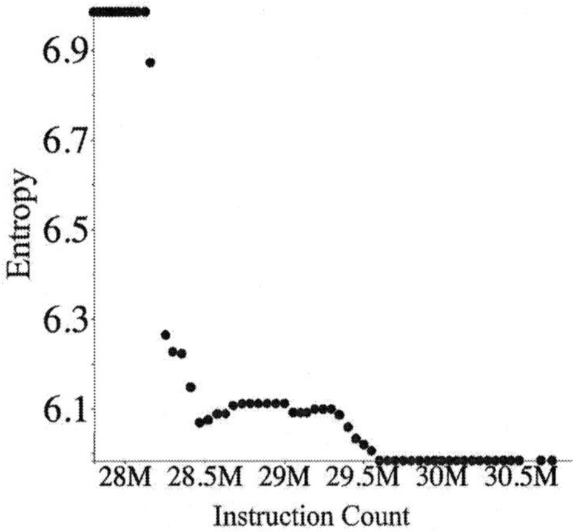

3) Transitioning to Ghidra: Our transition to Ghidra begins by establishing a connection to ghidra_bridge. We do this through the use of ghidra_bridge, a Python 3 module for Remote Procedure Calls (RPC) to Ghidra using their Jython interface. When we establish a connection through ghidra_bridge we declare the namespace to be globals(). This populates our main namespace with RPC variables and allows us to do scripting with Ghidra in a very similar manner to normal Ghidra scripting. Next, we run our replay until we reach the instruction count selected by the user. At this point we can to move our program's virtual memory to Ghidra. This is a fairly simple process. In PyPANDA, we simply use our OSI capabilities to list the virtual memory mappings for our program and read them. In Ghidra, we establish a memory transaction, create a memory segment per virtual memory mapping, and then populate it with our data. Lastly, we take the program counter at this point in time and set cursor position in Ghidra to that program counter and perform an auto-analysis of the program.

[7]https://flask.palletsprojects.com

[8]https://github.com/justfoxing/ghidra_bridge

TABLE III
Runtime of PANDA vs PyPANDA analyses, averaged (n=10).

Replay	Analysis	Total Callbacks Run	PANDA Runtime	PyPANDA Runtime	% Difference
grep (4M insns.)	no-op	0	$0.88s \pm 0.03$	$0.93s \pm 0.05$	$6\% \pm 7$
	asid_logger	14	$0.86s \pm 0.01$	$0.93s \pm 0.03$	$8\% \pm 4$
	unique_bbs	0.94M	$0.92s \pm 0.03$	$1.40s \pm 0.03$	$53\% \pm 6$
wget (8M insns.)	no-op	0	$1.02s \pm 0.02$	$1.08s \pm 0.04$	$5\% \pm 5$
	asid_logger	21	$1.04s \pm 0.03$	$1.08s \pm 0.03$	$4\% \pm 4$
	unique_bbs	1.83M	$1.10s \pm 0.03$	$2.02s \pm 0.03$	$83\% \pm 5$
sleep (426M insns.)	no-op	0	$8.20s \pm 0.16$	$8.28s \pm 0.25$	$1\% \pm 4$
	asid_logger	108	$8.36s \pm 0.24$	$8.23s \pm 0.23$	$2\% \pm 4$
	unique_bbs	89.45M	$13.46s \pm 0.24$	$51.67s \pm 0.35$	$284\% \pm 7$

TABLE IV
Source Lines of Code for Simple Analyses

Analysis	PANDA (C++)	PyPANDA
unique_bbs	20	9
asid_logger	18	8

4) Summary: In this section we described a PyPANDA script which performs graphs the entropy of a binary in real time and allows a user to transition program state from any point in time into Ghidra for subsequent analysis. This integration between Ghidra and PANDA allows PyPANDA users to leverage Ghidra's decompiler and its analyses. PyPANDA enables such integrations by easily synchronizing state between PANDA and other projects with Python interfaces. This integration between a disprate set of tools shows the value of using Python for a scripting language. This analysis was built in under 250 lines of Python code.

D. Performance comparision of PyPANDA to PANDA

Unfortunately, the case studies presented are too complex to reasonably reimplement without PyPANDA. To compare PyPANDA's performance to that of PANDA, we developed two simple plugins in both PANDA and PyPANDA. The first plugin, unique_bbs, tracks every distinct program counter executed by storing it in a set. At the end of the execution, the size of the set is printed. The second, asid_logger, reports every time the ASID changes by printing out the new ASID. The lines of source code for each plugin are presented in Table IV.

Three PANDA recordings were captured on an i386 guest (using PyPANDA for convenience):

1) wget downloading from example.com.
2) grep searching through /etc/passwd.
3) sleep running for 20 seconds.

For each recording, we ran both the PANDA plugin and the PyPANDA plugin 10 times and recorded the time taken[9]. We also run each recording through PANDA and PyPANDA with no analyses enabled (labeled no-op). The average run time along with standard deviation for each plugin is presented in Table III.

[9]We use the Linux time utility and combine the CPU time with the kernel time to capture how long the process was actually executing.

Unsurprisingly, PyPANDA runs slower than compiled PANDA plugins. There are additional costs when running PyPANDA: a fixed startup cost to launching a Python interpreter, loading the Python module, and a cost for each time PANDA switches into PyPANDA (i.e., in a callback). It is this last cost which is the most significant to consider when developing PyPANDA scripts. As can be seen in Table III the no-op and asid_logger analyses have near-identical run times to native C. Only when the number of callbacks run increases dramatically do we see a significant performance cost. We believe this performance is sufficient to enable many analyses to be completed in PyPANDA.

When high-speed analyses are desired (i.e., for algorithmically complex analyses of live systems) we tend to consider two avenues. First, a PyPANDA prototype could be developed and then transitioned into C or C++ to meet specific performance needs. Second, move more speed-critical portions of code into a C or C++ plugin. We have found that for many callbacks there is a series of conditions (e.g. not in kernel, in specific process, etc.) for the machine which must be met before complex analysis is done. Writing a simple C plugin which handle this more primitive initial checking before calling into Python can lead to drastic performance improvements. For examples of plugins of this type consider hooks, which calls a callback when a program counter reaches a particular value and mem_hooks which calls a callback when a memory transactions takes place that meet specified criteria.

VII. Discussion

Having successfully used PyPANDA to enable three distinct dynamic analyses, we now consider if PyPANDA met our design goals.

1) High Performance Scripting: PyPANDA's meets our goal of enabling high performance scripting as shown in §VI-D. The core runtime overhead of PyPANDA with few callbacks enabled is consistently below 10%. However, there is a slight performance difference between callbacks implemented in C/C++ code vs Python code. Generally, compiled code will execute faster than Python code implementing the same behaviors. As the complexity of the logic run in a callback increases or the number of times callbacks are run increases, the PyPANDA overhead will grow more

pronounced. As previously shown in Table III, we see an overhead as high as 284% when running nearly a simple callback 90 million callbacks, but much lower overhead for callbacks that run less frequently. This performance trade-off fits well within our objective.

2) Unified Perspective: We sought to build a system to unify the interfaces to interact with a guest and to control its analysis. This is a shift in perspective from the plugin system normally used for analysis with PANDA. Traditionally PANDA is run from the command line with various arguments which dictate the plugins to be loaded and their various settings. Instead of compiling in an interpreter to a plugin in PANDA we intentionally inverted the normal control structure of a plugin. We accomplished this through compiling PANDA as a shared object. In doing so we made PyPANDA encapsulate PANDA and provided a path for other languages to encapsulate PANDA as well through our PANDA API. In PyPANDA the process begins with a Python script executed which sets up an emulated machine, various plugins and their arguments, its own python callbacks, and then chooses to either run the machine or a replay. PyPANDA maintains the ability to interact with and control the emulated machine through a separate thread which can interact with various PANDA interfaces including the PANDA monitor and the serial console. In doing so we have provided a reproducible mechanism to simultaneously control guest behavior and analyze it from a single script.

3) Ease of Use: Through building PyPANDA, we took several steps to improve the usability of PANDA. The largest change is that we provided "generic" QCOW images for every PANDA supported architecture which are automatically downloaded along with a PANDA OSI profile prior to use. All the required settings to run each generic image are built into PyPANDA so only the image's name must be specified by a user. Another significant improvement is that we created a docker container and Python package for PyPANDA that can be installed through the Python package manager, pip.

4) Integrations: A goal of this project was to enable integrations between PANDA other software projects. By selecting Python as our scripting language, we found a significant number of relevant projects that could be easily imported. As described in § VI, VEX, PyPCODE, Flask, and Ghidra were all seamlessly integrated with PyPANDA to enable program analyses.

5) Access to Internal PANDA Data Structures: By using CFFI with the PANDA shared libraries and autogenerated headerfiles, PyPANDA can present parsed structures as Python objects. This allows for nested structure access as well as easy modification of structure elements by name.

VIII. Related Work

There are many projects which are closely related to PyPANDA. Other emulators have Python bindings to enable program analysis but focus on execution of shellcode of single binaries as opposed to a whole system. For example, the Unicorn Engine [34] is another QEMU fork with Python bindings capable of running shellcode from many architectures. The Qiling framework [33, 20] is a binary emulation framework built on top of Unicorn with Python bindings which supports running individual binaries in an analysis platform, but not a full operating system.

Many dynamic analysis tools have been created with Python interfaces. Frida [36] injects custom hooking and tracing logic into compiled binaries using a Python interface. Angr [47] is a Python-based framework that enables static analyses of binaries and symbolic execution. Recent advances to Angr [14] allow transfering state to and from concrete execution environments (e.g., QEMU) which enables transitioning between concrete and symbolic executions.

Volatility [12] and Libvmi [49] enable virtual machine introspection from Python which is akin to PANDA's OSI plugin. Both systems have OS-specific profiles which are used to bridge the semantic gap [18] to provide meaningful information about an operating system running in an emulator.

avatar^2 [26] is an orchestration platform designed to transfer the state of a whole system between different analysis platforms or a physical system. It initially supported transferring state into and out of PANDA as well as limited interactions with both the guest through PANDA's gdbstub as well as PANDA itself (loading plugins, recording/replaying) through the PANDA monitor. Recent updates to avatar^2 have added support for a "PyPANDA target" which enables avatar^2 scripts to use the PANDA API and callback system. Through this interface, the avatar^2 developers used PyPANDA's hooks plugin for what they describe as a "huge speedup" as compared to avatar^2's traditional, GDB-based hook system [16].

Another related project to PyPANDA is PyREBox, a dynamic analysis system built on top of QEMU with Python-based callbacks. Although similar on the surface, there are three significant differences between PyREBox and PyPANDA. First, PyREBox is built on QEMU so it cannot leverage PANDA's plugin system, callbacks, nor its record/replay system. Beyond this, PyREBox is implemented by embedding a Python interpreter within the emulator. As previously discussed in §III, this apparoch is limiting as it prevents both our unified perspective of dynamic analysis and access to emulator internal structures. Finally, PyREBox currently supports only Python 2 for scripting and is limited to the x86 and x86_64 architectures.

IX. Conclusions

Through this work, we identified that existing whole-system dynamic analysis platforms largely lack scripting interfaces, and have a split view of guest behavior and analyses. We designed PyPANDA to provide a Python interface to the PANDA dynamic analysis platform and to unify the analysts view of a system. Using PyPANDA, we describe the process of implementing 3 distinct whole-system dynamic analyses: evaluating binary analysis frameworks, tracking heap allocations in all processes, and dynamically moving program state into the Ghidra reverse engineering framework. We examine the analyses and discuss how PyPANDA achieved the requisite goals. PyPANDA has been merged into the PANDA project and is now publicly available at https://github.com/panda-re/panda. We hope this platform will make the field of dynamic analysis more welcoming for beginners while allowing experts to conduct complex analyses and integrations.

Acknowledgements

The authors wish to acknowledge the following individuals for their contributions and support: Chris Connelly, Marius Muench, Wesley Van Pelt, Andrew Mueller, and Michael Rusnak.

This research was supported in part by National Science Foundation (NSF) Award 1657199. Any opinions, findings, conclusions, or recommendations expressed are those of the authors and not necessarily of the NSF.

References

[1] Fabrice Bellard. "QEMU, a fast and portable dynamic translator." In: USENIX Annual Technical Conference, FREENIX Track. Vol. 41. 2005, p. 46.

[2] Binary Ninja Intermediate Language Series, Part 0: Overview. url: https://docs.binary.ninja/dev/bnil-overview.html.

[3] Derek Bruening and Qin Zhao. "Practical memory checking with Dr. Memory". In: International Symposium on Code Generation and Optimization (CGO 2011). IEEE. 2011, pp. 213–223.

[4] David Brumley, Ivan Jager, Thanassis Avgerinos, and Edward J. Schwartz. "BAP: A Binary Analysis Platform". In: Proceedings of the 23rd International Conference on Computer Aided Verification. CAV'11. Snowbird, UT: Springer-Verlag, 2011, pp. 463–469. isbn: 9783642221095.

[5] Prashanth P. Bungale and Chi-Keung Luk. "PinOS: A Programmable Framework for Whole-System Dynamic Instrumentation". In: Proceedings of the 3rd International Conference on Virtual Execution Environments. VEE '07. San Diego, California, USA: Association for Computing Machinery, 2007, pp. 137–147. isbn: 9781595936301. doi: 10.1145/1254810.1254830. url: https://doi.org/10.1145/1254810.1254830.

[6] Juan Caballero, Gustavo Grieco, Mark Marron, and Antonio Nappa. "Undangle: early detection of dangling pointers in use-after-free and double-free vulnerabilities". In: Proceedings of the 2012 International Symposium on Software Testing and Analysis. 2012, pp. 133–143.

[7] Cisco-Talos. Cisco-Talos/pyrebox: Python scriptable Reverse Engineering Sandbox, a Virtual Machine instrumentation and inspection framework based on QEMU. url: https://talosintelligence.com/pyrebox.

[8] Couverture. url: http://www.open-do.org/projects/couverture/.

[9] Cyber Grand Challenge (CGC). url: https://www.darpa.mil/program/cyber-grand-challenge.

[10] Brendan Dolan-Gavitt, Josh Hodosh, Patrick Hulin, Tim Leek, and Ryan Whelan. "Repeatable reverse engineering with PANDA". In: Proceedings of the 5th Program Protection and Reverse Engineering Workshop. 2015, pp. 1–11.

[11] Brendan Dolan-Gavitt, Tim Leek, Michael Zhivich, Jonathon Giffin, and Wenke Lee. "Virtuoso: Narrowing the semantic gap in virtual machine introspection". In: 2011 IEEE symposium on security and privacy. IEEE. 2011, pp. 297–312.

[12] The Volatility Foundation. Volatility. url: https://www.volatilityfoundation.org/.

[13] Isaac Gouy and B Fulgham. The computer language benchmarks game. 2017. url: https://benchmarksgame-team.pages.debian.net/benchmarksgame/index.html.

[14] Fabio Gritti, Lorenzo Fontana, Eric Gustafson, Fabio Pagani, Andrea Continella, Christopher Kruegel, and Giovanni Vigna. "SYMBION: Interleaving Symbolic with Concrete Execution". In: 2020 IEEE Conference on Communications and Network Security (CNS). IEEE. 2020, pp. 1–10.

[15] Andrew Henderson, Aravind Prakash, Lok Kwong Yan, Xunchao Hu, Xujiewen Wang, Rundong Zhou, and Heng Yin. "Make it work, make it right, make it fast: building a platform-neutral whole-system dynamic binary analysis platform". In: Proceedings

of the 2014 International Symposium on Software Testing and Analysis. 2014, pp. 248–258.

[16] Grant Hernandez, Marius Muench, Tyler Tucker, Hunter Serle, Weidong Zhu, Patrick Traynor, and Kevin Butler. Emulating Samsung's Baseband for Security Testing. Blackhat. 2020.

[17] John D Hunter. "Matplotlib: A 2D graphics environment". In: Computing in science & engineering 9.3 (2007), pp. 90–95.

[18] Bhushan Jain, Mirza Basim Baig, Dongli Zhang, Donald E Porter, and Radu Sion. "Sok: Introspections on trust and the semantic gap". In: 2014 IEEE symposium on security and privacy. IEEE. 2014, pp. 605–620.

[19] G. Jeong, E. Choo, J. Lee, M. Bat-Erdene, and H. Lee. "Generic unpacking using entropy analysis". In: 2010 5th International Conference on Malicious and Unwanted Software. 2010, pp. 98–105. doi: 10.1109/MALWARE.2010.5665789.

[20] Lau KaiJern. Qiling Framework. url: https://www.qiling.io/.

[21] Soomin Kim, Markus Faerevaag, Minkyu Jung, SeungIl Jung, DongYeop Oh, JongHyup Lee, and Sang Kil Cha. "Testing Intermediate Representations for Binary Analysis". In: Proceedings of the 32nd IEEE/ACM International Conference on Automated Software Engineering. ASE 2017. Urbana-Champaign, IL, USA: IEEE Press, 2017, pp. 353–364. isbn: 9781538626849.

[22] David Korczynski. Building a custom malware sandbox with PANDA - Part 1. 2019. url: https://adalogics.com/blog/Building-a-custom-malware-sandbox-with-PANDA-Part-1.

[23] Robert Lyda and James Hamrock. "Using Entropy Analysis to Find Encrypted and Packed Malware". In: IEEE Security and Privacy 5.2 (Mar. 2007), pp. 40–45. issn: 1540-7993. doi: 10.1109/MSP.2007.48. url: https://doi.org/10.1109/MSP.2007.48.

[24] Lorenzo Martignoni, Roberto Paleari, Giampaolo Fresi Roglia, and Danilo Bruschi. "Testing System Virtual Machines". In: Proceedings of the 19th International Symposium on Software Testing and Analysis. ISSTA '10. Trento, Italy: Association for Computing Machinery, 2010, pp. 171–182. isbn: 9781605588230. doi: 10.1145/1831708.1831730. url: https://doi.org/10.1145/1831708.1831730.

[25] Mark Mossberg, Felipe Manzano, Eric Hennenfent, Alex Groce, Gustavo Grieco, Josselin Feist, Trent Brunson, and Artem Dinaburg. "Manticore: A user-friendly symbolic execution framework for binaries and smart contracts". In: 2019 34th IEEE/ACM International Conference on Automated Software Engineering (ASE). IEEE. 2019, pp. 1186–1189.

[26] Marius Muench, Dario Nisi, Aurélien Francillon, and Davide Balzarotti. "Avatar2: A multi-target orchestration platform". In: Proc. Workshop Binary Anal. Res.(Colocated NDSS Symp.) Vol. 18. 2018, pp. 1–11.

[27] Marius Muench, Jan Stijohann, Frank Kargl, Aurélien Francillon, and Davide Balzarotti. "What You Corrupt Is Not What You Crash: Challenges in Fuzzing Embedded Devices." In: NDSS. 2018.

[28] Markus FXJ Oberhumer. UPX the Ultimate Packer for eXecutables. 2004. url: https://upx.github.io/.

[29] John K Ousterhout. "Scripting: Higher level programming for the 21st century". In: Computer 31.3 (1998), pp. 23–30.

[30] P-Code Reference Manual. url: https://ghidra.re/courses/languages/html/pcoderef.html.

[31] PyPCODE. url: https://github.com/angr/pypcode.

[32] PyVEX. url: https://github.com/angr/pyvex.

[33] Nguyen Anh Quynh and Lau KaiJern. QiLing. 2019.

[34] NGUYEN Anh Quynh and DANG Hoang Vu. "Unicorn: Next generation cpu emulator framework". In: BlackHat USA (2015).

[35] Norman Ramsey and Mary F. Fernandez. "Specifying Representations of Machine Instructions". In: ACM Trans. Program. Lang. Syst. 19.3 (May 1997), pp. 492–524. issn: 0164-0925. doi: 10.1145/256167.256225. url: https://doi.org/10.1145/256167.256225.

[36] Ole Andrè Ravnas. Frida. url: https://www.frida.re/.

[37] Bob Joyce Reed Hastings. "Purify: Fast detection of memory leaks and access errors". In: In proc. of the winter 1992 usenix conference. Citeseer. 1991.

[38] Goldwyn Rodrigues. Poke-a-hole and friends. June 2009. url: https://lwn.net/Articles/335942/.

[39] Triton: A Dynamic Symbolic Execution Framework. SSTIC, 2015, pp. 31–54.

[40] Giorgio Severi, Tim Leek, and Brendan Dolan-Gavitt. "Malrec: compact full-trace malware recording for retrospective deep analysis". In: International Conference on Detection of Intrusions and Malware, and Vulnerability Assessment. Springer. 2018, pp. 3–23.

[41] Julian Seward and Nicholas Nethercote. "Using Valgrind to Detect Undefined Value Errors with Bit-Precision." In: USENIX Annual Technical Conference, General Track. 2005, pp. 17–30.

[42] Manolis Stamatogiannakis, Herbert Bos, and Paul Groth. "PANDAcap: a framework for streamlining collection of full-system traces". In: Proceedings of the 13th European workshop on Systems Security. 2020, pp. 1–6.

[43] Frederick Ulrich. "Exploitability Assessment with TEASER". MA thesis. Northeastern University, 2017.

[44] Using Valgrind to troubleshoot possible ndsd memory leaks. url: https://support.microfocus.com/kb/doc.php?id=7005905.

[45] Sébastien Valat, Andres S Charif-Rubial, and William Jalby. "MALT: a Malloc tracker". In: Pro-

ceedings of the 4th ACM SIGPLAN International Workshop on Software Engineering for Parallel Systems. 2017, pp. 1–10.

[46] Pauli Virtanen, Ralf Gommers, Travis E. Oliphant, Matt Haberland, Tyler Reddy, David Cournapeau, Evgeni Burovski, Pearu Peterson, Warren Weckesser, Jonathan Bright, Stéfan J. van der Walt, Matthew Brett, Joshua Wilson, K. Jarrod Millman, Nikolay Mayorov, Andrew R. J. Nelson, Eric Jones, Robert Kern, Eric Larson, C J Carey, İlhan Polat, Yu Feng, Eric W. Moore, Jake VanderPlas, Denis Laxalde, Josef Perktold, Robert Cimrman, Ian Henriksen, E. A. Quintero, Charles R. Harris, Anne M. Archibald, Antônio H. Ribeiro, Fabian Pedregosa, Paul van Mulbregt, and SciPy 1.0 Contributors. "SciPy 1.0: Fundamental Algorithms for Scientific Computing in Python". In: Nature Methods 17 (2020), pp. 261–272. doi: 10.1038/s41592-019-0686-2.

[47] Fish Wang and Yan Shoshitaishvili. "Angr-the next generation of binary analysis". In: 2017 IEEE Cybersecurity Development (SecDev). IEEE. 2017, pp. 8–9.

[48] David Wheeler. SLOCCount. 2001. url: http://www.dwheeler.com/sloccount/.

[49] Haiquan Xiong, Zhiyong Liu, Weizhi Xu, and Shuai Jiao. "Libvmi: a library for bridging the semantic gap between guest OS and VMM". In: 2012 IEEE 12th International Conference on Computer and Information Technology. IEEE. 2012, pp. 549–556.

Effects of Precise and Imprecise Value-Set Analysis (VSA) Information on Manual Code Analysis

Laura Matzen, Michelle A Leger, Geoffrey Reedy
Sandia National Laboratories
lematze@sandia.gov, maleger@sandia.gov, gereedy@sandia.gov

Abstract—**Binary reverse engineers combine automated and manual techniques to answer questions about software. However, when evaluating automated analysis results, they rarely have additional information to help them contextualize these results in the binary. We expect that humans could more readily understand the binary program and these analysis results if they had access to information usually kept internal to the analysis, like value-set analysis (VSA) information. However, these automated analyses often give up precision for scalability, and imprecise information might hinder human decision making.**

To assess how precision of VSA information affects human analysts, we designed a human study in which reverse engineers answered short information flow problems, determining whether code snippets would print sensitive information. We hypothesized that precise VSA information would help our participants analyze code faster and more accurately, and that imprecise VSA information would lead to slower, less accurate performance than no VSA information. We presented hand-crafted code snippets with precise, imprecise, or no VSA information in a blocked design, recording participants' eye movements, response times, and accuracy while they analyzed the snippets. Our data showed that precise VSA information changed participants' problem-solving strategies and supported faster, more accurate analyses. However, surprisingly, imprecise VSA information also led to increased accuracy relative to no VSA information, likely due to the extra time participants spent working through the code.

I. Introduction

Many static analysis frameworks (e.g., Infer, angr, S2E, BAP) support building automated binary analyses for tasks like bugfinding, trigger detection, and malware analysis [7], [11], [15]–[17], [36], [37]. However, humans must understand the results from these analyses to use them, and that requires some manual reverse engineering (RE) to put the results in their proper context. Can we reuse the work done by the automated analyses to effectively support that RE effort?

Many automated static analyses perform some form of value-set analysis (VSA) [3], over-approximating what values memory and register locations can take on at runtime at each program point [26]. Binary analyses particularly lean on VSA because it does not require distinguishing between addresses and integers [4]. Instead of discarding this VSA information, we would like to make it available to reverse engineers to help them contextualize the analysis results.

Workshop on Binary Analysis Research (BAR) 2021
21 February 2021, Virtual

https://dx.doi.org/10.14722/bar.2021.23002
www.ndss-symposium.org

However, these analyses trade off between precision and scalability [18]. Some analysis techniques are very precise, e.g., symbolic execution produces path-, context-, and flow-sensitive VSA information [5]. Other techniques use approximation to gain scalability, often by omitting some of these sensitivities. For example, data structure analysis (DSA) accepts imprecision through unification-based tracking and flow-insensitivity [25], and Parfait's demand-driven framework finds bug candidates using fast, imprecise analyses but filters candidates using slower, precise analyses [12]. The effects of these tradeoffs between approximation and scalability have been well studied within automated workflows, particularly for pointer analysis [21]. But before building a system to assist human reverse engineers, we need to understand the effects of these tradeoffs on the reverse engineers. We do not want to build a system that ends up impairing human reasoning — and approximate VSA information might do just that [26], [27].

To explore the effects of these tradeoffs on reverse engineers, we designed a human studies experiment asking people to solve a series of information flow problems. Information flow problems are core to many types of security questions (e.g., How could this binary leak a password? When does input influence this critical decision?), and they require reverse engineers to understand how data flows between specific sources and sinks. In our experiment, we crafted 24 simple C snippets that looked somewhat like code from a decompiler (e.g., Ghidra's, Ida's, or DREAM [1], [20], [50]). In each snippet, we defined "PUBLIC" and "SENSITIVE" information, moved this information through memory (sometimes conditionally), and then printed the value of one memory location. We asked participants to tell us whether each snippet would **always**, **sometimes**, or **never** print SENSITIVE information.

Figure 1a shows one information flow problem used in the experiment. In this example, SENSITIVE is written into the allocation to `note`; that memory is pointed to by `sams`, the memory pointed to by `katies`, and `delivery`. The printed memory, referenced through `delivery`, always points to SENSITIVE information, so the answer is **always**. Although this example used whimsical variable names, half of our examples used less meaningful names like `eax`.

We want to understand the effects of having different types of VSA information on reverse engineers' performance in solving simple information flow problems. Will reverse engineers use VSA information if they have it? Does the VSA information help? Does the precision of the information affect their performance? We know of no structured investigation into how this kind of imprecision affects a person's understanding of a program during analysis-assisted RE.

```
note = alloc();
*note = SENSITIVE;
sams = note;
note = alloc();
*note = PUBLIC;
katies = alloc();
*katies = sams;
delivery = *katies;
print(*delivery);
```

(a) Code Snippet

```
note: ->Mem1,->Mem2
sams: ->Mem1
katies: ->Mem3
delivery: ->Mem1

Mem1: SENSITIVE
Mem2: PUBLIC
Mem3: ->Mem1
```

(b) Precise VSA Information

```
note: ->Mem1, ->Mem2
sams: ->Mem1, ->Mem2
katies: ->Mem3
delivery: ->Mem1,->Mem2

Mem1: PUBLIC,SENSITIVE
Mem2: PUBLIC,SENSITIVE
Mem3: ->Mem1, ->Mem2
```

(c) Imprecise VSA Information

Fig. 1. One code snippet (information flow problem) from our experiment and its associated precise and imprecise VSA information. This code snippet **always** prints sensitive information.

To answer these questions, we asked our study participants to answer 24 information flow problems in a blocked design across three conditions (presented in a random order): eight problems with only an image of code, eight with images of code and precise VSA information (see Figure 1b), and eight with images of code and imprecise VSA information (see Figure 1c). Our precise and imprecise VSA information reflected that produced by sound may-analyses for the print statement, i.e., both included the correct values, but imprecise VSA information was an over-approximation and also included some incorrect values. Precise VSA information trivially revealed each problem's answer given the print statement. (The print above dereferences `delivery`; in the precise VSA information, `delivery` only points to `Mem1`, which contains SENSITIVE, resulting in an **always** answer.) However, imprecise VSA information never revealed the answer.

We collected eye tracking data to answer our first question (Will people use the information?) and to reveal strategies used.[1] We also collected behavioral data (timing and accuracy) to answer the latter two questions (Does it help? Does precision affect performance?). We hypothesized that participants would have the highest accuracy and fastest response times when they had precise VSA information to aid their analysis. We also hypothesized that imprecise VSA information would produce performance equal to or worse than that with no VSA information. If participants ignored the imprecise VSA information, their performance should be equivalent to the no VSA information condition. Alternatively, if participants spent time trying to understand the imprecise VSA information, which provided very little detail, they should be slower and perhaps less accurate than when they had no VSA information.

In this paper, we describe our experiment to determine whether VSA information (precise or imprecise) can aid a reverse engineer's understanding of a program, present and discuss our results, and briefly touch on implications for static analysis tool builders. Our contributions include:

- presentation and analysis of behavioral and eye tracking data from a human subjects research study, showing that fully precise VSA information *does* improve speed and accuracy of reverse engineers in small information flow problems, and that imprecise VSA information (as compared to no VSA information) improves accuracy but decreases speed;
- an analysis of this data comparing results between less and more experienced participants, showing that VSA information (both precise and imprecise) raised the accuracy of less experienced participants to be comparable to more experienced participants', and that precise VSA information led less experienced participants to adopt strategies similar to those of highly experienced participants; and
- the stimuli and experimental framework used to gather this data, which we release to support reproducibility.

[1] To facilitate eye-tracking data collection, we presented both code and VSA information as static images rather than using a RE platform like Ghidra. Some participants noted that they missed Ghidra's taint highlighting.

II. Related Works

A rich body of work over the past several decades looks to characterize the workflows and cognitive processes in reverse engineering (RE), program understanding, and defect discovery. This work explores both possible and actual interactions between human analysts and automated analyses. Many, but not all, of these studies focus on source code. Here, we mention a few publications specifically related to human studies.

Some of the studies that characterize RE directly are more applied, using metrics related to achieving a realistic RE goal. Example study goals in this category of study include characterizing the processes and reasoning [8] (even without human studies [46]), defining appropriate approaches to RE tasks [29], and identifying effective functional allocation between humans and automated analyses [38]. Our study falls into the other category, using metrics focused on the cognitive processes. Study goals in this category include determining what support humans need for gaining program understanding [42], and, in the programming domain, determining information needs when addressing interruption-caused memory failures [30].

Human studies in this domain have used a range of techniques to gain process insights, including post-hoc analysis or surveys as in [9] (potentially missing automatic decisions), think-aloud protocols or semi-structured interviews as in [45] (potentially changing analysts' approaches), or in situ data collection (potentially losing information about the relevance of actions). Other studies, like ours, take the general approach used in cognitive science research: developing a task that explores the cognitive processes of interest but is controlled enough to support understanding the data. This latter approach can provide interesting insights, even though the stimuli may not be realistic, and it supports the collection of fine-grained physical evidence using tools like fMRI [39] or eye tracking.

Eye tracking data has been used to identify differences between experts and novices during program comprehension tasks, e.g., learning to mitigate software vulnerabilities [14]. [34] provides a review of studies using eye-tracking to study source code understanding. In code comprehension tasks, the relationship between expertise and number or location of fixations is task dependent. When asked to make trustworthiness judgments, experts make more fixations within a piece of code than novices, although their comprehension of the code does not differ [22]. In bug detection, though, experts make more vertical eye movements than novices up-front [31] and achieve faster bug detection later [35], [44]. In code or print statement characterization, experts spend more time viewing task-relevant lines of code, and they tend to focus on *beacons* in the code [13], but novices spend more time reading comments [6]. We are using eye tracking data to evaluate how reverse engineers will use automated analysis results to help them understand code, and whether experts and novices use those results differently.

Many user studies evaluate existing tooling to explore how automation might support RE. The goals of these studies include comparing specific tools [49], understanding why available tools are not used [23], [40], evaluating the utility of a single tool [2], [28], and discovering information requirements of would-be users [41]. Although our study is similar in that we are evaluating the utility of a single type of information, our evaluation focuses on *potential* information prior to tool development rather than information from an existing tool.

Detailed studies like these have taken us a long way, but we still have much to learn about the cognitive processes supporting RE tasks, and what information and automation would best support RE [10], [43]. Thus, we take another small step in this basic research to understand how binary analyses can help humans better understand programs; specifically, we use eye-tracking to understand in detail how cognitive processing and strategies change in decompiled binary RE given different VSA information approximations.

III. Methods

Prior to data collection, this study was reviewed and approved by the Human Subjects Board at Sandia National Laboratories, in accordance with the Federal Policy for the Protection of Human Subjects.

A. Materials

In this experiment, we asked participants to evaluate a set of 24 information flow problems (reasoning about source to sink relationships). Each problem required analyzing a code snippet that moved PUBLIC and SENSITIVE information through memory (sometimes conditionally) and then printed the value of one memory location. We asked participants to tell us whether each snippet would **always**, **sometimes**, or **never** print SENSITIVE information. The stimuli consisted of these 24 code snippets, each of which could be paired with precise VSA information, imprecise VSA information, or no VSA information. All images of code problems, VSA information, and problem descriptions are available in our supplemental materials.[2] An example of one of the problems, and its layout, is shown in Figure 3.

Each hand-crafted snippet was written in basic C to reflect decompiler code; half of the problems used semantically relevant names like those a reverse engineer might apply (Figure I), and half used less semantically meaningful names more like those a decompiler might apply by default (Figure 3).[3] Our snippets used two C types, pointers and integers; integers could be either an enumeration value of PUBLIC or SENSITIVE, or 0 through 3. Each snippet allocated memory, explicitly initialized memory to PUBLIC or SENSITIVE or to point to other memory, moved values through memory (using dereferences, assignments, and conditional statements testing for equality), and ultimately dereferenced a variable to print the value from one memory location. Because the snippets did not use arithmetic, VSA information in this study devolved to points-to information.

The hand-crafted precise and imprecise VSA information showed *at least* all possible values of variables and memory at the print statement, reflecting results from an over-approximate, may-points-to value-set analysis. Precise VSA information was always sufficient to answer the information flow problem (given the print), and imprecise VSA information was never sufficient to answer the problem. Thus, the memory printed always pointed to both PUBLIC and SENSITIVE in imprecise VSA information, but it only pointed to both in precise VSA information when the answer was **sometimes**.

All problems reflect this structure, but we further classify the problems into four different types, "flow," "path," "field," and "callsite," so named to reflect our inspiration for the problems.[4] We created six problems of each type: three were intended to be easy, and three were intended to be more difficult. More difficult problems used more statements, indirection, or oddly ordered conditionals than easier problems. In each difficulty level, we created one problem that **always** printed SENSITIVE information, one that **never** did, and one that **sometimes** did. Thus, overall, half of the problems were easy, and half were more difficult; and each of the three possible answers was correct for 1/3 of the problems.

Flow problems, like that seen in Figure I, used multiple assignments to the same location (memory or variables) to cause imprecise approximations. **Sometimes** flow problems additionally used a conditional statement.

Path problems additionally used conditional assignments. We define these conditional code regions to be either *Conditional Sources*, where each branch assigns from a different source location to the same destination, or *Conditional Destinations*, where each branch assigns from the same source to a different destination. (Figure 11 shows these two types of code regions in a callsite-inspired problem.) More difficult path problems used multiple related conditionals.

Field problems used at least two levels of memory indirection along with *Conditional Sources*. See Figure 2 for an example of an easy field problem. More difficult field problems used more levels of indirection.

Callsite problems, like that seen in Figure 3, used *Conditional Sources*, paired *Conditional Destinations* (i.e., the conditions between the two were identical), and straightline code between the two with direct information flow from the shared destination of the *Conditional Source* to the shared source of the *Conditional Destination*. More difficult callsite problems presented the paired conditionals in reverse order.

[2]Supplemental materials: https://github.com/maleger/vsa4infoflowstudy

[3]Because novices are less accurate when using semantically meaningless variable names [31], and because we had some imbalance in which problem types had which variable name types, our use of both meaningful and meaningless variable names could have been problematic. However, these differing name types did not appear to be problematic in this case. Labeling variable name types as "letter" or "word," participants averaged 81.4% correct for "letter" variables and 81.2% for "word" variables. Given this, and given that we provided no type information, we further believe that presenting disassembled code rather than source would not impact the shape of our results (although it might slow the process). However, our problems did not give us any insight into the effects of reused variable names.

[4]These names are notional and do not reflect a formal use of flow-, path-, callsite-, and field-sensitivity. However, we constructed imprecise VSA information to reflect the results of an analysis that lacked at least one critical sensitivity (flow- or path-, for these problems), and we constructed the precise VSA information to reflect flow- and path-sensitive results.

```
// assume o is 2
f1 = alloc();
f2 = alloc();
b = alloc();
*b = f1;
**b = SENSITIVE;
*b = f2;
**b = PUBLIC;
if (o == 1) {
    *b = f1; }
if (o == 2) {
    *b = f2; }
res = *b;
print(*res);
```
(a) Code Snippet

```
f1: ->Mem1
f2: ->Mem2
b: ->Mem3
o: 2
res: ->Mem2

Mem1: SENSITIVE
Mem2: PUBLIC
Mem3: ->Mem2
```
(b) Precise VSA Information

```
f1: ->Mem1
f2: ->Mem2
b: ->Mem3
o: ?
res: ->Mem1, ->Mem2

Mem1: SENSITIVE, PUBLIC
Mem2: SENSITIVE, PUBLIC
Mem3: ->Mem1, ->Mem2
```
(c) Imprecise VSA Information

Fig. 2. An example of the easy field problem, where the code **never** prints sensitive data, along with its precise and imprecise VSA information.

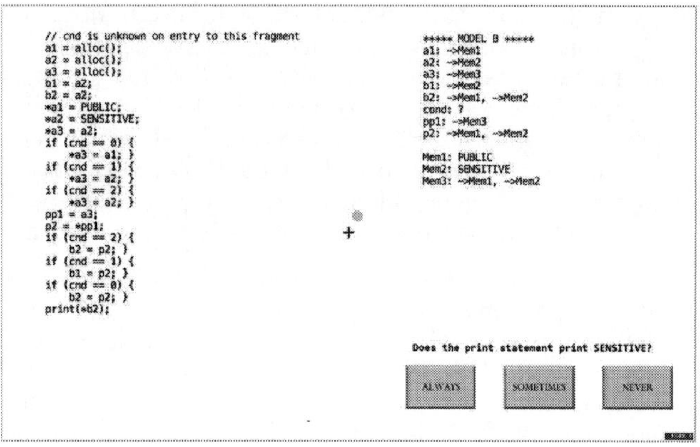

Fig. 3. An example of the problem layout. This example is a callsite problem paired with precise VSA information. The correct answer is **sometimes**.

Pairing each of the 24 snippets with each of the three possible VSA information types, we had a total of 72 stimuli. We organized the stimuli into counterbalanced blocks of trials, where each block had eight different problems paired with the same type of VSA information. Within each block, the stimuli were placed in a fixed random order (i.e., the same order for each participant). We also counterbalanced the order of the blocks: across participants, the block containing each VSA information type appeared equally often first, second, or third. This counterbalancing procedure resulted in nine experimental lists, where every problem appeared in every condition, and every block appeared in every position across lists. Each participant saw one of the nine experimental lists.

B. Procedure

After completing the informed consent process, participants filled out a basic demographic questionnaire, providing their age, highest level of education, and level of experience with C and similar programming languages, information leakage, pointer analysis, and reverse engineering.

Participants sat in a dimly lit, sound-attenuating booth, with their eyes approximately 60 cm from the computer monitor displaying the stimuli. We asked participants to sit as still as possible throughout the experiment and to avoid leaning forward or backward. A Fovio eye tracker recorded participants' eye movements during the task. After participants were seated comfortably, the eye tracker was calibrated using a five point calibration screen. Then participants read the instructions for the task.[5] The instructions explained that the participant would be using code snippets and three types of VSA information (precise, imprecise, or no VSA information) to determine whether each code snippet would **always**, **sometimes**, or **never** print sensitive information. The instructions gave examples to illustrate the nature and format of the precise and imprecise VSA information, and they demonstrated how PUBLIC and SENSITIVE information could be traced through the code snippets to the print. We instructed participants to prioritize accuracy but to answer the questions as quickly as possible.

As described above, we presented the stimuli in blocks of eight problems, displaying the same type of VSA information for all problems in a block. Before each block, a screen of instructions indicated whether the trials in that block would have precise, imprecise, or no VSA information. Participants were given breaks between the blocks.

We used E-Prime 3.0 software to present the experimental stimuli. Each trial began with a fixation cross "+" presented in black 48 point font on a white background. We instructed participants to stare at the cross until the code and VSA information appeared; it was displayed alone on the screen for 2 seconds and remained on the screen when the images appeared. The code always appeared on the left side of the screen, and, when present, the VSA information appeared on the right. Three response buttons, labeled **ALWAYS**, **SOMETIMES**, and **NEVER**, appeared in the lower right-hand corner of the screen (see Figure3). Each stimulus remained on the screen until the participant clicked on one of the response buttons with the mouse. Then, a new screen appeared with a button that said "Continue to next problem." Participants clicked on that button when they were ready to advance to the next trial. Most participants completed the self-paced experiment within 45 minutes, although a handful took longer.

C. Participants

Twenty Sandia employees (four female) participated in the experiment. They were compensated for their time at their normal hourly rate. The mean age of the participants was 32 (range 22-49). Four of the participants held bachelor's degrees, twelve held master's degrees, and four held Ph.Ds.

Of the twenty participants, eleven reported having 8-20 years of experience with C and similar programming languages. All but three of these participants indicated that they had experience with answering questions about information leakage, and all but one indicated that they had experience with pointer analysis. All of them reported that they had experience with reverse engineering.

The other nine participants were less experienced. They reported having 2-5 years of experience with C, but minimal or no experience with answering information leakage questions. One participant rated themselves as being knowledgeable about pointer analysis and two rated themselves as being knowledgeable about reverse engineering. The rest of the participants indicated that they had little or no experience in those areas.

IV. Behavioral Results

Before analyzing our results, we assessed whether the difficulty level, information leakage type, and problem type impacted participants' responses as we intended. If we were

[5]The complete instructions are provided in our supplemental materials.

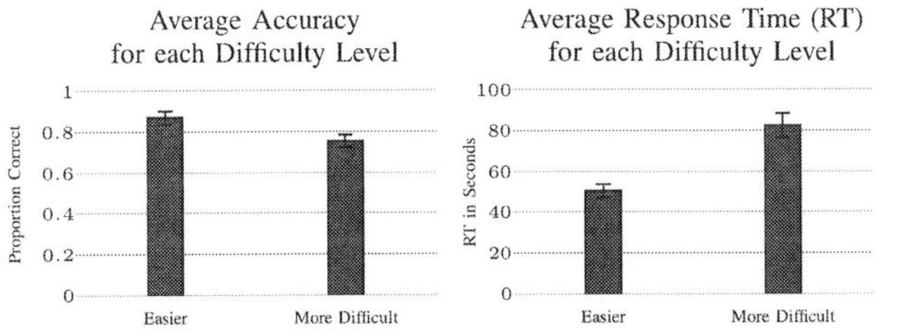

Fig. 4. Average accuracy (left) and response times (right) by difficulty level. Error bars in all figures represent the standard error of the mean.

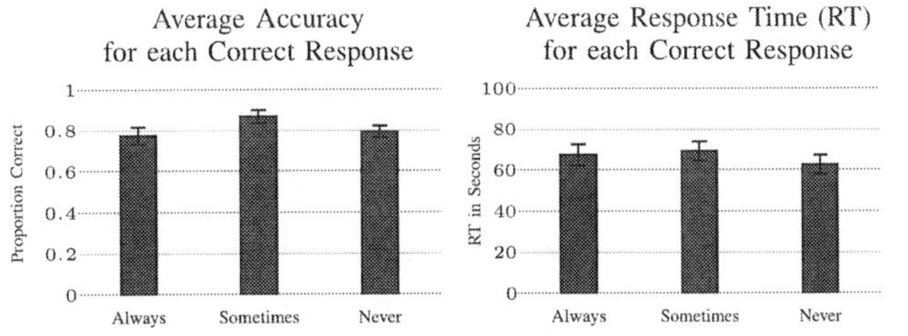

Fig. 5. Average accuracy (left) and response times (RTs, right) for problems where **always**, **sometimes** or **never** was the correct response.

		Participants' Answer		
		Always	**Never**	**Sometimes**
Correct Answer	**Always**	124	9	27
	Never	2	127	31
	Sometimes	5	16	139

TABLE I. COUNT OF PARTICIPANTS' ANSWERS BY CORRECT ANSWER.

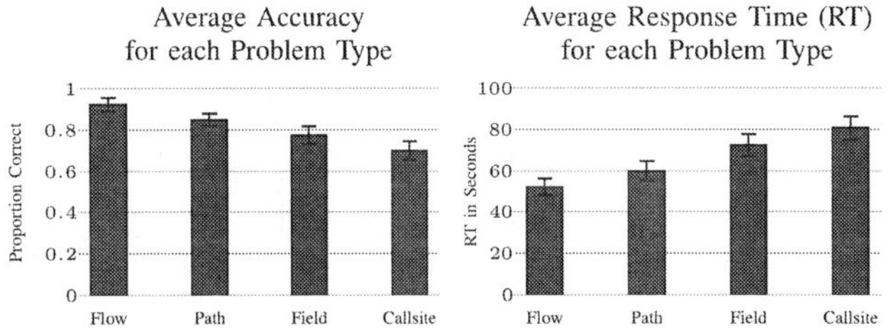

Fig. 6. Average accuracy (left) and RTs (right) by problem type.

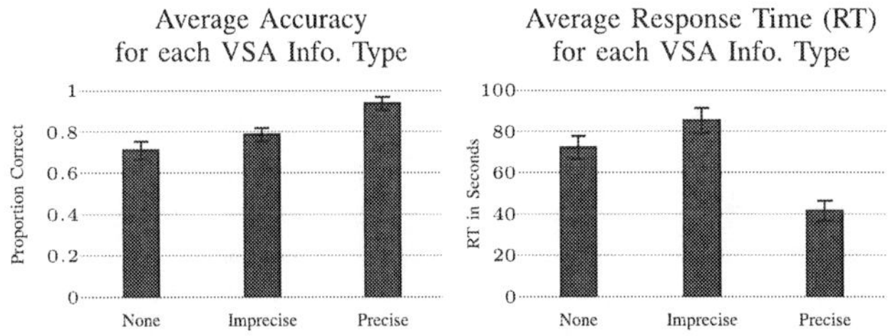

Fig. 7. Average accuracy (left) and RTs (right) by VSA information type.

successful in stimulus design, participants should have faster, more accurate responses to easier problems than to more difficult problems, and the type of information leakage (i.e., whether the answer was **always**, **sometimes**, or **never**) should not have affected accuracy or response time (RT).

Figure 4 shows the average accuracy and response times (RTs) for each problem difficulty level. We used paired t-tests to determine whether difficulty level impacted participants' performance. As predicted, participants had significantly higher accuracy for easier problems ($t(19) = 3.91, p < 0.001$), and they spent significantly more time on more difficult problems ($t(19) = 7.88, p < 0.001$). These results indicate that our easy and more difficult problems functioned as intended.

Figure 5 shows the average accuracy and RTs for each information leakage condition. These problems were intended to be equivalent in difficulty to one another - problems that **never** printed sensitive information should not be more difficult than problems that **always** or **sometimes** did. One-way ANOVAs [24] showed no significant differences in accuracy ($F(2, 57) = 2.02$, $p = 0.14$) or RTs ($F(2, 57) = 0.51$, $p = 0.60$) across the three conditions. These results show that we successfully developed problems that were similar in difficulty for each information leakage condition.

Although participants' performance did not differ significantly across the information leakage conditions, we observed that participants chose the **sometimes** response most often (see Table I), even though all responses were correct equally often. When the correct answer was **always** or **never**, participants were likely to choose **sometimes** if they answered the problem incorrectly, perhaps answering **sometimes** when they were unsure. In the future, we suggest having an additional response, **unsure**, to distinguish between answers that are confidently **sometimes** and those that are not.

We also assessed the effect of problem type on participants' performance. Figure 6 shows the average accuracy and RTs for each problem type. One-way ANOVAs showed that problem type had a significant effect on accuracy and RTs (both Fs > 6.49, both ps < 0.001). Paired t-tests showed that participants had significantly higher accuracy and significantly faster RTs for flow problems than for any other problem type (all ts > 1.82, all ps < 0.05). Participants performed next best on path problems, with significantly better accuracy and significantly faster RTs than on field and callsite problems (all ts > 1.90, all ps < 0.04). Participants performed most poorly on field and callsite problems. While the participants' RTs were significantly faster for field problems than for callsite problems ($t(19) = 2.12$, $p = 0.02$), their average accuracy for these two types of problems did not differ significantly ($t(19) = 1.53$, $p = 0.07$, one-tailed). These results showed that flow problems were easiest for participants, while callsite and field problems were the most difficult.

A. *Impact of VSA Information Type*

The results above indicate that our stimuli showed the intended variations in difficulty across conditions. Participants had better performance for easier problems and similar performance across information leakage conditions (although they answered **sometimes** more frequently). The different problem types varied in difficulty, producing a range of performance.

Our primary goal in this experiment was to assess the impact of different VSA information types on participants' accuracy, RTs, and patterns of eye movements. To do this, we first analyzed the impact of each VSA information type (precise, imprecise, and no VSA information) on participants' overall performance, and we then assessed the impact of the different VSA information types on participants' performance across the two difficulty levels and the four problem types.

Figure 7 shows participants' overall accuracy and RTs in the three VSA information conditions. One-way ANOVAs

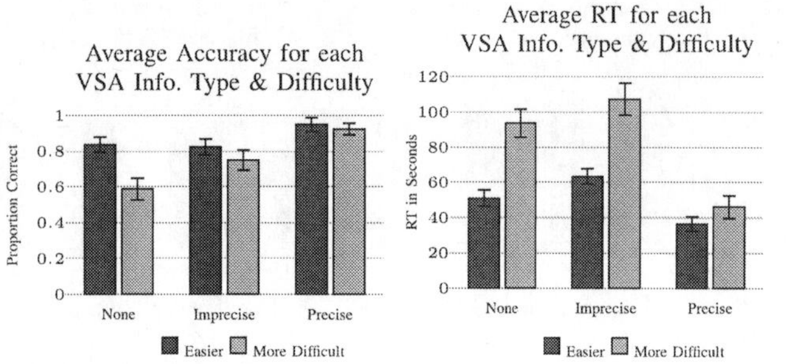

Fig. 8. Average accuracy (left) and response times (RTs, right) by VSA information type and difficulty level.

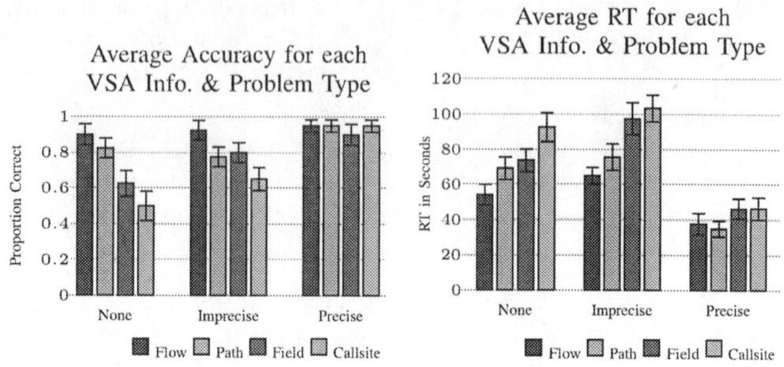

Fig. 9. Average accuracy and RTs by VSA information and problem type.

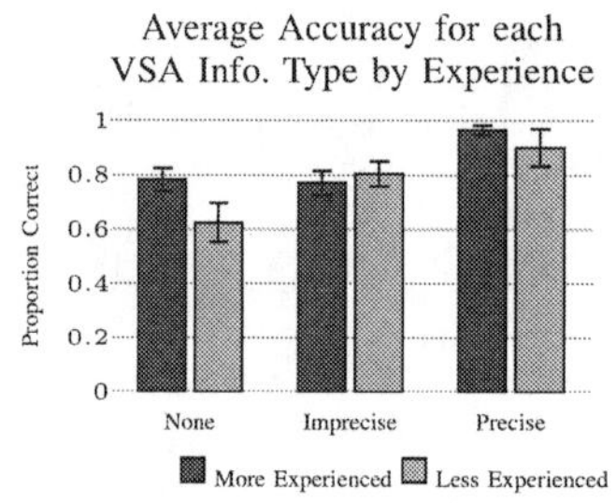

Fig. 10. Average accuracy by VSA information type, participant experience.

showed that VSA information type had a significant effect on the participants' accuracy and RTs (both Fs > 10.24, both ps < 0.001). Paired t-tests showed that participants were significantly more accurate when given precise VSA information than when given imprecise or no VSA information (both ts > 3.93, both ps < 0.001). Surprisingly, they were also significantly more accurate when given imprecise VSA information than when given no VSA information ($t(19) = 1.79$, $p = 0.04$, one-tailed). For the RT data, paired t-tests showed that participants responded significantly faster when given precise VSA information than when given imprecise or no VSA information (both ts > 6.29, both ps < 0.001), and significantly slower when given imprecise VSA information than when given no VSA information ($t(19) = 2.01$, $p = 0.03$, one-tailed). Overall, the results showed that precise VSA information improved both the speed and accuracy of participants' decisions. Contrary to our predictions, imprecise VSA information also led to improved accuracy, but that improvement came at a cost: participants were much slower in the imprecise VSA condition than in any other condition.

Figure 8 shows the average accuracy and RTs for each VSA information type, broken down by problem difficulty. A two-way repeated measures ANOVA showed that accuracy was significantly affected by VSA information type ($F(2, 95) = 15.09$, $p < 0.001$) and by difficulty level ($F(1, 95) = 11.74$, $p < 0.01$). There was also a significant interaction between VSA information type and difficulty level ($F(2, 95) = 4.01$, $p = 0.02$). RTs were similarly affected by VSA information type ($F(2, 95) = 39.03$, $p < 0.001$) and by difficulty level ($F(1, 95) = 59.25, p < 0.001$), and the ANOVA again showed significant interaction between the two ($F(2, 95) = 7.29$, $p < 0.01$). When no VSA information was shown, participants had much lower accuracy and much longer RTs on more difficult problems relative to easier problems. Showing participants imprecise VSA information eliminated the difference in accuracy between easier and more difficult problems, but the difference in RTs remained. Showing participants precise VSA information eliminated the accuracy difference and nearly eliminated the RT difference. Paired t-tests confirmed this, showing a significant difference in accuracy between easier and more difficult problems when no VSA information was shown ($t(19) = 4.16$, $p < 0.001$), but not when imprecise or precise VSA information was shown (both ts < 1). The average RTs for easier and more difficult problems were significantly different for all three VSA information conditions (all ts > 2.05, all ps < 0.03), but the magnitude of the difference was much smaller when precise VSA information was shown. This pattern indicates that the presence of VSA information was particularly helpful for more difficult problems, making participants' accuracy on more difficult problems comparable to their accuracy on easier problems.

We also assessed the interplay between problem type and VSA information type (Figure 9). For the accuracy data, a two-way repeated measures ANOVA showed a significant main effect of problem type ($F(3, 209) = 10.52$, $p < 0.001$), a significant main effect of VSA information type ($F(2, 209) = 19.64$, $p < 0.001$), and a significant interaction between the two ($F(6, 209) = 3, 51$, $p < 0.01$). Similarly, the RT data showed a significant main effect of problem type ($F(3, 209) = 17.41$, $p < 0.001$), a significant main effect of VSA information type ($F(2, 209) = 72.85$, $p < 0.001$), and a significant interaction between the two ($F(6, 209) = 2.28$, $p = 0.04$).

One-way ANOVAs comparing the four problem type conditions within each VSA information type condition showed a significant effect of problem type on accuracy and RTs when there was no VSA information or imprecise VSA information (all Fs> 3.76, all ps< 0.02). However, when participants had precise VSA information, there was no longer a significant effect of problem type for either accuracy ($F(3, 76) = 0.35$) or RTs ($F(3, 76) = 0.36$). Once again, the presence of precise VSA information mitigated the impact of problem difficulty, allowing participants to perform equally well for all four problem types (with no significant differences in accuracy or RTs). We expected that precise VSA information would reduce all problem types to the same kind of question; this confirmed our expectation.

B. *Impact of Experience*

To assess the impact of the participants' prior experience with information leakage questions, pointer analysis, and reverse engineering on their performance, we compared the aver-

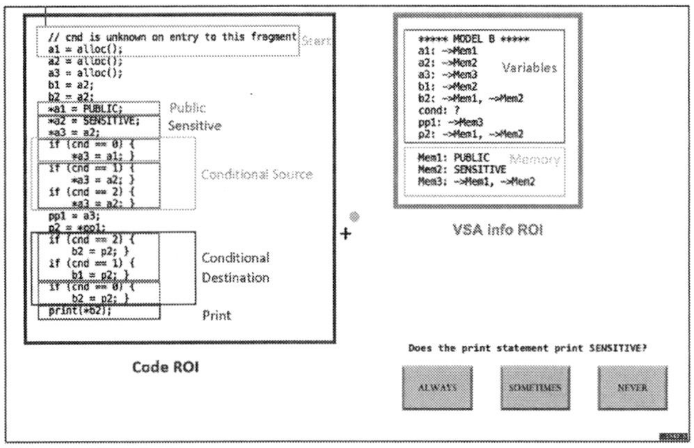

Fig. 11. An example of the ROIs for one stimulus. Blue regions within the Code ROI are Public ROIs, and red regions are Sensitive ROIs.

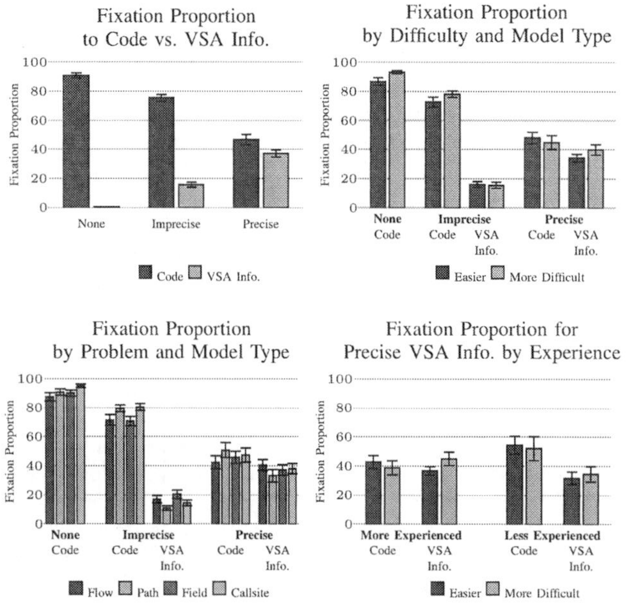

Fig. 12. Average proportion (percentage) of fixations to the Code and VSA Information Regions of Interest (ROIs) for each VSA information type condition, additionally broken down by problem difficulty, by problem type, and, for the precise VSA information condition only, by experience.

age accuracy of participants who had professional experience in those areas (11 participants) to those who did not (9 participants) for each VSA information type. A two-way ANOVA with VSA information type and experience level as factors showed a significant interaction between VSA information type and experience ($F(2, 36) = 3.29$, $p < 0.05$). Post-hoc t-tests showed that more experienced participants had significantly higher accuracy than less experienced participants when given no VSA information ($t(13) = 1.91$, $p = 0.04$). However, the difference between the two groups was eliminated when either precise VSA information or imprecise VSA information was available (both $ts < 1$). As shown in Figure 10, the presence of either type of VSA information enabled the less experienced participants to perform at the same level as the more experienced participants.

V. Eye Tracking Results

Due to a technical problem impacting eye tracking data from five participants, only 15 participants (eight experienced and seven less experienced) were included in the eye tracking analysis. Human eye movements consist of saccades (fast eye movements from one location to another) and fixations (where the eyes are relatively stationary). Virtually all visual information processing occurs during fixations [32], [33]. In our analysis, we used the default algorithm in the EyeWorks software to calculate fixations, using one degree of visual angle for the spatial parameter (estimated at 52 pixels based on the distance from the participants' eyes to our computer monitor). We divided each stimulus into regions of interest (ROIs) for the eye tracking analysis. We defined two high-level ROIs: one for the code, on the left side of the screen, and one for the VSA information, on the right side. We also conducted a more fine-grained analysis, subdividing the code and VSA information ROIs into smaller regions. We split the VSA information region into two ROIs: Variables and Memory. We identified seven possibly overlapping subdivisions in the Code ROI: Start, Memory Initialization, Conditional Source, Conditional Destination, Sensitive, Public, and Print. Not every stimulus had all of these seven ROIs, and each line of code was included in all relevant ROIs. Figure 11 shows example ROIs for one stimulus. A more detailed explanation of the ROIs is provided in the supplemental materials.

A. *Fixations to the Code and VSA Information Regions of Interest*

For our high-level analysis, we calculated the total number of fixations for each trial, then calculated the average proportion of fixations to the Code and VSA Information ROIs. Changes to the distribution of fixations to the different ROIs reflect changes in the participants' information processing strategies, since people tend to fixate on the information that they consider to be most relevant to their current task [19], [48]. Figure 12a shows the results of this analysis. As expected, participants did not fixate in the VSA Information ROI when no VSA information was present. When the imprecise VSA information was shown, approximately 18% of participants' fixations (on average) were in the VSA Information ROI, and when the precise VSA information was shown, approximately 37% of participants' fixations were in the VSA Information ROI. This shows that participants did use the VSA information, and that they relied more heavily on the precise VSA information than on the imprecise VSA information.

We found that problem difficulty had no impact on how much participants fixated on the imprecise VSA information (Figure 12b). When given precise VSA information, participants had a numerically higher proportion of fixations to the VSA information for more difficult problems than for easier problems. However, this difference did not reach statistical significance ($t(14) = 1.43$, $p = 0.08$).

Incorporating participants' experience levels, our analysis showed that the more experienced participants drove this trend toward fixating more on the precise VSA information for difficult problems. As shown in Figure 12d, the less experienced participants looked at the Code ROI more often than they looked at the Precise VSA Information ROI. This difference was significant for easier problems ($t(11) = 3.00$,

$p < 0.001$) and marginally significant for more difficult problems ($t(10) = 1.80$, $p = 0.05$). In contrast, the more experienced participants had more similar proportions of fixations to the Code and VSA Information ROIs. For easier problems, they had a slightly higher proportion of fixations to the Code ROI than to the VSA Information ROI. This pattern switched for more difficult problems, with experienced participants having a higher proportion of fixations to the VSA Information ROI than to the Code ROI. This switch indicates that the more experienced participants tended to rely more on the VSA information for the more difficult problems.

When we considered the different problem types, we observed again that when precise VSA information was available, participants had a lower proportion of fixations to the Code ROI and a higher proportion of fixations to the VSA Information ROI (Figure 12c). The problem type did not impact the proportion of fixations to the precise VSA information ($F(3, 56) = 0.58$); participants devoted 33-40% of their fixations to the VSA Information ROI across all four problem types. However, problem type did have an impact on the proportion of fixations to the imprecise VSA information ($F(3, 56) = 2.99$, $p < 0.04$).

B. *Fixations to the Smaller ROIs Within the Code and VSA Information Regions*

We next examined the patterns of fixations to the smaller ROIs that marked specific features within the code or VSA information. The VSA Information ROI contained Variables and Memory ROIs (see Figure 11). We did not observe any differences in the proportions of fixations to those ROIs across any of the experimental conditions. For all conditions in which VSA information was present, participants devoted approximately equal proportions of fixations to the Variables ROI and the Memory ROI.

When looking at the smaller ROIs within the Code ROI, we considered each problem type separately because some ROIs were specific to certain problem types. The results for each problem type are shown in Figure 13. As expected, we observed a reduced proportion of fixations to each of the ROIs in the code region when VSA information was present. In most cases, the magnitude of the reduction was similar for all ROIs, producing similar distributions of fixations across all VSA information types. For example, in flow problems, the Sensitive ROI always had the highest proportion of fixations and the Public ROI always had the second highest proportion of fixations, regardless of VSA information type. This indicates that the presence of VSA information decreased participants' fixations to the ROIs in the code region in general, rather than having a disproportionate impact on some ROIs over others.

We saw one exception to this general pattern. In callsite and path problems, participants had a higher proportion of fixations to the Conditional Source ROIs than to the Conditional Destination ROI when given no VSA information or imprecise VSA information. That pattern reversed when they were given precise VSA information; participants then had numerically higher proportions of fixations to the Conditional Destination ROI than to the Conditional Source ROIs. In these two problem types, the relationship between the conditional source and the conditional destination is critical to determining whether or

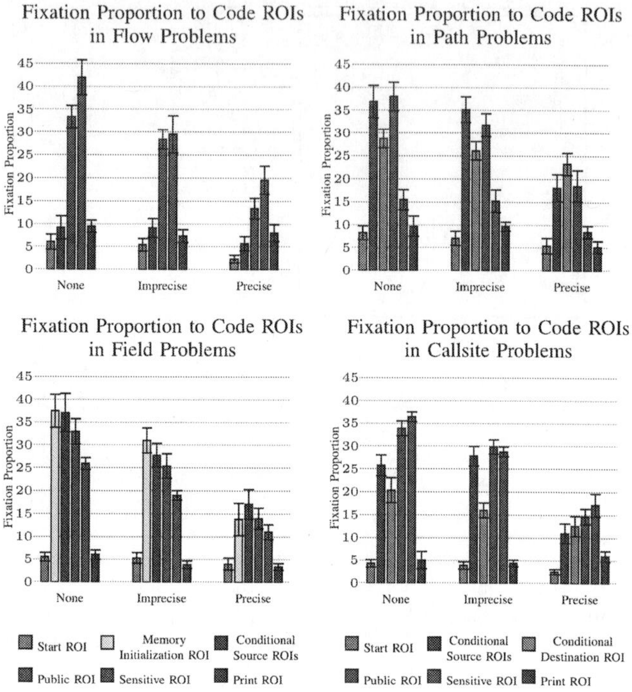

Fig. 13. Average proportion of fixations to the line-by-line ROIs in the Code region for the four problem types. Callsite problems are shown in (a), field problems in (b), flow problems in (c), and path problems in (d).

not the code will print sensitive information. The fact that participants spent less time studying the Conditional Source ROIs when precise VSA information was present indicates that they were using the information from the VSA information when reasoning about these problems. With the assistance of the VSA information, they did not need to spend as much time studying the information in the Conditional Source ROIs. Instead, they could study the VSA information and then check their understanding of the VSA information against the information in the Conditional Destination ROI. The VSA information reduced the overall amount of time needed to understand the code, but it also changed how participants interacted with specific parts of the code.

C. *Order of Fixations to ROIs*

We next assessed the order in which participants fixated on various regions in the code to determine whether their level of experience or the type of VSA information presented had an impact on their strategies. Given precise VSA information, participants could have answered the question of whether the code **always**, **sometimes**, or **never** printed sensitive information by looking only at the print statement and the VSA information, ignoring the rest of the code. The eye tracking data revealed that some participants did just that, as shown in Figure 14. A trace of all of the gaze points on this trial shows that this participant started at the fixation cross, looked at the VSA information, then the print statement in the code, then back to the VSA information, and finally to the correct response button at the bottom of the screen before clicking on that button.

To assess how often participants used this strategy, we analyzed the time between trial onset and each participant's

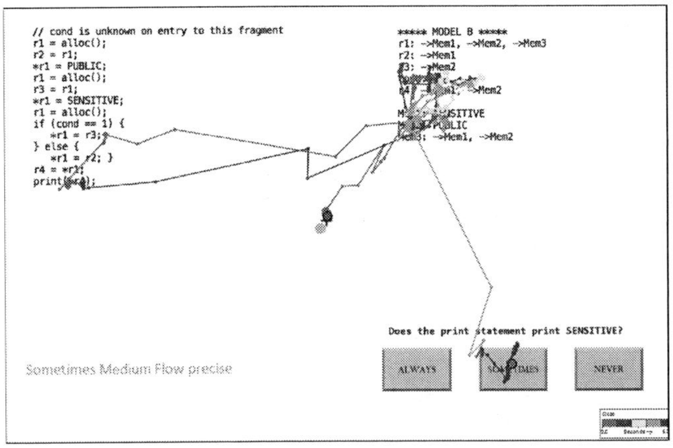

Fig. 14. Gaze data for one participant on one trial. The green circle shows the position of the participant's gaze at the beginning of the trial, and the color coding shows how the participant's eye movements unfolded over time.

first fixation on the VSA Information ROI, the Start ROI in the code region, and the Print ROI in the code region. If participants read the code from top to bottom, we would expect a shorter time to first fixation for the Start ROI relative to the Print ROI. If a participant started from the Print ROI and worked backwards through the code, we would expect the Print ROI to have a shorter time to first fixation than the Start ROI.

We found that most participants generally read the code from top to bottom, fixating on the Start ROI before the Print ROI. Given no VSA information, the average time between trial onset and the first fixation on the Start ROI was 6.44 seconds ($SD = 6.55s$), while the average was 19.5 seconds for the Print ROI ($SD = 11.28s$). Only three participants fixated on the Print ROI before the Start ROI (as determined by average time to first fixation). All three of those participants were from the highly experienced group.

Given imprecise VSA information, the average time to first fixation across all participants was shortest for the Start ROI at 7.98 seconds ($SD = 6.41s$), slightly longer for the VSA Information ROI at 9.49 seconds ($SD = 7.18$), and longest for the Print ROI at 19.27 seconds ($SD = 17.20$). This indicates that participants often started reading the code from the top, glancing back and forth between the code and the VSA information as they worked their way to the bottom. However, the overall averages obscure the fact that different participants used different strategies. While seven participants followed the pattern observed when averaging across all participants, eight did not. A group of four participants consistently fixated on the VSA Information ROI first, then on the Print ROI, and later on the Start ROI. Once again, all four were in the highly experienced group. Another two highly experienced participants tended to fixate on the Print ROI first, then on the Start ROI, and later on the VSA Information ROI, after working their way backwards through the code. Finally, two participants, both among the least experienced, had unique patterns. One of these tended to fixate on the VSA Information ROI first, then on the Start ROI, and then on the Print ROI. The other tended to fixate on the Print ROI first, then on the VSA Information ROI, and later on the Start ROI.

The average times to first fixation in our three regions of interest were quite different when participants were shown precise VSA information. Here, when averaging across all participants, the average time to first fixation was lowest for the VSA Information ROI at 4.86 seconds ($SD = 2.97$), somewhat longer for the Start ROI at 9.83 seconds ($SD = 9.32s$), and longest for the Print ROI at 15.14 seconds ($SD = 17.12s$). A total of eleven participants (six highly experienced and five less experienced) consistently fixated on the VSA Information ROI first. Seven of those eleven, including five of the highly experienced participants, tended to fixate on the Print ROI next and the Start ROI last (although one highly experienced participant never fixated on the Start ROI at all in trials with precise VSA information), while the other four participants tended to fixate on the Start ROI before the Print ROI. Another group of three participants tended to fixate on the Start ROI first, the VSA Information ROI later, and the Print ROI last. Finally, one of the less experienced participants tended to fixate on the Start ROI first, the Print ROI next, and the VSA Information ROI last.

One takeaway from the differences across VSA information conditions is that precise VSA information made the less experienced participants' eye movements more like those of the highly experienced participants. When given no VSA information or imprecise VSA information, none of the less experienced participants consistently used a strategy of starting from the print statement and working backwards through the code. In addition, when given imprecise VSA information, none of the less experienced participants started by looking at the VSA Information, whereas half of the more experienced participants started there. Yet when given precise VSA information, the majority of participants (11 of 15) tended to use a strategy where they started from the VSA Information ROI, and two of the less experienced participants adopted the experts' strategy of looking at the Print ROI before looking at the Start ROI.

VI. Discussion

In our experiment, we found that providing participants with precise VSA information improved their speed and accuracy in assessing information flow through code. We also found that providing imprecise VSA information improved participants' accuracy relative to having no VSA information, but it decreased participants' speed. The speed-accuracy tradeoff is a common finding in research on cognition [47], so it is likely that the additional time spent on imprecise VSA problems led to the accuracy improvement.[6]

We also found an interaction between problem difficulty and the three VSA information conditions. Participants performed reasonably well on easier code problems when given no VSA information, but they struggled for more difficult problems, spending much more time on each problem and providing incorrect responses an average of 40% of the time. When given imprecise VSA information, participants were still slower for more difficult problems than for easier problems,

[6]We have noticed that reverse engineers often avoid using imprecise automated analyses for support when they can perform a task manually. We wonder if reverse engineers make this trade-off because their tools do not meet their information needs, like developers [23], or because their analyses are time-limited and they can identify and correct classification errors later. This remains interesting future work.

but the difference in average accuracy was eliminated. When given precise VSA information, participants had equally good accuracy for both easy and difficult problems, and the difference in response times (RTs) was nearly eliminated as well.[7]

We saw a similar pattern when considering different problem types (flow, path, field, and callsite problems). Precise VSA information was particularly beneficial for the more difficult problem types. We observed significant effects of problem type on participants' accuracy and RTs when there was no VSA information or imprecise VSA information, but providing precise VSA information eliminated these differences, leading to near-ceiling accuracy across all four types of problems. Recall that our stimuli were fully counterbalanced, so the same code problems appeared equally often with each type of VSA information across all participants. This allows us to conclude that the differences between VSA information types are driving these results.

Our analysis of participants' eye movements provided further evidence that the precise VSA information was helpful to participants, particularly for more difficult problems. The eye tracking data confirm that participants used the VSA information, particularly the precise VSA information. All participants had a higher proportion of fixations to the VSA Information region of interest (ROI) when given precise VSA information than when given imprecise VSA information. For more experienced participants, the proportion of fixations to the precise VSA information grew even higher when the problems were more difficult. We also observed that the presence of precise VSA information could change which parts of the code participants looked at most. For callsite and path problems, participants had a high proportion of fixations to the Conditional Source ROIs when there was no VSA information or imprecise VSA information. When precise VSA information was shown, the relative proportion of fixations to the Conditional Source ROIs dropped substantially, while the relative proportion of fixations to the Conditional Destination ROIs increased. This pattern indicates that participants may have changed their strategies for reasoning about the code when precise VSA information was available.

Finally, our analysis of the order of participants' fixations showed that more experienced participants often used different strategies for approaching the code problems than less experienced participants. Some of the most experienced participants tended to start from the print statement and work their way up the code when given no VSA information. When given imprecise VSA information, the majority of the more experienced participants used this strategy, looking at the print statement first, referring to the VSA information, and then working their way through the rest of the code. When given precise VSA information, the majority of participants looked at the VSA information first, then checked the contents of the VSA information against the print statement. In this case, several of the less experienced participants adopted this strategy as well, leading to more similar patterns of eye movements for the more and less experienced participants. This echoes the behavioral results, which showed that the VSA information helped the less experienced participants to improve their accuracy to the point where it was comparable to that of the more experienced participants.

Although we greatly simplified this binary reverse engineering task to fit the constraints of a small human study using eye-tracking, we believe that the cognitive aspects observed are similar to those in realistic tasks. However, additional research is needed to determine whether our results generalize to more complex VSA information beyond points-to information (i.e., that obtained for more complex code snippets).

[7]RTs remained relatively consistent for each VSA information condition regardless of block order, indicating no significant learning effect.

VII. Conclusion

Overall, the results of this experiment show that fully precise memory VSA information improves the speed and accuracy of reverse engineers reasoning about information flow problems. Precise VSA information was particularly helpful for more difficult problems and for less experienced participants. Given precise memory VSA information, participants changed the ways in which they worked through the problems, and several of the less experienced participants adopted the same strategies as the more experienced participants. Participants did not rely as heavily on imprecise VSA information, but even that VSA information was helpful in improving accuracy. Participants spent the most time on problems with imprecise VSA information, and their accuracy there was significantly higher than when there was no VSA information available. Like precise VSA information, imprecise VSA information was particularly helpful for the more difficult problems and for the less experienced participants, although it did not improve the participants' accuracy as much as precise VSA information did.

Our findings show that aiming for more precision in VSA information is useful for reverse engineers, and also that full precision is not necessary for improving their accuracy. However, having imprecise VSA information does slow reverse engineers. In situations limited by the human reverse engineers' time where accuracy does matter, fully precise analyses like symbolic execution may be more appropriate. In situations limited by human time where accuracy is not as important, it may be better to have no supporting analyses than an imprecise analysis. Further study is necessary to understand which situations require accuracy in spite of the long time scales required by realistic reverse engineering tasks today.

Acknowledgments

We would like to thank Breannan Howell, David Hannasch, Denis Bueno, our editors and reviewers, and the RAMSeS team for their comments and support; we would also like to thank the reverse engineers who made time to be our study's subjects.

This work was supported by the Laboratory Directed Research and Development program at Sandia National Laboratories, a multimission laboratory managed and operated by National Technology and Engineering Solutions of Sandia LLC, a wholly owned subsidiary of Honeywell International Inc. for the U.S. Department of Energy's National Nuclear Security Administration under contract DE-NA0003525. This paper describes objective technical results and analysis. Any subjective views or opinions that might be expressed in the paper do not necessarily represent the views of the U.S. Department of Energy or the United States Government.

References

[1] N. S. Agency, "Ghidra - software reverse engineering framework," https://www.nsa.gov/resources/everyone/ghidra/, 2019.

[2] M. Angelini, G. Blasilli, L. Borzacchiello, E. Coppa, D. C. D'Elia, C. Demetrescu, S. Lenti, S. Nicchi, and G. Santucci, "Symnav: Visually assisting symbolic execution," in *2019 IEEE Symposium on Visualization for Cyber Security (VizSec)*, 2019, pp. 1–11.

[3] G. Balakrishnan and T. Reps, "Analyzing memory accesses in x86 executables," in *International conference on compiler construction*. Springer, 2004, pp. 5–23.

[4] ——, "Wysinwyx: What you see is not what you execute," *ACM Trans. Program. Lang. Syst.*, vol. 32, no. 6, Aug. 2010. [Online]. Available: https://doi.org/10.1145/1749608.1749612

[5] R. Baldoni, E. Coppa, D. C. D'Elia, C. Demetrescu, and I. Finocchi, "A survey of symbolic execution techniques," *ACM Comput. Surv.*, vol. 51, no. 3, 2018.

[6] T. Beelders and J.-P. du Plessis, "The influence of syntax highlighting on scanning and reading behaviour for source code," in *Proceedings of the Annual Conference of the South African Institute of Computer Scientists and Information Technologists*, ser. SAICSIT '16. New York, NY, USA: Association for Computing Machinery, 2016. [Online]. Available: https://doi.org/10.1145/2987491.2987536

[7] D. Brumley, I. Jager, T. Avgerinos, and E. J. Schwartz, "Bap: A binary analysis platform," in *Computer Aided Verification*, G. Gopalakrishnan and S. Qadeer, Eds. Berlin, Heidelberg: Springer Berlin Heidelberg, 2011, pp. 463–469.

[8] A. R. Bryant, R. Mills, G. Peterson, and M. Grimaila, "Software reverse engineering as a sensemaking task," 2012.

[9] K. Butler, M. Leger, D. Bueno, C. Cuellar, M. Haass, T. Loffredo, G. Reedy, and J. Tuminaro, *Creating a User-Centric Data Flow Visualization: A Case Study*, 06 2019, pp. 174–193.

[10] G. Canfora, M. Di Penta, and L. Cerulo, "Achievements and challenges in software reverse engineering," *Commun. ACM*, vol. 54, no. 4, p. 142–151, Apr. 2011. [Online]. Available: https://doi.org/10.1145/1924421.1924451

[11] V. Chipounov, V. Kuznetsov, and G. Candea, "The s2e platform: Design, implementation, and applications," *ACM Trans. Comput. Syst.*, vol. 30, no. 1, pp. 2:1–2:49, Feb. 2012. [Online]. Available: http://doi.acm.org/10.1145/2110356.2110358

[12] C. Cifuentes and B. Scholz, "Parfait: designing a scalable bug checker," in *SAW '08: Proceedings of the 2008 workshop on Static analysis*. New York, NY, USA: ACM, 2008, pp. 4–11.

[13] M. Crosby, J. Scholtz, and S. Wiedenbeck, "The roles beacons play in comprehension for novice and expert programmers," in *PPIG*, 2002.

[14] D. Davis and F. Zhu, "Understanding and improving secure coding behavior with eye tracking methodologies," in *Proceedings of the 2020 ACM Southeast Conference*, ser. ACM SE '20. New York, NY, USA: Association for Computing Machinery, 2020, p. 107–114. [Online]. Available: https://doi.org/10.1145/3374135.3385293

[15] D. Distefano, M. Fähndrich, F. Logozzo, and P. W. O'Hearn, "Scaling static analyses at facebook," *Commun. ACM*, vol. 62, no. 8, p. 62–70, Jul. 2019. [Online]. Available: https://doi.org/10.1145/3338112

[16] Y. Fratantonio, A. Bianchi, W. Robertson, E. Kirda, C. Kruegel, and G. Vigna, "Triggerscope: Towards detecting logic bombs in android applications," 05 2016, pp. 377–396.

[17] GrammaTech, "Codesonar for binaries," https://www.grammatech.com/codesonar-sast-binary.

[18] N. Grech, G. Fourtounis, A. Francalanza, and Y. Smaragdakis, "Shooting from the heap: Ultra-scalable static analysis with heap snapshots," in *Proceedings of the 27th ACM SIGSOFT International Symposium on Software Testing and Analysis*, ser. ISSTA 2018. New York, NY, USA: Association for Computing Machinery, 2018, p. 198–208. [Online]. Available: https://doi.org/10.1145/3213846.3213860

[19] J. M. Henderson, "Human gaze control during real-world scene perception," *Trends in Cognitive Sciences*, vol. 7, no. 11, pp. 498 – 504, 2003. [Online]. Available: http://www.sciencedirect.com/science/article/pii/S1364661303002481

[20] Hex-Rays, "Ida hex-rays decompiler," https://www.hex-rays.com/products/decompiler/.

[21] M. Hind, "Pointer analysis: Haven't we solved this problem yet?" *ACM SIGPLAN/SIGSOFT Workshop on Program Analysis for Software Tools and Engineering*, 07 2001.

[22] S. A. Jessup, S. M. Willis, G. M. Alarcon, and M. A. Lee, "Using eye-tracking data to compare differences in code comprehension and code perceptions between expert and novice programmers," in *54th Hawaii International Conference on System Sciences*, Conference Proceedings.

[23] B. Johnson, Y. Song, E. Murphy-Hill, and R. Bowdidge, "Why don't software developers use static analysis tools to find bugs?" in *Proceedings of the 2013 International Conference on Software Engineering*, ser. ICSE '13. IEEE Press, 2013, p. 672–681.

[24] J. Kaufmann and A. Schering, *Analysis of Variance ANOVA*, 09 2014.

[25] C. Lattner, A. Lenharth, and V. Adve, "Making context-sensitive points-to analysis with heap cloning practical for the real world," in *Proceedings of the 28th ACM SIGPLAN Conference on Programming Language Design and Implementation*, ser. PLDI '07. New York, NY, USA: Association for Computing Machinery, 2007, p. 278–289. [Online]. Available: https://doi.org/10.1145/1250734.1250766

[26] J. Lin, L. Jiang, Y. Wang, and W. Dong, "A value set analysis refinement approach based on conditional merging and lazy constraint solving," *IEEE Access*, vol. 7, pp. 114 593–114 606, 2019.

[27] E. Loftus, D. Miller, and H. Burns, "Semantic integration of verbal information into a visual memory," *Journal of experimental psychology. Human learning and memory*, vol. 4, pp. 19–31, 02 1978.

[28] R. Mangal, X. Zhang, A. V. Nori, and M. Naik, "A user-guided approach to program analysis," in *Proceedings of the 2015 10th Joint Meeting on Foundations of Software Engineering*, ser. ESEC/FSE 2015. New York, NY, USA: Association for Computing Machinery, 2015, p. 462–473. [Online]. Available: https://doi.org/10.1145/2786805.2786851

[29] T. Nosco, J. Ziegler, Z. Clark, D. Marrero, T. Finkler, A. Barbarello, and W. M. Petullo, "The industrial age of hacking," in *USENIX Security Symposium*, 2020.

[30] C. Parnin and S. Rugaber, "Programmer information needs after memory failure," in *2012 20th IEEE International Conference on Program Comprehension (ICPC)*, 2012, pp. 123–132.

[31] N. Peitek, J. Siegmund, and S. Apel, "What drives the reading order of programmers? an eye tracking study," in *Proceedings of the 28th International Conference on Program Comprehension*, ser. ICPC '20. New York, NY, USA: Association for Computing Machinery, 2020, p. 342–353. [Online]. Available: https://doi.org/10.1145/3387904.3389279

[32] K. Rayner, "Eye movements in reading and information processing: 20 years of research." *Psychological bulletin*, vol. 124 3, pp. 372–422, 1998.

[33] ——, "The 35th sir frederick bartlett lecture: Eye movements and attention in reading, scene perception, and visual search," *Quarterly Journal of Experimental Psychology*, vol. 62, no. 8, pp. 1457–1506, 2009, pMID: 19449261. [Online]. Available: https://doi.org/10.1080/17470210902816461

[34] Z. Sharafi, Y.-G. Guéhéneuc, and Z. Soh, "A systematic literature review on the usage of eye-tracking in software engineering," *Elsevier Journal of Software and Information Technology (IST)*, 07 2015.

[35] B. Sharif, M. Falcone, and J. I. Maletic, "An eye-tracking study on the role of scan time in finding source code defects," in *Proceedings of the Symposium on Eye Tracking Research and Applications*, ser. ETRA '12. New York, NY, USA: Association for Computing Machinery, 2012, p. 381–384. [Online]. Available: https://doi.org/10.1145/2168556.2168642

[36] Y. Shoshitaishvili, R. Wang, C. Salls, N. Stephens, M. Polino, A. Dutcher, J. Grosen, S. Feng, C. Hauser, C. Kruegel, and G. Vigna, "Sok: (state of) the art of war: Offensive techniques in binary analysis," in *2016 IEEE Symposium on Security and Privacy (SP)*, 2016, pp. 138–157.

[37] Y. Shoshitaishvili, R. Wang, C. Hauser, C. Kruegel, and G. Vigna, "Firmalice - automatic detection of authentication bypass vulnerabilities in binary firmware," in *22nd Annual Network and Distributed System Security Symposium, NDSS 2015, San Diego, California, USA, February 8-11, 2015*. The Internet Society, 2015.

[38] Y. Shoshitaishvili, M. Weissbacher, L. Dresel, C. Salls, R. Wang, C. Kruegel, and G. Vigna, "Rise of the hacrs: Augmenting autonomous cyber reasoning systems with human assistance," in *Proceedings of the 2017 ACM SIGSAC Conference on Computer*

and Communications Security, ser. CCS '17. New York, NY, USA: Association for Computing Machinery, 2017, p. 347–362. [Online]. Available: https://doi.org/10.1145/3133956.3134105

[39] J. Siegmund, C. Kästner, S. Apel, C. Parnin, A. Bethmann, T. Leich, G. Saake, and A. Brechmann, "Understanding understanding source code with functional magnetic resonance imaging," in *Proceedings of the 36th International Conference on Software Engineering*, ser. ICSE 2014. New York, NY, USA: Association for Computing Machinery, 2014, p. 378–389. [Online]. Available: https://doi.org/10.1145/2568225.2568252

[40] J. Smith, L. Do, and E. Murphy-Hill, "Why can't johnny fix vulnerabilities: A usability evaluation of static analysis tools for security," in *SOUPS @ USENIX Security Symposium*, 2020.

[41] J. Smith, B. Johnson, E. Murphy-Hill, B. Chu, and H. R. Lipford, "Questions developers ask while diagnosing potential security vulnerabilities with static analysis," in *Proceedings of the 2015 10th Joint Meeting on Foundations of Software Engineering*, ser. ESEC/FSE 2015. New York, NY, USA: Association for Computing Machinery, 2015, p. 248–259. [Online]. Available: https://doi.org/10.1145/2786805.2786812

[42] M.-A. D. Storey, F. D. Fracchia, and H. A. Müller, "Cognitive design elements to support the construction of a mental model during software exploration," *J. Syst. Softw.*, vol. 44, no. 3, pp. 171–185, Jan. 1999. [Online]. Available: http://dx.doi.org/10.1016/S0164-1212(98)10055-9

[43] M. K. Tennor, "Reverse engineering cognition," 2015.

[44] R. Turner, M. Falcone, B. Sharif, and A. Lazar, "An eye-tracking study assessing the comprehension of c++ and python source code," in *Proceedings of the Symposium on Eye Tracking Research and Applications*, ser. ETRA '14. New York, NY, USA: Association for Computing Machinery, 2014, p. 231–234. [Online]. Available: https://doi.org/10.1145/2578153.2578218

[45] D. Votipka, S. Rabin, K. Micinski, J. S. Foster, and M. L. Mazurek, "An observational investigation of reverse engineers' process and mental models," in *Extended Abstracts of the 2019 CHI Conference on Human Factors in Computing Systems*, ser. CHI EA '19. New York, NY, USA: Association for Computing Machinery, 2019, p. 1–6. [Online]. Available: https://doi.org/10.1145/3290607.3313040

[46] K. A. Weigand and R. Hartung, "Abduction's role in reverse engineering software," in *2012 IEEE National Aerospace and Electronics Conference (NAECON)*, 2012, pp. 57–62.

[47] W. A. Wickelgren, "Speed-accuracy tradeoff and information processing dynamics," *Acta Psychologica*, vol. 41, no. 1, pp. 67 – 85, 1977. [Online]. Available: http://www.sciencedirect.com/science/article/pii/0001691877900129

[48] J. Wolfe, "Guided search 2.0 a revised model of visual search," *Psychonomic Bulletin and Review*, vol. 1, pp. 202–238, 06 1994.

[49] K. Yakdan, S. Dechand, E. Gerhards-Padilla, and M. Smith, "Helping johnny to analyze malware: A usability-optimized decompiler and malware analysis user study," in *2016 IEEE Symposium on Security and Privacy (SP)*, 2016, pp. 158–177.

[50] K. Yakdan, S. Eschweiler, E. Gerhards-Padilla, and M. Smith, "No more gotos: Decompilation using pattern-independent control-flow structuring and semantic-preserving transformations," in *NDSS*, 2015.

JMPscare: Introspection for Binary-Only Fuzzing

Dominik Maier, Lukas Seidel
TU Berlin
{dmaier@sect, seidel.1@campus}.tu-berlin.de
Both authors contributed equally to this paper

Abstract—**Researchers spend hours, or even days, to understand a target well enough to harness it and get a feedback-guided fuzzer running. Once this is achieved, they rely on their fuzzer to find the right paths, maybe sampling the collected queue entries to see how well it performs. Their knowledge is of little help to the fuzzer, while the fuzzer's behavior is largely a black box to the researcher. Enter JMPscare, providing deep insight into fuzzing queues. By highlighting unreached basic blocks across all queue items during fuzzing, JMPscare allows security researchers to understand the shortcomings of their fuzzer and helps to overcome them. JMPscare can analyze thousands of queue entries efficiently and highlight interesting roadblocks, so-called frontiers. This intel helps the human-in-the-loop to improve the fuzzer, mutator, and harness. Even complex bugs, hard to reach for a generalized fuzzer, hidden deep in the control flow of the target, can be covered in this way. Apart from a purely analytical view, its convenient built-in binary patching facilitates forced execution for subsequent fuzz runs. We demonstrate the benefit of JMPscare on the ARM-based MediaTek Baseband. With JMPscare we gain an in-depth understanding of larger parts of the firmware and find new targets in this RTOS. JMPscare simplifies further mutator, fuzzer, and instrumentation development.**

I. Introduction

Emulators and dynamic binary instrumentation frameworks are very flexible tools. As some of these solutions introduce very little overhead, they can be used for performant feedback-guided fuzzing of binary-only code [7], [14], [16], [17], [23]. Modern binary-only instrumentation only lacks behind source-based instrumentation slightly, incorporating most modern mutation schemes and improvements. State-of-the-art binary instrumentation for fuzzing splits multi-byte comparisons at emulation time to be able to report successful hits of single bytes (*cmpcov* or LAF-intel [15]). It may even supply the fuzzer with feedback about compare results (*cmplog* [5], [9]) or inject address sanitization in an efficient way [7], [10]. Still, they are far from perfect and still get stuck on trivial checksums, complex floating-point calculations, and more complex formats like XML.

While fuzzers get smarter and smarter, being enriched with introspection, better instrumentation, and even symbolic execution [21], [28], it is still common for successful fuzzing campaigns to require lots of manual effort. On top of developing a functioning harness, the researcher collects common tokens and seeds, writes custom mutators [11] and grammars [2], [13] or may even actively guide the fuzzer with waypoints [4].

Especially for binary-only fuzzing, after the initial setup runs, getting deeper knowledge about the fuzzer's actual performance, and figure out shortcomings and roadblocks, can be a daunting task. Often, reverse engineers will look at the resulting coverage maps, debug hand-picked, interesting-looking inputs, and load up several collected traces in existing tools like Lighthouse [12] and Dragondance [1]. However, with thousands of queue entries for a fuzzer like AFL++, the tools reach their limits. Even if loading all traces as once succeeds, it is hard to spot interesting unreached jumps. A fuzzing queue, or corpus, is commonly used in feedback-based fuzzers and collects interesting test cases that led to new coverage or otherwise new feedback during execution. We deem insights into this queue important to improve the overall harness and fuzzer performance. It shows us which parts of the harness the fuzzer explored and at which branches it got stuck. On complex targets, like a full-blown RTOS, a complete view of basic-blocks (not) reached would not provide the researcher with the same insights. No harness covers all basic blocks in the target: reaching some of the branches may rely on the target to be in a different state. Non-covered basic blocks may be reached with better harnessing and mutations or be completely unreachable. The human-in-the-loop has no chance to see this difference immediately just by looking at a coverage map.

To improve this situation, we developed JMPscare, an analysis toolkit that takes all traces in a fuzzer queue into account. The goal is to provide reverse engineers with full insight into their fuzzing campaigns. JMPscare efficiently uncovers never-taken branches, so-called frontiers. To guide the human-in-the-loop towards interesting frontiers, it performs a *Potential New Coverage* (PNC) analysis, surfacing frontiers that can lead to large new control flows if traversed., leading to additional corner cases. JMPscare offers a quick solution to overcome simple frontiers through a single click binary patching to force execution in this direction. With this, the fuzzer traverses any roadblocks but triggers false positives if the prior condition is directly responsible for a crash. While JMPscare will work with any target, as long as a program counter trace of the executions can be acquired, JMPscare features a stand-alone trace collection with native *unicornafl* [11], *BaseSAFE* [17], and qiling [22] support. For the course of this paper, we evaluate JMPscare using the publicly available MediaTek harness and test case corpus of *BaseSAFE*. We are able to gather further knowledge about the harness that the original work could not collect and use, for the lack of JMPscare.

Workshop on Binary Analysis Research (BAR) 2021
21 February 2021, Virtual

https://dx.doi.org/10.14722/bar.2021.23003
www.ndss-symposium.org

A. Contributions

The contributions of this work are as follows:

- We design, implement, and open-source JMPscare, an introspection toolkit suited for the analysis of fuzzer queues with thousands of traces at the same time, with support for *ARM32*, *MIPS*, and *X86_64* targets.
- JMPscare helps researchers to guide their fuzzers better through deep insights, useful analyses, binary ninja integration, and forced execution through binary patching.
- We evaluate JMPscare on the publicly available MediaTek Baseband harness and released corpus of BaseSAFE [18].

B. Structure

In the following, we will discuss related work around fuzzing insights and forced execution. In Sect. III we will outline the design of JMPscare, including its included trace collector, the analyses, and its binary ninja plugin. Further, we evaluate it on the BaseSAFE MediaTek harness and corpus. In Sect. VI, we discuss these results and further use cases for fuzzer development. After highlighting the next steps for JMPscare, we conclude with Sect. VIII.

II. Background

The workflow we ultimately target with the binary-only JMPscare analysis is influenced by Ned Williamson's talk on *Modern Source Fuzzing* [27]. By the example of the XNU kernel source, he proposes, as an initial step, to patch out obstacles in source code for quick results while at the same time working to improve harnessing for sound results. Although forcefully skipping over certain conditional jumps, read *checks*, can lead to subsequent false-positive bugs, the additional insights can help guide the researcher's manual analysis towards real bugs. To properly evaluate coverage data on binary-only runs, we may use Lighthouse [12] for IDA and Binary Ninja and Dragon Dance [1] for Ghidra. Both tools are not targeted towards fuzzing introspection or designed for the quick processing of thousands of files. In contrast to them, JMPscare's PNC analysis can guide the researcher towards very interesting frontiers. One of the few actual fuzzing introspection tools discussed publicly, although yet to be released, is the unnamed source-code fuzzer introspection tool by Aschermann and Schumilo [3].

In contrast to this almost unexplored field of fuzzer insights, *forced execution* has been well-researched. For forced execution, the target's control flow is artificially altered to overcome frontiers by patching or instrumenting branches. Wilhelm and Chiueh load and emulate kernel rootkits for Windows while tracing multiple possible branches through forced sampled execution [26]. This allows them to explore the behavior of the rootkit with ease, even code paths and functionality deeply hidden within the code. In the past, forced execution has also been applied to fuzzing, e.g., by Wang et al. [25]. Their fuzzer *TaintScope* uses dynamic taint analysis and symbolic execution and can bypass checksums by altering the control flow of the target. Peng et al. remove fuzzing roadblocks from the target binary through program transformation. They minimize the potential false positives using a symbolic-execution-based post-processing step [20]. As early as 2007, Will Drewry and Tavis Ormandy proposed the use of control flow alteration for binary-only fuzzing, with their *Valgrind*-based *Flayer* [8]. While advanced for its time, Flayer does not work together with modern coverage-guided fuzzers. Its overall fuzzing performance is further hindered by the slow speed of Valgrind.

III. Design

In the following, we present the design and functionality of JMPscare. JMPscare is a collection of tools aiding researchers to unearth bugs hidden deeply within modern black-box binaries through fuzzing. Our goal with JMPscare was to create an easy-to-use analysis suite for multi-execution jump coverage introspection on a large dataset. Reverse engineers can use it to inspect fuzzing results and specifically see which important jumps were not taken by the fuzzer. As illustrated in Fig. 1, JMPscare contains tools for every step of the way: from trace collection to analysis and reasoning, to visualization and binary patching.

A. Working on Execution Traces

While the JMPscare analysis is geared towards fuzzing, it does not operate on the fuzzer queue or related tools like *afl-showmap* of the original *AFL* [29] directly. Instead, JMPscare uses simple instruction-counter traces and is thus suited for the analysis of execution traces from various sources. The rationale behind this is simple: most binary-only fuzzers only hash edges. This hash may collide and hence cannot be reversed. A perfect 1:1 mapping of taken jumps will be impossible, making the default AFL coverage map useless. The instruction-counter traces used by JMPscare are simple to get for targets that support coverage-guided fuzzing. The expected format is a list of all addresses executed for each input, or at least of all jump sources and targets, in order of execution. These files are called program counter traces, or PC-traces, in the following.

B. Automated JMPscare Analysis

The automated JMPscare analysis is the core component of our contribution. It takes the PC-traces of each fuzzer corpus item and the original binary as input.

1) Finding Frontiers: Our goal is to find basic block edges that the fuzzer was not able to overcome, so-called frontiers, see Fig. 2. For each conditional jump in a trace, we extract the jump's target address and store the jump's information (e.g., condition, target address, instruction size). Subsequently, the jmp analysis disassembles the next address in the trace, i.e., the next executed instruction, and checks whether it matches the last jump's target address. If so, the jump was taken (the condition was true), else it was not taken. After all collected PC-traces were parsed to
jmp's internal map, all conditional branches with multiple executed targets are filtered out. As a result, all remaining branches have been executed for only one truth value.

Example: We have encountered a `beq #0x2000` (*branch if equal*) and the condition was never met during all of our fuzz runs, i.e., the jump was never taken. We only ever encountered the instruction's immediate successor. For the branch at address

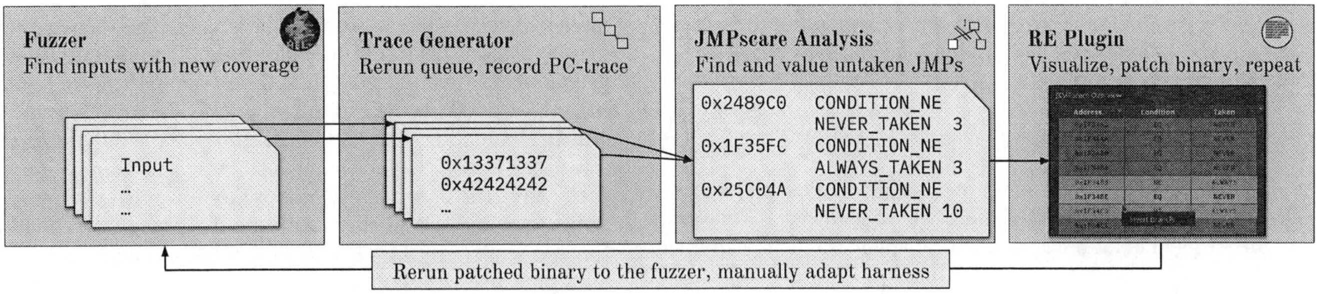

Fig. 1: The Trace Generator reruns the target for each interesting input the fuzzer found up to this point. The JMPscare Analysis then merges all found basic blocks, analyzes the taken and non taken branches and weights blocks that were not reached. The researcher can display them in Binary Ninja, and choose to auto-patch jumps or adapt the harness for the next fuzz run.

`0x1000` the next instruction in any trace was always `0x1004`. By following the branch, we find that the basic block starting at address `0x2000` already has coverage because it was reached in at least one PC-trace on another control flow path. It, therefore, becomes uninteresting for further analyses.
Collecting all taken and non-taken jumps, we can reconstruct all basic blocks the fuzzer reached over time. We uncover conditional jumps with unsatisfied conditions, so branches that were always, or never, taken across all PC-traces.

2) Potential New Coverage Analysis: Additionally, for supported platforms (ARM32 and *thumb* mode at the time), we perform the PNC analysis, a deeper analysis run on the control flow graph, recreated by following branches. In Fig. 2, the *hero branch* will get the highest PNC value. None of the basic blocks behind the frontier were previously touched by any other input. The more new blocks a never-taken branch may reach, the more interesting it may be to the reverse engineer. The PNC analysis assigns a value to each non-traversed frontier, guiding the analyst: a higher score may indicate a potentially more interesting branch, yielding a high amount of new coverage in comparatively little time. This PNC value gets displayed in the Binary Ninja plugin and can be used to prioritize these frontiers for manual analysis, see Sect. IV-C. Up to N edges for each of the previously found uni-directional jumps are traversed. The parameter N is user-specified. Basic blocks are reconstructed again, visited blocks are tainted, and each previously unseen branch target

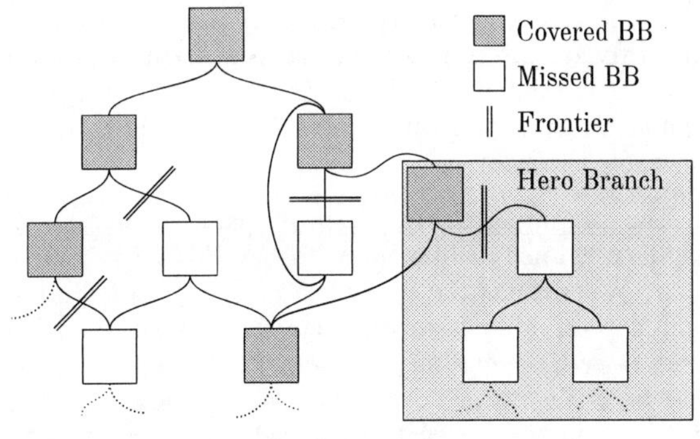

Fig. 2: Basic Blocks, as seen by JMPscare. White blocks have no coverage in the analyzed PC-traces.

gets registered and added to the list of edges to traverse next. After performing N traversals, we are left with information about potential new coverage hidden behind this roadblock jump, measured as the number of basic blocks without previous coverage. Each basic block can either have 0 (in case of a function return, cf. Listing 1), 1 (in case of an unconditional jump, cf. Listing 2) or 2 (in case of a conditional branch, cf. Listing 3) new edges.

Listing 1: Basic Block with no (resolvable) outgoing edge.

```
0x25ec74  add    r3, #0x174
0x25ec76  pop    {r4, r5, pc}
```

Listing 2: Basic Block with one (static) outgoing edge.

```
0x25d68a  mov    r0, r4
0x25d68c  ldr    r1, [pc, #0x1e0]
0x25d68e  b      #0x6c484c
```

Listing 3: Basic Block with two (conditional) outgoing edges.

```
0x1f34ae  cmp    r0, #0xa
0x1f34b0  beq    #0x1f3514
```

In the last iteration, i.e., after taking N jumps, unseen edges are still registered but not traversed. This leaves us with an upper bound of

$$b = 2^{N+1} - 1 \tag{1}$$

and a lower bound of 1 for the amount of possible new edges reachable in N jumps per initial roadblock jump.

C. Reverse Engineering Suite Integration

Finally, the JMPscare toolkit offers integration with reverse engineering software suites. The JMPscare plugins can import and display analysis in programs such as Binary Ninja [24], thus seamlessly integrating with the reverse engineering workflow. We aim to facilitate a researcher's workflow, visualizing the outcome and insights of the analysis step in a comprehensive way. The plugin is designed for visual guidance and allows to quickly navigate to points of interest. Researchers can order by e.g., the PNC score to quickly assess which jumps may lead to especially interesting hero frontiers in order to continue manual reverse engineering there. The plugin also allows the researcher to negate jumps at this point, forcing control flow down this path for subsequent fuzz runs. The mostly platform-agnostic, stand-alone approach in the design of the other parts of JMPscare theoretically allows for an integration in various software solutions, not limiting the researcher in the selection of their preferred tool.

IV. Implementation

After discussing the ideas and design philosophy behind JMPscare in the previous section, we will now go over some of the implementation details and challenges of the provided toolkit.

A. Stand-Alone Trace Collection

The JMPscare toolkit currently offers example implementations in Python library and Rust, generating program counter (PC) traces in the appropriate format, i.e., a file with one address per line. The Python library and Rust crate can be easily imported and used with *unicornafl*, *BaseSAFE* and *qiling* harnesses. They all make use of the *Unicorn* multi-architecture CPU emulator framework [19] for binary-only instrumentation for black-box fuzzing with AFL++ [11]. Traces are generated for each input of the to-be-analyzed fuzzing queue. To keep up with a large number of queue entries, JMPscare can make use of the harnesses forkserver to speed up trace collection. As constantly writing trace files back to disc will slow down fuzzing, the trace collection should only be executed on-demand, independently of the actual fuzzing run. In order to guide the disassembler during the analysis of ARM binaries, the addresses of instructions that were executed in *thumb* mode are expected to have their Least Significant Bit (LSB) set to 1. Whenever the researcher needs introspection, they will run the PC-trace collection on the current queue to then continue with the JMPscare analysis step.

B. JMPscare Analysis

The JMPscare analysis tool is written in Rust and heavily relies on the widely-used *Capstone* [6] disassembler. At the moment, x86_64, MIPS, and 32 bit ARM (incl. thumb2) architectures are supported. By disassembling instructions at all traced addresses, the initial analysis pass determines which jumps were taken and which basic blocks were reached, taking into account all basic blocks across multiple runs taken from the fuzzer queue. Addresses in execution traces are used to read from the provided binary file and disassemble the instruction at the corresponding location using *Capstone*. An offset can be specified in case the binary blob was not loaded at $0x0$ during execution. As the last step during analysis, noise reduction is performed by only retaining those roadblock jumps in our list, which, when following the non-observed branch, do not immediately lead to a basic block that already has coverage. The JMPscare analysis works quickly on thousands of traces (cf. Sect. V-A).

During PNC analysis, function calls are usually treated as conditional jumps: The function, as well as the code after the call, will be treated as a new edge. For unresolvable branches, i.e., branches featuring register targets such as `blx r3`, the user has the option to guide the analyzer on how to treat them. Such jumps present no problem during the first analysis step, as we simply disassemble at a given address following an input PC-trace. However, resolving them during PNC analysis is not trivially possible as we would have to infer register contents during a static pass. The tool features a `weight` flag, specifying to what degree the observation of an unresolvable function call should be counted towards unseen basic blocks. With the default value of 1, each of these calls will be counted as one new block, even if the edge cannot be traversed. Specifying a weight of 0 leads to simply ignoring such calls. The user can also choose to make them count more. The reasoning behind this would be that in certain situations, function calls may be of increased interest, and huge weights allow the user to spot them more easily. While the function might have been seen before or might quickly terminate, it could also lead to a large previously undiscovered part of the binary. Multi-targeted jumps, such as callbacks or jump tables, are not being handled at the moment. These, too, are non-trivial to resolve during static analysis. While we considered using the capabilities of an external tool, such as Binary Ninja, for indirect jump resolution, we decided to design and implement the tool in a self-contained way for now. This enables the development of plugins for other RE suites, such as Ghidra, in a straightforward way.

In the current design, the analysis tool expects and works on a single binary blob or code segment. This has the shortcoming that the tool would encounter a problem if it is presented with the PC-trace of e.g., an ELF, as it may contain jumps into code segments not being present in the loaded binary, e.g., into shared libraries.

After JMPscare completes its analyses on all trace files in the queue, it outputs a single file. This file contains details about all uni-directional jumps. Every line describes one such jump, specifying the address in the binary, the jump's condition, whether it is taken always or never. For PNC, it also includes the number of previously unseen basic blocks reachable within a user-specified amount of edge traversals, as discussed in Sect. III-B1, e.g.:

```
0x1172 CONDITION_LT NEVER_TAKEN 15
```

This generated analysis output summary can then be imported with the provided disassembler plugin, as discussed in the following.

C. Binary Ninja Plugin

The JMPscare toolkit comes with a Python plugin for use with the Binary Ninja [24] reverse engineering software. While plugins for other popular RE suites, such as Ghidra, are planned, we chose Binary Ninja for our initial development. The software offers powerful and user-friendly scripting- and plugin environment. At the same time, the tool lays the focus on concise visualizations and was hence well-suited for what we wanted to achieve.

The plugin, see Fig. 3, provides a tabular overview of results previously obtained with the JMPscare analysis tool. Each row presents the user with all the information available for a certain address in the analysis summary and is colored green or red, depending on whether the jump was observed to have been always or never taken, respectively. Lines featuring found roadblock instructions are also colored respectively in the disassembly view, providing visual aid in navigating the graph view while looking into analysis results. The overview can be used for quick navigation and automatic patching.

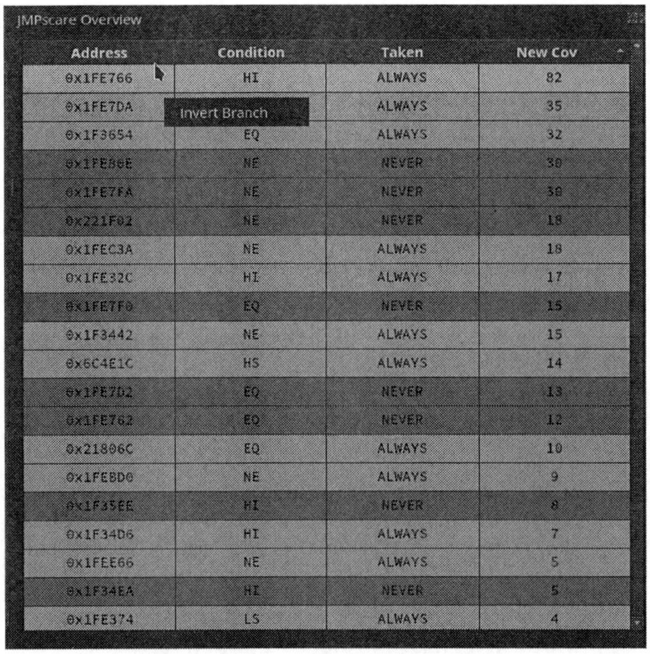

Fig. 3: JMPscare UI in Binary Ninja

Using Binary Ninja's built-in API capabilities, inverting a branch, e.g., from `beq #0x1000` to `bne #0x1000`, can be achieved via a single context-menu-click on any list entry, see the blue (activated) entry in Fig. 3. This alters the control flow quickly for forced execution. In the course of our work, we patched Binary Ninja to support this auto-patching feature for ARM's *thumb* mode, as it was formerly missing for this architecture. We consequently opened a pull request to get this patch upstreamed.

V. Evaluation

A. Analysis of Baseband Firmware PC-Traces

In the following, we show the application of JMPscare by analyzing 3580 traces, obtained by fuzzing the ARM firmware for MediaTek's Helio X10 (MT6795) baseband processor for 24 hours. The evaluated harness was taken from the BaseSAFE's repository queue and fuzzes the `errc_event_handler_main` function, including various ASN.1 parsers. We conducted the following experiments on an Intel Core i7-1065G7 CPU @ 1.3 GHz with a maximum frequency of 3.8 GHz on a 512 GB M.2 NVMe SSD. Averaged over 5 runs each, analyzing 5000 files in
jmp takes 17 seconds on this machine. 2500 files take 8 seconds to analyze. Analyzing 250 files never surpassed 1.2 seconds. Initially, we emulated and fuzzed the firmware using *unicornafl* with AFL++. We fuzzed the target for 24 hours with *cmpcov* level 1 (splitting multi-byte compares during emulation [15]), resulting in 3580 queue entries. To collect coverage information, we plugged the JMPscare-col Rust crate into the existing Rust BaseSAFE harness [18]. The executions on all 3580 fuzzing inputs generated an equal amount of execution traces, each with one address per line corresponding to each executed instruction. The obtained traces feature 8400 executed instructions on average. As no instructions are added by the *unicornafl* instrumentation, this is the total count of target instructions. File input/output dominates execution time of JMPscare analysis runs. In total, the 3580 execution traces contain 3599027 jumps, making up for about 12% of all encountered instructions. Of those, 1099 jumps are unique. 270 are uni-directional, i.e., representing frontiers for the fuzzer that the harness did not overcome in 24 hours. Here, the branching condition was always true or always false in all the traces. We performed PNC deep analysis in two modes: following the next $N = 8$ jumps and with $N = 1000$ jumps. The top ten roadblock jumps with the most edges behind them for $N = 8$ offer between 14 and 340 new basic blocks without coverage in the analyzed traces, with the median being 120.

B. Fuzzer Exploration, Graphed

Additionally, we conducted an experiment to see how the numbers of uni-directional jumps and potential new edges being blocked by them correlate with the number of input PC-traces in the queue. For this, we let the fuzzer run for 24 hours to get an initial corpus. We then removed the newest trace for each round, ran the JMPscare analysis on all remaining traces, and picked the next trace, with a depth of $N = 8$ and $N = 1000$ for PNC analysis. Figure 4(a) shows the amount of unique frontier jumps in correlation to the number of execution traces on a logarithmic scale. As expected, after an initial increase, the growth stagnates as it becomes more and more difficult for the fuzzer to find inputs that lead to new program parts. In Figure 4(b), the number of uni-directional jumps is illustrated. Additional execution traces reflect broader coverage, consequently containing more paths with more jumps. At some point, the fuzzer finds more condition-switching inputs than previously unknown jumps. The relation saturates before finally decreasing. In other words, in the beginning, a lot of totally new jumps are found and taken into one direction until the right inputs are found to switch the condition and follow the second edge. From here on, the jump is no longer considered to be uni-directional, resulting in the observed decrease. Fig. 4(c) shows the Coverage Score, i.e., the number of previously unknown basic blocks behind all frontiers with a depth of up to $N = 8$. As long as the analyzed traces themselves only provide marginal coverage, every new uni-directional jump may lead to huge increases in potential new coverage. Increased coverage through provided input cases leads consequently to earlier termination during traversal of unseen edges while performing PNC analysis, as the probability of encountering a block that already has coverage increases. Instead, we may also follow up to $N = 1000$ branches, analyzing the binary almost fully from the start. While we initially aimed for smaller static analysis, our tests showed that the analysis speed is still sufficient for day-to-day use when analyzing the binary fully.

VI. Discussion

In this section, we interpret our evaluation results. First, we discuss the direct positive impact JMPscare has on fuzzing harnesses, and specifically on the MediaTek Baseband harness. Then, we quickly describe an additional use-case: the improvement of fuzzers and instrumentation.

A. Improving Harnesses Through JMPscare

Naturally to the domain, many of the found frontiers turn out to be false positives. For example, the largest amount of

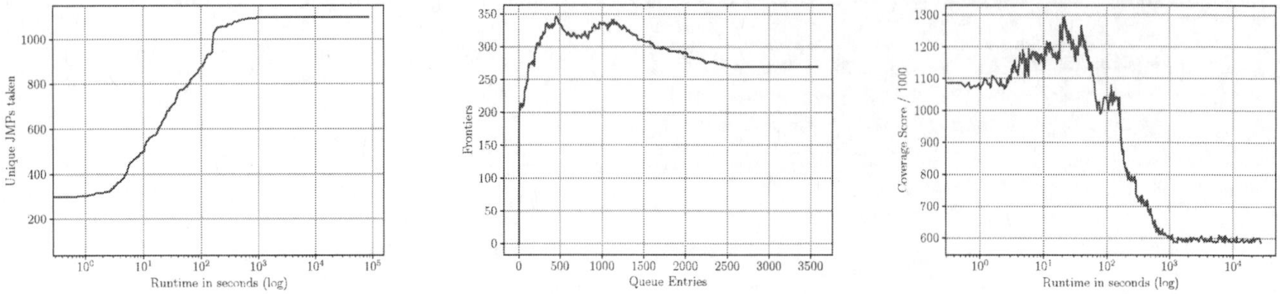

(a) Over time, the number of unique jump comes to a halt. The fuzzer takes less and less new unique jumps.

(b) The JMPscare frontier count increases sharply at the beginning when the fuzzer finds new paths. Once it explored the target, the amount of unexplored branches decreases slowly

(c) With $N = 8$, the coverage peaks after exploring most of the program and reaches a saturated corpus.

new basic blocks was found to be behind a double roadblock. Following a full 4 byte compare (`cmp r3, r2`), we first encounter a branch if equal, which is never taken, followed by a branch if (unsigned) higher, which is always taken. Upon closer inspection and reverse engineering of the code surrounding these branches, it turned out that this was the check for a so-called *Message-ID*, widely used throughout the firmware to guide incoming messages through different stages of baseband processing. As these Message-IDs were hardcoded within the fuzzing harness, it is clear why the code behind this check could not be reached. We analyzed recovered uni-directional jumps and prove that about 92% of them were either Message-ID checks or error handling, e.g., bounds checks, resulting in assertion failures. This shows that we reached good coverage for the BaseSAFE harness in 24 hours. Very few reachable blocks remain behind complex frontiers. Given the nature of the target, a low-powered embedded device with a space-saving message format, this is unsurprising [17]. As the evaluation shows, in Sect. V-B, at an earlier point of time, a lot of blocks were not yet uncovered JMPscare, the reverse engineer could have taken a short-cut using JMPscare. By adjusting the aforementioned Message-ID in the harness, it is possible to reach different parts of the program.

Although it is not surprising that fuzzing a different part of the program, which was previously purposefully ignored, leads to greatly increased coverage, the additional insights aid us to find our next target. The `errc_event_handler_main` contains checks for more than 20 different Message-IDs of which not all may be equally interesting. The combination of JMPscare analysis and direct integration with a reverse engineering suite, such as Binary Ninja, enables us to effectively evaluate which target might be the most promising to fuzz next, leading to new coverage or large functions the quickest.

B. Basic Block Classification

Inspired by the insights and by further looking into the results of our analyses, we arrive at the following conclusion: After a fixed amount of fuzzing executions, given an arbitrary but fixed harness and initial state (e.g., a snapshot), every basic block in the target falls into one of the following categories:

1) *Reached:* The fuzzer has already produced an input to the harness, which leads to or has a path containing the basic block. This block is in one of the traces.

2) *Reachable:* A basic block falls into this category if the fuzzer has the capabilities to reach this block in a reasonable time. It simply needs additional cycles to find input satisfying some conditions or to find a certain, presumably long, path.

3) *Reachable Behind Frontier:* While still reachable in theory, a roadblock may not be solvable by the current fuzzer in any reasonable time. Manual aid, binary patching, or an improvement of the fuzzer itself, will be needed to overcome this frontier. This can be the case, when the control flow altering state becomes too complex, e.g., through deeply nested structs with multiple pointer indirections or cryptography. JMPscare is especially valuable for reachable blocks behind frontiers.

4) *Reachable Altering Precondition:* Cases in which control flow to the block exists but are hidden behind state that cannot be changed by mutating the input. This may be the case if we start fuzzing from a snapshot and the socket in question has not been opened before snapshotting. Another example is the Message-ID we had hardcoded in the harness in Sect. VI-A. To overcome this issue, we either have to change the harness or start over with a different setup or snapshot. While altering the Message-ID is well in scope, it may be impractical to manually set up memory to mimic concepts such as whole file systems or open socket connections. For simple cases, forced execution can also help to reach these branches.

5) *Unreachable:* Of course, a block could be completely unreachable. In the case of a baseband, most parts of the baseband will never be reached from a given entry point. However, the block may become reachable with the first memory corruption the fuzzer finds.

C. Improving Fuzzers Through JMPscare

Improving the harness over and over throughout a fuzzing campaign, patching out checksums, adding tokens to the input, and so on, greatly improves the success chance. It is the norm to have a human in the loop, and it is still the major use case for fuzzers. However, we strive to make fuzzing available to a broader audience. This can only be achieved by keeping the complexity of the harness low. Instead, the fuzzer needs to be improved. For individual fuzzer and instrumentation engineering purposes, JMPscare can also deliver valuable insights. To give one example, *unicornafl* supports the splitting of compare operations for ARM and X86(_64), often called *cmpcov*, or *laf-intel* [11]. When fuzzing with *cmpcov* enabled, we see that the fuzzer traverses checks of two bytes more easily, which are quite common in baseband firmware, for tags and Message-IDs. On the flip side, the overall speed decreased slightly, from around $1.65k$ executions per second to $1.4k$ exec/s on the machine used during the evaluation. A deeper analysis of fuzzing performance goes beyond the scope of this paper. This anecdotal observation, however, suggests that researchers can directly measure and evaluate novel fuzzing mechanisms and their effect using the JMPscare analysis.

VII. Future Work

In the future, JMPscare can be extended in multiple directions. Using JMPscare analysis, binary-only fuzzing can be improved, and recent advancements can be benchmarked in-depth, as briefly discussed in Sect. VI-C. A straightforward addition to our work will be support for additional reverse engineering platforms, such as IDA and Ghidra, and tracers to support additional instrumentation methods, for example, *qemu-mode*. During analysis, additional heuristics for interesting basic blocks can be implemented, and the GUI representation can even be enriched with taint and dataflow-data in order to provide the reverse engineer a better overview. Similarly, the JMPscare approach can be enriched with symbolic execution, in a similar fashion to *Driller* [28] and *QSYM* [28], however with additional human guidance. Apart from binary-only progress, the concept of JMPscare can be adapted to source-based fuzzing, for example, by analyzing *gcov* output for each test case and then deducting basic block interestingness on a language level or on the compiled binary.

As the last research point, deeper static analysis can enhance the quality of the PNC analysis. Currently, indirect jumps to unknown locations are not handled by JMPscare in a precise way. The reverse engineer simply sets a weight factor, a rough estimate of how to count these indirect branches, when encountered. Additional analysis could resolve these indirect jumps to better approximate the actual potential new coverage hidden behind them.

VIII. Conclusion

With the wave of published fuzzing research in recent years, it is surprising to see close to no existing tools for further introspection into the actual fuzzing runs. While fuzzers work on vast amounts of data and an increase of the overall performance can be statistically proven, deeper insight into the fuzz runs will immediately show the fine-grained roadblocks. With tools such as JMPscare, far better results can be achieved, as they aid researchers during manual reviews. While automated analyses improve steadily, putting the human in the loop can still greatly enhance the overall bug-finding performance. Forced execution allows the reverse engineer to potentially overcome hard challenges, such as checksums or cryptographic operations, without going through the trouble of rewriting the test case. At the same time, information gained through introspection via JMPscare can be used to aid a researcher in their decision where to continue fuzzing. In the case of fuzzing the MediaTek baseband firmware, we were able to make an informed decision on which message type, specified by the Message-ID, would be a promising next target without requiring large changes to our harness. We will use JMPscare to improve binary-only instrumentation in the future.

Availability

JMPscare and all related source code is available open-source at https://github.com/fgsect/JMPscare.

Acknowledgments

The authors would like to thank Jiska Classen for her valuable feedback and insights.

References

[1] 0ffffffffh, "Dragon dance," Jan 2021, [Online; accessed 7. Jan. 2021]. [Online]. Available: https://github.com/0ffffffffh/dragondance

[2] C. Aschermann, T. Frassetto, T. Holz, P. Jauernig, A. Sadeghi, and D. Teuchert, "NAUTILUS: fishing for deep bugs with grammars," in *26th Annual Network and Distributed System Security Symposium, NDSS 2019, San Diego, California, USA, February 24-27, 2019*. The Internet Society, 2019. [Online]. Available: https://www.ndss-symposium.org/ndss-paper/nautilus-fishing-for-deep-bugs-with-grammars/

[3] C. Aschermann and S. Schumilo, "What the fuzz," Black Hat Europe 2019, Dec. 2019. [Online]. Available: https://www.blackhat.com/eu-19/briefings/schedule/#what-the-fuzz-18031

[4] C. Aschermann, S. Schumilo, A. Abbasi, and T. Holz, "Ijon: Exploring deep state spaces via fuzzing," in *2020 IEEE Symposium on Security and Privacy, SP 2020, San Francisco, CA, USA, May 18-21, 2020*. IEEE, 2020, pp. 1597–1612.

[5] C. Aschermann, S. Schumilo, T. Blazytko, R. Gawlik, and T. Holz, "Redqueen: Fuzzing with input-to-state correspondence." in *NDSS*, vol. 19, 2019, pp. 1–15.

[6] Capstone, "The Ultimate Disassembly Framework," Nov 2020, [Online; accessed 9. Jan. 2021]. [Online]. Available: https://www.capstone-engine.org

[7] S. Dinesh, N. Burow, D. Xu, and M. Payer, "Retrowrite: Statically instrumenting COTS binaries for fuzzing and sanitization," in *2020 IEEE Symposium on Security and Privacy, SP 2020, San Francisco, CA, USA, May 18-21, 2020*. IEEE, 2020, pp. 1497–1511.

[8] W. Drewry and T. Ormandy, "Flayer: Exposing application internals," in *First USENIX Workshop on Offensive Technologies, WOOT '07, Boston, MA, USA, August 6, 2007*, D. Boneh, T. Garfinkel, and D. Song, Eds. USENIX Association, 2007. [Online]. Available: https://www.usenix.org/conference/woot-07/flayer-exposing-application-internals

[9] A. Fioraldi, D. C. D'Elia, and E. Coppa, "Weizz: Automatic grey-box fuzzing for structured binary formats," in *Proceedings of the 29th ACM SIGSOFT International Symposium on Software Testing and Analysis*, 2020, pp. 1–13.

[10] A. Fioraldi, D. C. D'Elia, and L. Querzoni, "Fuzzing binaries for memory safety errors with qasan," in *IEEE Secure Development, SecDev 2020, Atlanta, GA, USA, September 28-30, 2020*. IEEE, 2020, pp. 23–30.

[11] A. Fioraldi, D. Maier, H. Eißfeldt, and M. Heuse, "AFL++ : Combining incremental steps of fuzzing research," in *14th USENIX Workshop on Offensive Technologies, WOOT 2020, August 11, 2020*, Y. Yarom and S. Zennou, Eds. USENIX Association, 2020. [Online]. Available: https://www.usenix.org/conference/woot20/presentation/fioraldi

[12] gaasedelen, "Lighthouse - a code coverage explorer for reverse engineers," Jan 2021, [Online; accessed 7. Jan. 2021]. [Online]. Available: https://github.com/gaasedelen/lighthouse

[13] R. Gopinath and A. Zeller, "Building fast fuzzers," *CoRR*, vol. abs/1911.07707, 2019. [Online]. Available: http://arxiv.org/abs/1911.07707

[14] E. Gustafson, M. Muench, C. Spensky, N. Redini, A. Machiry, Y. Fratantonio, D. Balzarotti, A. Francillon, Y. R. Choe, C. Kruegel, and G. Vigna, "Toward the analysis of embedded firmware through automated re-hosting," in *22nd International Symposium on Research in Attacks, Intrusions and Defenses (RAID 2019)*. Chaoyang District, Beijing: USENIX Association, Sep. 2019, pp. 135–150. [Online]. Available: https://www.usenix.org/conference/raid2019/presentation/gustafson

[15] laf intel, "Circumventing Fuzzing Roadblocks with Compiler Transformations," Aug. 2016, [Online; accessed 11. Jan. 2021]. [Online]. Available: https://lafintel.wordpress.com

[16] D. Maier, B. Radtke, and B. Harren, "Unicorefuzz: On the viability of emulation for kernelspace fuzzing," in *13th USENIX Workshop on Offensive Technologies, WOOT 2019, Santa Clara, CA, USA, August 12-13, 2019*, A. Gantman and C. Maurice, Eds. USENIX Association, 2019. [Online]. Available: https://www.usenix.org/conference/woot19/presentation/maier

[17] D. Maier, L. Seidel, and S. Park, "BaseSAFE: baseband sanitized fuzzing through emulation," in *WiSec '20: 13th ACM Conference on Security and Privacy in Wireless and Mobile Networks, Linz, Austria, July 8-10, 2020*, R. Mayrhofer and M. Roland, Eds. ACM, 2020, pp. 122–132. [Online]. Available: https://doi.org/10.1145/3395351.3399360

[18] ——. (2021, Jan) BaseSAFE: Open source framework. [Online; accessed 7. Jan. 2021]. [Online]. Available: https://github.com/fgsect/BaseSAFE

[19] A. Q. Ngyuen and H. V. Dang. (2020) Unicorn: Next generation CPU emulator framework. [Online]. Available: http://www.unicorn-engine.org/BHUSA2015-unicorn.pdf

[20] H. Peng, Y. Shoshitaishvili, and M. Payer, "T-fuzz: Fuzzing by program transformation," in *2018 IEEE Symposium on Security and Privacy (SP)*, 2018, pp. 697–710.

[21] S. Poeplau and A. Francillon, "Symbolic execution with symcc: Don't interpret, compile!" in *29th USENIX Security Symposium, USENIX Security 2020, August 12-14, 2020*, S. Capkun and F. Roesner, Eds. USENIX Association, 2020, pp. 181–198. [Online]. Available: https://www.usenix.org/conference/usenixsecurity20/presentation/poeplau

[22] qilingframework, "Qiling advanced binary emulation framework," Jan 2021, [Online; accessed 12. Jan. 2021]. [Online]. Available: https://github.com/qilingframework/qiling

[23] J. Ruge, J. Classen, F. Gringoli, and M. Hollick, "Frankenstein: Advanced wireless fuzzing to exploit new bluetooth escalation targets," in *29th USENIX Security Symposium, USENIX Security 2020, August 12-14, 2020*, S. Capkun and F. Roesner, Eds. USENIX Association, 2020, pp. 19–36. [Online]. Available: https://www.usenix.org/conference/usenixsecurity20/presentation/ruge

[24] Vector 35 Inc., "Binary Ninja," Jan 2021, [Online; accessed 7. Jan. 2021]. [Online]. Available: https://binary.ninja/

[25] T. Wang, T. Wei, G. Gu, and W. Zou, "Checksum-aware fuzzing combined with dynamic taint analysis and symbolic execution," *ACM Trans. Inf. Syst. Secur.*, vol. 14, no. 2, Sep. 2011. [Online]. Available: https://doi.org/10.1145/2019599.2019600

[26] J. Wilhelm and T.-c. Chiueh, "A forced sampled execution approach to kernel rootkit identification," in *Recent Advances in Intrusion Detection*, C. Kruegel, R. Lippmann, and A. Clark, Eds. Berlin, Heidelberg: Springer Berlin Heidelberg, 2007, pp. 219–235.

[27] N. Williamson, "Modern source fuzzing [talk]," OffensiveCon19, Feb. 2019.

[28] I. Yun, S. Lee, M. Xu, Y. Jang, and T. Kim, "QSYM : A practical concolic execution engine tailored for hybrid fuzzing," in *27th USENIX Security Symposium, USENIX Security 2018, Baltimore, MD, USA, August 15-17, 2018*, W. Enck and A. P. Felt, Eds. USENIX Association, 2018, pp. 745–761. [Online]. Available: https://www.usenix.org/conference/usenixsecurity18/presentation/yun

[29] M. Zalewski, "American Fuzzy Lop - Whitepaper," https://lcamtuf.coredump.cx/afl/technical_details.txt, 2016.

icLibFuzzer: Isolated-context libFuzzer for Improving Fuzzer Comparability

Yu-Chuan Liang
National Taiwan University
jasonliang30115@gmail.com

Hsu-Chun Hsiao
National Taiwan University
hchsiao@csie.ntu.edu.tw

Abstract—**libFuzzer is a powerful fuzzer that has helped find thousands of bugs in real-world programs. However, fuzzers that seek to compare with libFuzzer and its variants face two significant limitations. First, they are restricted to use the time-to-first-crash metric rather than the code-coverage metric because libFuzzer will abort whenever the fuzzing target crashes. Second, even if libFuzzer in the *ignore-crash mode* can continue after finding a crash, it may produce wrong results for programs expecting a clean global context. Thus, fuzzers wishing to compare with libFuzzer are restricted to use carefully modified programs or programs without global-context dependency. To solve this context pollution problem and enhance comparability between libFuzzer and other fuzzers, we present a new libFuzzer mode called *isolated-context mode* (icLibFuzzer) that isolates the contexts of each fuzzer instance and fuzzing target, allowing to reinitialize the fuzzing target's context after each execution efficiently. To implement icLibFuzzer, we modify libFuzzer's in-process infrastructure into a lightweight forkserver infrastructure inspired by AFL's design and propose *structure packing*, which speeds up the fuzzing speed by about 2x. We compare icLibFuzzer with four state-of-the-art fuzzers (AFL, Angora, QSYM, and Honggfuzz) using several real-world programs. The experiment result shows that icLibFuzzer outperforms these four fuzzers in most target programs after 24 hours of fuzzing and maintains the lead from 24 to 72 hours. To demonstrate that we can easily keep up with libFuzzer's updates, we upgrade icLibFuzzer to using the latest libFuzzer (from LLVM9 to LLVM11) with no change to our code base. Our preliminary evaluation hints at icLibFuzzer-LLVM11's promising improvement compared with icLibFuzzer-LLVM9 and AFL++, one of the latest fuzzers in the AFL family. We hope icLibFuzzer can serve as another baseline for fuzzing research. Our source code is available at GitHub.**

I. Introduction

Fuzzing is a popular technique for automatically finding bugs. To fuzz a computer program, which can be a standalone executable or a library function, a fuzzing tool (called a fuzzer) feeds random inputs into the program and reports inputs that cause unexpected behaviors such as hangs or crashes. These interesting inputs can further help uncover bugs in the program.

Workshop on Binary Analysis Research (BAR) 2021
21 February 2021, Virtual

https://dx.doi.org/10.14722/bar.2021.23013
www.ndss-symposium.org

AFL [20] and libFuzzer [14] are two of the most successful fuzzers with different design goals and have been evolving separately for several years. AFL aims to continuously fuzz executables, while libFuzzer targets library functions and stops whenever hitting a crash. As a result, fuzzers in the AFL and libFuzzer families mainly consider the code-coverage and time-to-first-crash metrics, respectively. It is challenging to compare them directly with each other over the same metrics.

This comparability issue is solved partially by enabling the *ignore-crash mode* in libFuzzer. The ignore-crash mode spawns multiple fuzzer instances and fuzzes a target executable in different processes parallelly. Whenever a fuzzer instance exits or finds a crash, libFuzzer will restart the fuzzer instance. Although libFuzzer in the ignore-crash mode can fuzz continuously and restart after a crash, the fuzzing results may be incorrect when previous non-crash runs pollute the global context because of libFuzzer's in-process infrastructure. Therefore, most fuzzers were compared with libFuzzer only on few manually tuned datasets (e.g., fuzzer-test-suite [9]) that allow both fuzzer families to operate correctly.

Due to the lack of comparability, the advances in libFuzzer seem to be left unnoticed in the state-of-the-art academic papers, which predominantly consider the code-coverage metric. For example, libFuzzer has integrated advanced instrumentation features such as CMP tracing since 2017, but similar features were unavailable in AFL-based fuzzers until 2019 in RedQueen [2] (which is later integrated into AFL++ [7]). To this end, we believe a *bridge* between these two fuzzer families is needed to foster knowledge accumulation and sharing in the community.

In this work, we present *isolated-context libFuzzer (icLibFuzzer)*, a new libFuzzer mode that bridges the two fuzzer families and allows them to be compared over commonly seen metrics on arbitrary programs. To solve the context pollution problem, icLibFuzzer runs in the AFL-like forkserver architecture and correctly manages the global context between executions. As speed is a crucial requirement of fuzzers, we further optimize icLibFuzzer's implementation via *structure packing*, achieving similar performance to other forkserver-based implementation while preserving libFuzzer's advanced instrumentation features.

To demonstrate that icLibFuzzer improves fuzzer comparability, we compare icLibFuzzer with four state-of-the-art fuzzers (AFL, Angora, Honggfuzz, and QSYM) using the code-coverage metric on several real-world programs. icLibFuzzer outperforms all of the tested fuzzers in most target programs after 24 hours of fuzzing. Moreover, icLibFuzzer maintains the lead and continues to increase the code coverage from 24 to 72 hours[1].

To incentivize adoption, we provide a compiler wrapper to compile standalone programs without modifying the source code. As libFuzzer is under active development and new features may appear in the future, we also provide a guideline for adding its new features into icLibFuzzer. To demonstrate that we can easily keep up with libFuzzer's updates, we upgrade icLibFuzzer to using the latest libFuzzer (i.e., upgrading from LLVM9 to LLVM11) with no change to our code base. Our preliminary evaluation hints at icLibFuzzer-LLVM11's promising improvement compared with icLibFuzzer-LLVM9 and AFL++, one of the latest fuzzers in the AFL family that integrates multiple enhanced techniques.

This paper makes the following contributions:

1) We design and implement icLibFuzzer, a new libFuzzer mode that isolates the contexts of each fuzzing target and fuzzer instance, enabling continuous fuzzing on arbitrary programs while inheriting libFuzzer's advanced instrumentation features and analysis techniques.
2) We propose the structure packing technique to improve the running speed of icLibFuzzer by roughly 2x.
3) We evaluate icLibFuzzer using several real-world programs and find that icLibFuzzer outperforms all of the tested fuzzers in most target programs, implying that icLibFuzzer is a competitive fuzzing tool and may serve as another evaluation baseline for fuzzing research.
4) We release our source code at https://github.com/csienslab/icLibFuzzer.

II. Background

libFuzzer supports several advanced instrumentation features that have not been fully adopted by other fuzzers, but it is challenging to compare libFuzzer with others due to its in-process design. We briefly introduce libFuzzer in this section and explain the comparability issues in the next section.

A. libFuzzer Overview

Similar to AFL, libFuzzer is a *coverage-guided* fuzzer, which collects coverage information through *instrumentation*, selects interesting inputs (called *seeds*) based on the collected information, and mutates seeds to generate new inputs.

For example, to collect program branches covered by inputs, code-coverage instrumentation inserts instructions to the target binary to record the current program counter right after each conditional branch, exemplified by the following C code:

```
if (a > 0) {
   bitmap[current_program_ctr] += 1;
   if (b > 0) {
      bitmap[current_program_ctr] += 1;
      do_something();
   }
}
```

[1]72 hours is the longest time budget that we can afford in our experiments.

After the program terminates, the `bitmap` array records the branches reached by the input. Thus, given a set of inputs, we can measure a fuzzer's branch coverage (a type of code-coverage metrics) by accumulating the information recorded in the bitmap.

While AFL mainly collects code-coverage information and keeps coverage-increasing inputs as seeds, libFuzzer collects additional information such as the branch condition via instrumentation and keeps inputs that make a variety kinds of "progress" (e.g., closer to pass a conditional branch), as we will see in the next subsection.

B. libFuzzer's Advanced Instrumentation Features

libFuzzer supports several advanced instrumentation features to assist fuzzing. Some of these features are unavailable in other fuzzers or appear years later. For example, libFuzzer implemented CMP tracing in 2017, but similar ideas were unavailable in other fuzzers until 2019 in RedQueen [2].

Below we choose and describe four advanced instrumentation features in libFuzzer which may impact code coverage significantly, and have also been ported to our icLibFuzzer: CMP tracing, value profiling, compare function, and dataflow trace. We also provide a guideline in Section VII to port new libFuzzer features to icLibFuzzer.

1) CMP tracing: Due to their random nature, fuzzers often struggle to discover inputs satisfying complex branch conditions, such as `x==65536` or `pwd=="secr3t"`. Instead of random guessing, libFuzzer supports a salient feature called CMP tracing, which hooks all of the `CMP` instructions (in the LLVM IR instruction set) at compile time and stores the two operands, indexed by their xored value. Take the following C code snippet as an example:

```
1      short int magic;
2      read(0, &magic, sizeof(short int));
3      if (magic == 0x1234)
4         bug();
```

The `if` branch in Line 3 will be compiled into a `CMP` instruction, so libFuzzer inserts instrumentation code to save the compared targets:

```
1      short int magic;
2      read(0, &magic, sizeof(short int));
3      save_compared_arguments();
4      if (magic == 0x1234)
5         bug();
```

When executing Line 3, the instrumentation code will store `magic` and `0x1234`, both indexed by `magic` $\oplus$ `0x1234`. These values will then be used when mutating seeds into new inputs, such as replacing `magic` in input into `0x1234`.

2) Value profiling: When value profiling is enabled, libFuzzer collects additional information to quantify the progress made toward passing each branch condition at runtime. Take the following code as an example:

initialize();
while *TRUE* **do**
    input = mutate();
    LLVMFuzzerTestOneInput(input, inputSize); ▷ User should implement this function.
end

Fig. 1: libFuzzer's in-process fuzzing

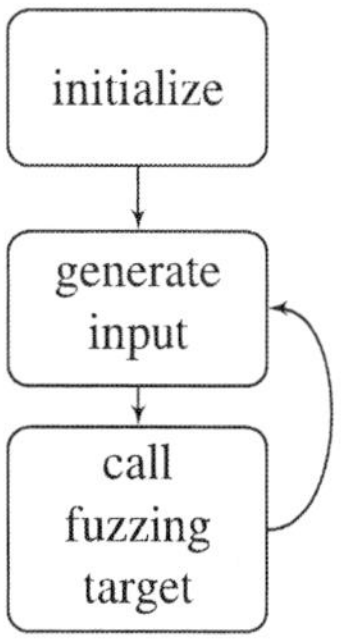

Fig. 2: libFuzzer's in-process fuzzing workflow

```
1     short int magic;
2     read(0, &magic, sizeof(short int));
3     if (magic == 0x1234)
4        bug();
```

In this example, though all `magic` values except `0x1234` will fail the branch condition at Line 3, some values are closer to passing the condition than others. Finding an input closer to passing the condition should be considered progress and saved as a new seed. For example, assuming that distance between two values is defined as the number of different bits, then if we mutate `magic` from `0x1237` to `0x1235`, `0x1235` should be saved as a seed because `0x1235` differs from the target (`0x1234`) by one bit, while `0x1237` has a two-bit difference.

When enabling value profiling, libFuzzer uses the program counter as an index to store the distance information calculated based on the xored value of the compared operands. For example, the distance can be defined as the number of zero bits in the xored value. If the distance indexed by the same program counter reduces, which means that we are closer to solving the branch, the input will become a new seed.

3) Compare function: Besides CMP tracing for the `CMP` instruction, libFuzzer also hooks functions related to string comparison (e.g., `strstr`, `memcmp`, and `strncasecmp`), and stores the function parameters for mutation later.

4) Dataflow trace: Hooking the compare instruction and string comparison functions allows libFuzzer to retrieve the compared values, but does not reveal the relationship between the input bits and the bits of the compared value. Dataflow trace taints an input to uncover the mapping between the input and compared value by checking the taint label.

C. libFuzzer's in-process infrastructure

libFuzzer adopts an *in-process* infrastructure for achieving high fuzzing speed (i.e., executions per second). In an in-process infrastructure, the fuzzer instance (libFuzzer) and the fuzzing target (LLVMFuzzerTestOneInput) work in the same context and share the same virtual memory space, as shown in Figure 1 and Figure 2. By contrast, AFL uses a *forkserver infrastructure*, in which each fuzzer instance and fuzzing target has an isolated context.

Despite the higher speed, the in-process infrastructure is more fragile and subject to the *context pollution problem* because the fuzzer instance may behave incorrectly due to bugs triggered in the fuzzing target, and the fuzzing target may behave incorrectly due to global context polluted in previous runs of fuzzing target.

The original libFuzzer can tolerate context pollution for two main reasons. First, it targets library functions (such as `png_sig_cmp` in `libpng`), and the fragility amplifies the impact of silent, non-crash bugs (e.g., memory leak), which are fatal in library functions.[2] Second, the impact of polluted context is limited because libFuzzer stops whenever encountering a crash, and the libFuzzer user is expected to fix the bug before finding the next one.

III. Comparability Issues

This section highlights two comparability issues when prior work compares libFuzzer with other fuzzers and explains why existing solutions are insufficient. These issues motivate our design and implementation of icLibFuzzer.

A. Lack support of common evaluation metrics

Fuzzers are often evaluated by how much code they covered in a fixed time, how many bugs they found in a fixed time, and how fast they found all intended bugs. However, it is hard to measure libFuzzer's progress using these metrics on arbitrary programs because libFuzzer terminates immediately whenever the fuzzing target crashes. Moreover, the crash may be triggered by a polluted global context rather than the program's bug. Thus, previous work is either limited to using the time-to-first-crash metric [21], compared on fine-tuned datasets [1], [9], or has to enable libFuzzer's ignore-crash mode, which restarts the fuzzer right after each crash [5].

Enabling the ignore-crash mode solves this comparability issue partially but also introduces additional problems. First, restarting a fuzzer is time-consuming, thus slowing down the fuzzing process. Worst yet, restarts may frequently happen because fuzzing often triggers the same crash repeatedly. Second, the context pollution problem is less tolerable when we are interested in metrics such as code coverage and the number of bugs found because the polluted context may result

[2] A memory leak bug may be tolerable in a standalone program with a short lifetime because the operating system will handle memory leaks after the program terminates. However, a memory leak is fatal in library functions since the memory leak will persist and exhaust memory eventually.

in an incorrect measurement of these metrics. Simply restarting the fuzzer after a crash is insufficient to avoid a broken context caused by non-crash bugs, which we will explain in the next subsection.

Some fuzzers [6], [21] avoid the context pollution problem by limiting their comparisons to a small set of manually crafted targets (e.g., Google's fuzzer-test-suite) or programs without global-context dependency, but again this limits the comparison scope.

B. Incorrect results due to context pollution

Even if libFuzzer in the ignore-crash mode can continue after finding a crash input to the fuzzing target, it may produce wrong results for targets expecting a clean global context. We identify two cases in which the ignore-crash mode may behave wrongly during fuzzing due to context pollution.

a) Programs depending on global variables: The first case is fuzzing from a *main* function that assumes correctly-initialized global variables before being called.

A C/C++ program can safely assume that global variables with no initial value will be set to zero. However, when fuzzing such a program, libFuzzer treats and calls the fuzzing target like a function, so the global variables are not reinitialized when libFuzzer fuzzes the target again. Thus, if the fuzzing target modifies these global variables during its execution, the fuzzing target may act incorrectly after running a few times.

For example, `getopt` is a widely used function parsing the command-line arguments. It relies on a global variable `optind`, which indicates the next element's index in the command-line arguments:

```
int getopt(int argc, char *const argv[],
   const char *optstring);
extern char *optarg;
extern int optind, opterr, optopt;
```

If the fuzzing target calls `getopt` and libFuzzer fuzzes the fuzzing target twice without reinitializing the global variable `optind`, `getopt` may behave unpredictably.

LibKluzzer [12] proposes to solve this problem by memorizing and replacing global variables every time the fuzzing target reruns. However, shared contexts other than the global variables, e.g., heap, are still polluted and will not be reset. Also, since their tool is not publicly available, it is unclear how LibKluzzer handles every possible global variable initialization, including some that can only be correctly reinitialized by calling the corresponding functions. Take the following C code as an example:

```
1  class Foo {
2  public:
3     Foo() {x = new char[10];}
4     ~Foo() {delete[] x;}
5     char *x;
6  };
7
8  Foo bar;
9
10 int LLVMFuzzerTestOneInput(uint8_t *data,
11    size_t size) {
12    memcpy(bar.x, data, 10);
13    parse(bar.x);
14    delete bar;
15 }
```

`bar` is a global variable. When LibKluzzer resets `bar` according to the previous snapshot after the function `LLVMFuzzerTestOneInput` exits, `bar.x` will be reinitialized to a memory address that has already been freed at line 14. Moreover, LibKluzzer cannot handle programs with memory leak, explained below.

b) Programs with memory leak: Another form of context pollution occurs when fuzzing programs that have memory leak bugs. Since the fuzzing target runs in the same context as the fuzzer instance, if the fuzzing target contains a memory leak, the memory leak will persist and keep consuming the memory until libFuzzer crashes and restarts.

IV. icLibFuzzer

This section presents icLibFuzzer's design and implementation. icLibFuzzer resolves the two comparability issues while achieving speed comparable to AFL. The key idea is to isolate each run of the fuzzing target and the fuzzer instance and implement this context isolation efficiently by changing libFuzzer's in-process infrastructure into a forkserver infrastructure. Additionally, we propose structure packing to improve fuzzing speed, set CPU affinity to ensure comparability, and provide a compiler wrapper to compile a standalone program without implementing the `LLVMFuzzerTestOneInput` function.

A. Efficient context isolation

There are two possible approaches to isolate context between each run of fuzzing target and fuzzing instance.

1) **Naive forkserver**: A straightforward yet expensive approach to ensuring a clean context would be forking from the fuzzer instance and running the fuzzing target every time. Since the `fork` call will spawn another process, the global context between each run of fuzzing target and fuzzing instance will be separated. However, this approach will introduce unnecessary overhead because many complicated logic and data structures in the fuzzer instance are unnecessary for the fuzzing target, and the main memory size impacts the forking speed significantly according to our experiment in Section V-D.
2) **Lightweight forkserer**: Inspired by AFL's infrastructure, instead of forking directly from the fuzzer instance, we can first `fork` and `execve` to create a forkserver, and `fork` from the forkserver. Because this approach requires less writable memory, it is faster than the native forkserver approach. The speed comparison is shown in Table V in Section V-C

Thus, we take the lightweight forkserver approach and separate the fuzzer instance into two components—*main controller* and *forkserver*. The pseudocode in Figure 3 and Figure 4

```
fork();
if inChild then
  | execv(forkserver);
end
while TRUE do
  input = mutate();
  tellForkServer(input);

  waitForForkServer();

end
```

Fig. 3: icLibFuzzer: main controller

```
while TRUE do
  input =
    FromMainCon-
    troller();

  fork();
  if inChild then
    call(fuzzingTarget,
      input);
    exit(0);
  else
    | waitForChild();
  end
  tellMainController();

end
```

Fig. 4: icLibFuzzer: forkserver

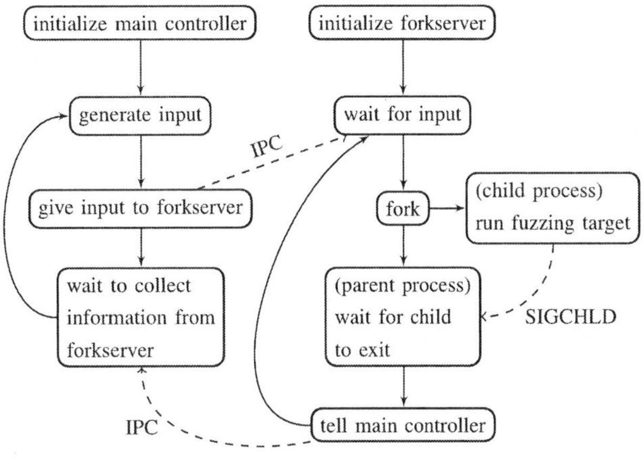

Fig. 5: icLibFuzzer's workflow.
The dashed lines represent the communication channel.

represent the *main controller* and *forkserver*, respectively, and Figure 5 illustrates how icLibFuzzer works.

The forkserver is spawned (`execve` after `fork`) from the main controller, and they communicate with each other through Inter-Process Communication (IPC). The main controller component is responsible for analyzing information collected from the instrumented program and generating inputs according to the collected information. For each input received from the main controller, the forkserver forks a child process to run the fuzzing target and collects instrumentation information. This design ensures that the fuzzing target always starts running from a clean context, free from the pollution of the previous runs, and is much faster than forking directly from fuzzing instance.

Moreover, we use shared memory as a fast IPC approach to pass instrumentation information back to the main controller from the forkserver. To achieve this, we move the data structure that stores instrumentation information into shared memory.

B. Structure Packing

Although this forkserver infrastructure is faster than forking directly from the *main controller*, it is still much slower than the original libFuzzer due to the resource-consuming fork procedure.

We observe that a primary factor affecting the forking speed is the writable memory size—the memory space that may be written to in the fuzzing target. Therefore, we propose *structure packing* to reduce the memory size and increase the forking speed.

The idea of structure packing is to pack all data collected from instrumentation into one compact structure to minimize the wasted space. For example, the following code snippet shows several data structures used in libFuzzer to store instrumentation data. The arrays `MemMemWords` and `Table` store the fuzzing target's information, collected through instrumentation at runtime.

```
template<size_t kMaxSize>
class FixedWord {
  public:
    ...
  private:
    uint8_t Size = 0;
    uint8_t Data[kMaxSize];
};
typedef FixedWord<64> Word;
struct Pair {
  Word A, B;
};
Word MemMemWords[1024];
struct Pair Table[32];
```

As these data structures store instrumentation information, they may be modified during the fuzzing target's execution. Instead of allocating space to them separately, icLibFuzzer packs all data into a compact structure in the shared memory to minimize the unused space:

```
Total = mmap(...);
MemMemWords = Total;
// ensure MemMemWords and Table
// don't overlap
Table = Total + Offset;
```

As shown in Section V-D, structure packing can double the running speed in several real-world binaries as we minimize the total memory pages that may be written to in the fuzzing target, allowing icLibFuzzer to fuzz at speed comparable to AFL.

This structure packing technique can be applied to speed up other forkserver-based fuzzers that use multiple data structures to pass information between the forkserver and main controller.

C. *Set CPU Affinity*

We set CPU affinity to each icLibFuzzer instance. Namely, we bind each fuzzer instance to a CPU/core. There are three reasons for doing this. First, binding a process to one CPU will improve cache locality and reduce cache miss for better performance. Second, since AFL binds its process to one CPU, most of its successors and family members do this too. Therefore, we eliminate a potential variation when comparing icLibFuzzer with fuzzers in the AFL family by following this convention. Third, binding a process to a CPU reduces interference between different fuzzing instances. Since one fuzzer instance can use at most one CPU, a fuzzer instance consisting of several processes (e.g., icLibFuzzer) will not interfere with other instances if we want to fuzz in parallel.

D. *Compiler wrapper*

icLibFuzzer comes with a compiler wrapper to automatically compile a standalone program for icLibFuzzer.

Recall that libFuzzer requires users to implement a `LLVMFuzzerTestOneInput` function as a callback in the fuzzer instance to identify the fuzzing target. This task can be laborious because users have to find out every input function in the fuzzing target and may accidentally introduce additional bugs. It is even more challenging when the fuzzing target reads inputs through non-standard methods or performs complex operations.

Take the following code snippet as an example:

```
read(0, buf1, size1);
read(0, buf2, size2);
```

One may implement the desired `LLVMFuzzerTestOneInput` function as follows.

```
int LLVMFuzzerTestOneInput(uint8_t*
  Data, size_t Size) {
   if (Size >= size1) {
      memcpy(buf1, Data, size1);
      if (Size >= size1 + size2)
         memcpy(buf2, Data + size1,
            size2);
      else
         memcpy(buf2, Data + size1,
            Size - size1);
   }
   else
      memcpy(buf1, Data, Size)
}
```

As the fuzzing target becomes more complex, the implementation of `LLVMFuzzerTestOneInput` may become harder and human errors may occur occasionally.

To simplify the procedure and avoid human errors, we provide a *clang* wrapper, *clang-fast*, which handles everything—just like *afl-clang-fast* in AFL. All a user needs to do is compile the target project using *clang-fast*; no need to modify any source code manually.

TABLE I: Fuzzers used in the evaluation and their versions

	version (or last-commit date)
AFL	2.52b (5 Nov 2017)
Angora	25 May 2019
Honggfuzz	22 May 2019
libFuzzer-LLVM9	LLVM 9 (22 April 2019)
libFuzzer-LLVM11	LLVM 11 (27 Sep 2020)
QSYM	15 October 2019
AFL++	11 Dec 2020
icLibFuzzer-LLVM9/11	follow libFuzzer-LLVM9/11

V. Evaluation

To demonstrate that icLibFuzzer improves fuzzer comparability, we compare icLibFuzzer with state-of-the-art fuzzers based on code coverage in real-world programs. The results will unveil how effective libFuzzer's advanced features are in comparison with other fuzzers. We also investigate icLibFuzzer's speed: how much is traded for comparability and how much we gain back by infrastructural and implementation optimizations.

Specifically, we ask the following three research questions:

RQ-1: Code-coverage comparison. Can icLibFuzzer achieve better code coverage compared with other state-of-the-art fuzzers?

RQ-2: Execution speed difference. What is icLibFuzzer's execution speed compared with AFL, libFuzzer, and a naive forkserver implementation?

RQ-3: The effectiveness of optimization. Does structure packing improve fuzzing speed, and by how much?

A. *Settings*

a) Fuzzers: Table I lists the fuzzers and their versions used in our experiments. We choose AFL and Honggfuzz because they are the core fuzzers (in addition to libFuzzer) used in OSS-Fuzz [16]. Speaking more specifically, we utilize the `afl-clang-fast` instead of `afl-gcc` as the execution speed of binaries compiled by `afl-clang-fast` is much faster. We also choose two strong fuzzers, QSYM and Angora, released in 2019. QSYM is a hybrid fuzzer that defeats AFL and previous hybrid fuzzers. It uncovers bugs in `ffmpeg` which has already been fuzzed by OSS-Fuzz for years. Angora uses multiple techniques, including taint tracking, to solve branch conditions without using symbolic execution. It shows notable improvement over AFL.

Our icLibFuzzer uses the same LLVM version as libFuzzer. Throughout the evaluation, we use LLVM9 by default (i.e., icLibFuzzer-LLVM9) unless specified otherwise. We include icLibFuzzer-LLVM11 (released in late 2020) mainly to demonstrate that one can effortlessly update icLibFuzzer whenever newer versions of LLVM and libFuzzer are available. Additionally, we include AFL++, whose latest version was released in December 2020. AFL++ assembles multiple optimization techniques and integrates them into the latest AFL. It shows a significant performance boost compared with the original AFL after enabling multiple optimizations simultaneously. However, due to the limited time before the sub-

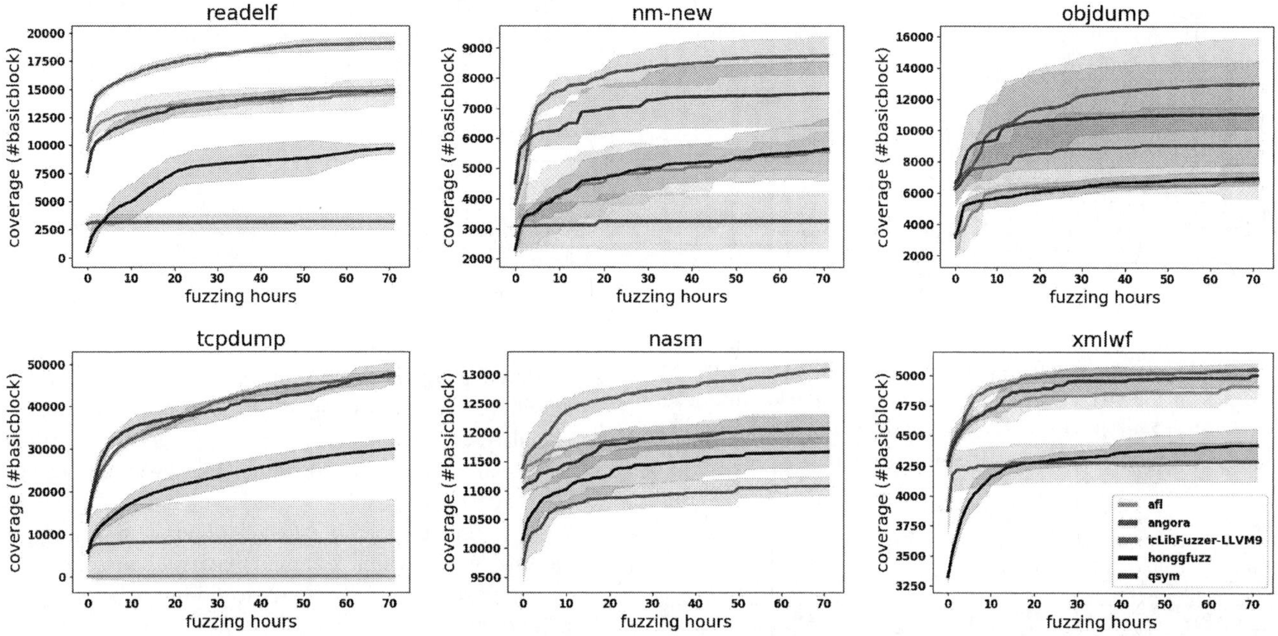

Fig. 6: Comparison between fuzzers. All the legend color mappings are the same as labeled in xmlwf.

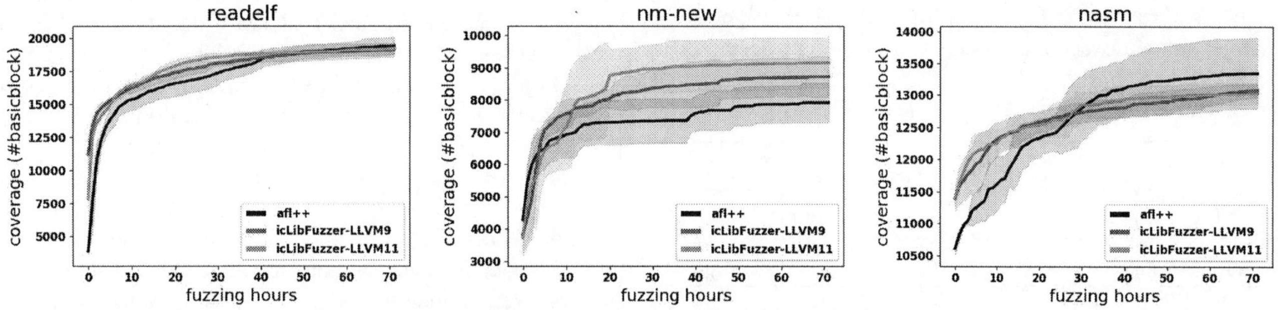

Fig. 7: Comparison among latest icLibFuzzer-LLVM11, state-of-the-art AFL++ and icLibFuzzer-LLVM9.

mission, we only compare icLibFuzzer-LLVM9, icLibFuzzer-LLVM11, and AFL++ with each other, not with the other fuzzers.

b) Datasets: We use two datasets: one contains real-world programs (objdump-2.35, readelf-2.35, nm-new-2.35, tcpdump-4.9.2, xmlwf-2.2.9, nasm-2.16rc0) and the other is the fuzzer-test-suite. The real-world program dataset is for coverage and speed comparison with icLibFuzzer, while the fuzzer-test-suite is only used for speed comparison with libFuzzer.

c) Time budget: We run every binary eight times and each for 72 hours, which is the longest we can do given our resource budget. We report the average code coverage and standard deviation. Because fuzzing in the real world often lasts long (e.g., more than one month), investigating the trend after 24 hours of fuzzing can hint at the fuzzer's ability to find new code coverage continuously.

d) Fuzzer configuration: To ensure fair comparisons, we assign no initial seeds to fuzzers because initial seeds may have a significant impact on fuzzing [11]. We discuss the effect of initial seeds in discussion section. We run all fuzzers with two threads to ensure a fair comparison with QSYM (which needs at least two threads). To further normalize the fuzzer's result, we calculate all the code coverage results using clang's source-based code coverage feature from interesting seeds reported by each fuzzers. We run our experiment on a machine with one AMD Ryzen Threadripper 2990WX 32-Core Processor and 64GB memory, running Ubuntu 18.04 LTS.

In our evaluation, we enable the first three advanced instrumentation features introduced in Section II but not dataflow trace because dataflow trace requires manual function labeling and may provide an unfair advantage to icLibFuzzer in our comparative evaluation.

TABLE II: Comparing each fuzzer's average speed (executions per second) on real-world programs after running 72 hours.

	readelf	nm-new	objdump	tcpdump	nasm	xmlwf
icLibFuzzer	1701	1667	1030	1603	359	2349
AFL	1708	1906	1032	2438	337	2983
qsym	1380	2990	1174	3087	430	4917
angora	1300	681	684	1068	419	1157
honggfuzz	86	96	116	108	76	126

TABLE III: Effect of structure packing. We run for 30 minutes in each cases to obtain a stable execution speed. `RSS` (Resident Set Size) is the RAM size consumed by the process, and `exec/s` stands for executions of fuzzing target per second.

	exec/s		RSS (Bytes)	
	no pack	pack	no pack	pack
objdump	1992	3740	7260K	3636K
readelf	2404	4426	7672K	3356K
nm-new	2083	3991	7544K	3324K
tcpdump	2168	4103	7504K	3492K

TABLE IV: Comparing each fuzzer's speed (executions per second) on the fuzzer-test-suite dataset. Version of libFuzzer and icLibFuzzer here is LLVM9. We run for 30 minutes in each case to get to a relatively stable execution speed.

	libFuzzer	icLibFuzzer	AFL	naive forkserver
boringssl-2016-02-12	26707	1722	1201	136
freetype2-2017	9210	927	1038	128
libpng-1.2.56	8707	2556	3340	69
openssl-1.1.0c	22460	512	560	164
sqlite-2016-11-14	20587	1112	881	63

TABLE V: Comparing naive forkserver with lightweight forkserver. We run for 30 minutes in each case to get to a relatively stable execution speed. `RSS` (Resident Set Size) is the RAM size consumed by the process, and `exec/s` stands for executions of fuzzing target per second.

Benchmark	light-weight forkserver		naive forkserver	
	exec/s	RSS (bytes)	exec/s	RSS (bytes)
boringssl-2016-02-12	1722	9M	136	335M
freetype2-2017	927	9M	128	388M
libpng-1.2.56	2556	6M	69	353M
openssl-1.1.0c	512	11M	164	276M
sqlite-2016-11-14	1112	6M	63	340M

B. RQ-1

To answer this question, we evaluate icLibFuzzer's code coverage on the real-world program dataset and compare the results with four state-of-the-art fuzzers (AFL [20], Angora [4], QSYM [19], and Honggfuzz [17]). Note that AFL, Honggfuzz, and libFuzzer have only been compared in the in-process mode (also called the *persistent mode* in AFL and Honggfuzz) in previous work. With icLibFuzzer, these three fuzzers can compare with each other on arbitrary programs.

Code coverage As shown in Figure 6, icLibFuzzer outperforms other fuzzers in most binaries.

We observe two interesting phenomena from the results.

1) **Bad performance of Angora**: Angora shows better performance than AFL in its original paper. However, we can see that Angora does not perform well in our experiment. One plausible reason may be that Angora highly relies on initial seeds, at least for these six programs we tested. Other fuzzers in our experiment seem to work reasonably despite an empty initial seed. It needs further investigation on selecting seeds wisely for Angora.
2) **Code coverage after 24 hours**: As suggested in [11], we should run fuzzers for 24 hours for a fair comparison. We can also see many papers [5], [7], [8] running experiments less than or equal to 24 hours. However, according to our experiment results, icLibFuzzer can still find new code coverage steadily after 24 hours, indicating that fuzzing results within 24 hours may still be insufficient to represent a fuzzer's capability to find new bugs or cover additional code.

Upgrade and compare with the latest fuzzers. To demonstrate that icLibFuzzer can easily update to incorporate newer libFuzzer versions, we update icLibFuzzer to LLVM 11 and compare it with icLibFuzzer-LLVM9 and a state-of-the-art fuzzer, AFL++ [7], released in late 2020.

As Figure 7 shows, icLibFuzzer-LLVM11 has competitive performance compared with AFL++. icLibFuzzer-LLVM11 performs better than icLibFuzzer-LLVM9 and AFL++ on `nm-new`. All three have similar code coverage on `readelf`, and AFL++ catches up after 24 hours on `nasm`. Due to our time budget, we can only run three binaries two times and 72 hours for each without initial seeds with these three fuzzers. We continue to run these experiments to evaluate the performance of the latest icLibFuzzer.

C. RQ-2

To answer this question, we run libFuzzer, icLibFuzzer, and AFL on the fuzzer-test-suite dataset and measure the number of executions per second. Using this dataset ensures libFuzzer can behave correctly.

As Table IV shows, icLibFuzzer is 4x to 50x slower than libFuzzer. However, when we compare icLibFuzzer with AFL, they run at almost the same speed even though icLibFuzzer supports more instrumentation than AFL.

We also compare the execution speed and main memory size of the naive forkserver and lightweight forkserver in Table V, as mentioned in Section IV. Since the naive forkserver approach forks directly from the fuzzer instance, it inherits the large memory space, slowing down the `fork` procedure and fuzzing target, thus the total execution speed of the fuzzer is 3x to 37x slower compared with icLibFuzzer.

D. RQ-3

As mentioned in Section IV, structure packing reduces the memory size in the forkserver and increases the speed. We evaluate the execution number per second with and without structure packing on four binaries, and Table III summarizes the results. On average, structure packing halves the memory usage and doubles the execution speed of icLibFuzzer.

VI. Discussion

This section discusses two crucial factors that influence the fuzzing results: initial seeds and the number of fuzzing threads. We view them as control variables in the evaluation to ensure fair comparison among fuzzers. Further investigation is needed to understand their impact on fuzzing.

A. *Initial seed selection*

Prior work shows that initial seeds may affect the fuzzing result drastically [11] and recommends that it may also be a good idea to assign no initial seed (i.e., starting a fuzzer with an empty seed pool). It hypothesizes that if one fuzzer can perform well across various programs without initial seeds, it is likely that this fuzzer can also perform well on other datasets without initial seeds. Therefore, in our experiments, we fuzz these real-world programs without assigning any initial seeds. Our experiment results on real-world programs conforms with this hypothesis, but we leave choosing initial seeds wisely and fairly, and evaluating fuzzing with these initial seeds for future work.

B. *The number of fuzzing threads*

Several fuzzers [4], [5], [7], [13], [14] support parallelism to utilize processing power better. Additionally, when conducting fuzzing experiments, one might run multiple fuzzer instances parallelly and compute the averaged results to reduce randomness.

However, we observe from our experiment that when running multiple fuzzers in parallel, the number of concurrent fuzzing threads affects the fuzzing speed. The reason might be that due to the Linux kernel's design nature, some system calls cannot run in parallel, which limits the scalability of parallel fuzzing.

Figure 8 provides an example, showing how AFL's execution speed decrease as number of fuzzer instances increases.

This observation coincides with the results reported in prior work [18] that AFL and LibFuzzer have little performance gain when using more cores in parallel fuzzing; the total execution time per second does not increase linearly with the number of cores used.

Hence, fuzzing experiments should control the number of fuzzer instances running simultaneously. For example, if we would like to run icLibFuzzer on objdump for 30 times and compute the average code coverage, we cannot split the experiment into 10 plus 20 times; otherwise, the execution speed will differ significantly, making the average value meaningless.

C. *Case Study*

Due to our time budget, we did not fuzz many real-world programs to find bugs (e.g., enabling the address sanitizer). Among those we tested, we found one crash on *nasm* after fuzzing it with icLibFuzzer for 15 hours.

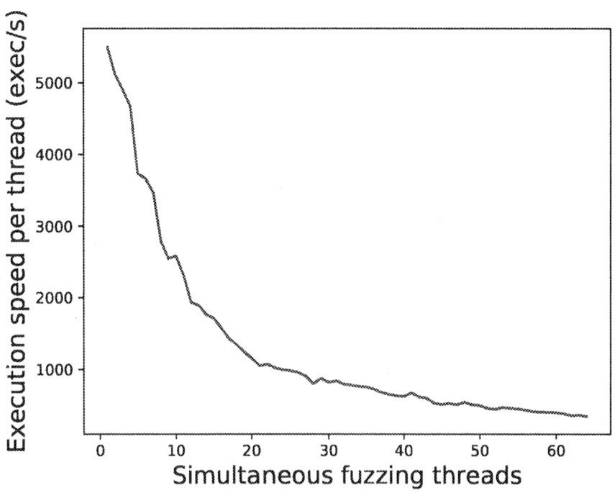

Fig. 8: Running multiple AFL fuzzer instances simultaneously. We run AFL on readelf with 1 to 64 fuzzer instances simultaneously. We spend 30 minutes in each case to wait for the execution speed to become rather stable and report the average speed.

The crash happens in the `paste_tokens` function:

```
1  p = buf = nasm_malloc(len + 1);
2  while (tok != next) {
3      p = mempcpy(p, tok_text(tok), tok->len);
4      tok = delete_Token(tok);
5  }
6  *p = '\0';
7  *prev_next = tok = t = tokenize(buf);
8  nasm_free(buf);
9
10 /*
11  * Connect pasted into original stream,
12  * ie A -> new-tokens -> B
13  */
14 while (t->next) {
15     t = t->next;
16 }
```

The object `t` returned by `tokenize` in line 7 is a link list, and in lines 14-16 it tries to find the tail of this link list. However, it fails to check if `t` is `NULL` or not. If `buf` in line 13 is `NULL`, then the returned `t` will be `NULL`, causing line 14 to crash as it tries to dereference a `NULL` pointer.

VII. Guideline for upgrading to newer libFuzzer

As libFuzzer evolves actively, we design icLibFuzzer to be generic enough to work with future libFuzzer updates and provide a guideline to port libFuzzer's new features to icLibFuzzer quickly.

1) **Non-instrumentation features**: Because the change we made in libFuzzer mainly affects how the fuzzer handles data structure that stores instrumentation information, libFuzzer updates that are irrelevant to instrumentation should work seamlessly without any modification to icLibFuzzer.

2) **Instrumentation features**: icLibFuzzer separates the fuzzer instance's context and fuzzing target's context, and we use shared memory to pass the information collected from instrumentation to the main controller. To add new data structure that stores instrumentation information, simply follow the two steps below:
   a) **Increase the allocated memory size**: The first step is increasing the allocated memory size to incorporate the new instrumentation information, but the increase should be as small as possible to minimize the impact on fuzzing speed. The member method `Initialize` in structure `TracePC` in `FuzzerTracePC.h` will allocate several contiguous shared memory pages storing every data structure related to instrumentation in order to share information between main controller and forkserver, One should try to minimize the required amount of increased memory because the memory size dominates icLibFuzzer's execution speed, as shown in Section V.
   b) **Map data structure to shared memory**: After allocating additional shared memory, we point the newly allocated shared memory to the data structure storing information collected from instrumentation. When the instrumentation code in the fuzzing target gathers new information, it will be passed to the main controller by the newly added data structure on the shared memory.

VIII. Related Work

Our work aims to improve comparability between libFuzzer-based fuzzers and other fuzzers in AFL family. In this section, we review related work that enhances, integrates, or compares with libFuzzer.

A. Enhancing libFuzzer

Several projects aim to improve libFuzzer [14], [15]. ParmeSan [21] implements sanitizer-oriented fuzzing on top of libFuzzer, aiming to optimize for bug coverage. FuzzerGym [6] applies reinforcement learning to improve seed mutation, implements the idea by combining OpenAI Gym with libFuzzer, and evaluates using the fuzzer-test-suite dataset.

Entropic [3] improves libFuzzer's seed scheduling algorithm. It quantifies the amount of information gained by each seed and chooses which seed to mutate first according to this value. Entropic is available in the latest libFuzzer (included in LLVM11, released in September 2020). As we show in the evaluation, icLibFuzzer can support this new libFuzzer feature easily, demonstrating the strength of our fuzzer. Moreover, icLibFuzzer-LLVM11 (using the latest libFuzzer) has competitive performance with AFL++ (v3), a powerful AFL-based fuzzer released in December 2020; this reconfirms the need to bridge the libFuzzer and AFL families, allowing new techniques to be shared transparently.

LibKluzzer [12] uses libFuzzer as a part of its hybrid fuzzer engine. To mitigate the context pollution problem, it identifies global variables, snapshots these global variables, and reinitializes these global variables in every fuzzing iteration. However, this approach may face several problems as mentioned in Section IV.

Our work differs from previous work in that we aim to improve libFuzzer's comparability with other fuzzers over a wide range of programs. Thus, we focus on solving the context pollution problem and reducing the manual efforts in modifying the target code. We also pay attention to implementation details to preserve libFuzzer's performance advantage.

B. Integrating or Comparing with libFuzzer

EnFuzz [5] combines fuzzers with diverse capabilities to increase overall code coverage, and one of the included fuzzers is libFuzzer. EnFuzz implements a monitor thread to restart libFuzzer whenever it crashes, which is similar to enabling the ignore-crash mode in libFuzzer. However, as mentioned in Section IV, EnFuzz's approach does not fully solve the comparability issue because the context may still be polluted and produce incorrect results.

OSS-Fuzz [16] is developed to find bugs in real-world programs and employs libFuzzer as one of its components. Instead of modifying libFuzzer, OSS-Fuzz modifies the fuzzing target to ensure libFuzzer works correctly.

IX. Conclusion

Although libFuzzer is under active development and supports advanced techniques such as CMP tracing and value profiling, its progress and success have not been thoroughly compared against other fuzzing tools.

In this work, we propose and implement icLibFuzzer, a new libFuzzer mode that can fuzz programs not designed to run continuously, including many real-world programs, without manually modifying them. icLibFuzzer achieves higher code coverage than several state-of-the-art fuzzers on most of the real-world programs we tested. Additionally, we design icLibFuzzer to be compatible with new features added in the future. We envision icLibFuzzer can serve as another baseline in fuzzing research.

We are currently working on integrating our compiler wrapper with FuzzGen [10], an automated tool to generate *LLVMFuzzerTestOneInput* for a library function, so that we can run icLibFuzzer not only on standalone programs but also library functions.

We are interested in three future research directions: (1) investigating factors critical to fuzzer comparability, such as initial seed selection; (2) improving icLibFuzzer's speed via infrastructural and implementation optimizations; and (3) exploring cache-aware structure packing to eliminate misalignment, a potential side-effect of structure packing.

Acknowledgment

This research was supported in part by the Ministry of Science and Technology of Taiwan (MOST 110-2628-E-002-002) and Delta Electronics. We gratefully thank Chun-Ying Huang, Shih-Kun Huang, Wei-Loon Mow, and Che-Yu Wu for seeding the idea and providing insightful feedback throughout the project execution.

References

[1] (2020) FuzzBench - Fuzzer benchmarking as a service. [Online]. Available: https://github.com/google/fuzzbench

[2] C. Aschermann, S. Schumilo, T. Blazytko, R. Gawlik, and T. Holz, "Redqueen: Fuzzing with input-to-state correspondence," in *Symposium on Network and Distributed System Security (NDSS)*, 2019.

[3] M. Böhme, V. J. Manès, and S. K. Cha, "Boosting fuzzer efficiency: An information theoretic perspective," in *Proceedings of the 28th ACM Joint Meeting on European Software Engineering Conference and Symposium on the Foundations of Software Engineering*, 2020, pp. 678–689.

[4] P. Chen and H. Chen, "Angora: Efficient fuzzing by principled search," in *2018 IEEE Symposium on Security and Privacy (SP)*, 2018, pp. 711–725.

[5] Y. Chen, Y. Jiang, F. Ma, J. Liang, M. Wang, C. Zhou, X. Jiao, and Z. Su, "Enfuzz: Ensemble fuzzing with seed synchronization among diverse fuzzers," in *28th USENIX Security Symposium (USENIX Security 19)*. Santa Clara, CA: USENIX Association, Aug. 2019, pp. 1967–1983. [Online]. Available: https://www.usenix.org/conference/usenixsecurity19/presentation/chen-yuanliang

[6] W. Drozd and M. Wagner, "Fuzzergym: A competitive framework for fuzzing and learning," 07 2018.

[7] A. Fioraldi, D. Maier, H. Eißfeldt, and M. Heuse, "Afl++ : Combining incremental steps of fuzzing research," in *14th USENIX Workshop on Offensive Technologies (WOOT 20)*. USENIX Association, Aug. 2020. [Online]. Available: https://www.usenix.org/conference/woot20/presentation/fioraldi

[8] V. Herdt, D. Große, J. Wloka, T. Güneysu, and R. Drechsler, "Verification of embedded binaries using coverage-guided fuzzing with systemc-based virtual prototypes," in *GLSVLSI*, 2020.

[9] G. Inc. (2016) A set of tests (benchmarks) for fuzzing engines (fuzzers). [Online]. Available: https://github.com/google/fuzzer-test-suite/

[10] K. Ispoglou, D. Austin, V. Mohan, and M. Payer, "Fuzzgen: Automatic fuzzer generation," in *29th USENIX Security Symposium (USENIX Security 20)*. USENIX Association, Aug. 2020, pp. 2271–2287. [Online]. Available: https://www.usenix.org/conference/usenixsecurity20/presentation/ispoglou

[11] G. Klees, A. Ruef, B. Cooper, S. Wei, and M. Hicks, "Evaluating fuzz testing," in *Proceedings of the 2018 ACM SIGSAC Conference on Computer and Communications Security*, ser. CCS '18. New York, NY, USA: Association for Computing Machinery, 2018, p. 2123–2138. [Online]. Available: https://doi.org/10.1145/3243734.3243804

[12] H. Le, *LLVM-based Hybrid Fuzzing with LibKluzzer (Competition Contribution)*, 04 2020, pp. 535–539.

[13] J. Liang, Y. Jiang, Y. Chen, M. Wang, C. Zhou, and J. Sun, "Pafl: Extend fuzzing optimizations of single mode to industrial parallel mode," in *Proceedings of the 2018 26th ACM Joint Meeting on European Software Engineering Conference and Symposium on the Foundations of Software Engineering*, ser. ESEC/FSE 2018. New York, NY, USA: Association for Computing Machinery, 2018, p. 809–814. [Online]. Available: https://doi.org/10.1145/3236024.3275525

[14] libfuzzer@googlegroups.com. (2019) LibFuzzer – a library for coverage-guided fuzz testing. [Online]. Available: http://llvm.org/docs/LibFuzzer.html

[15] K. Serebryany, "Continuous fuzzing with libfuzzer and addresssanitizer," in *2016 IEEE Cybersecurity Development (SecDev)*, 2016, pp. 157–157.

[16] K. Serebryany, "Oss-fuzz - google's continuous fuzzing service for open source software." Vancouver, BC: USENIX Association, Aug. 2017.

[17] R. Swiecki, "Honggfuzz: A general-purpose, easy-to-use fuzzer with interesting analysis options," 2017. [Online]. Available: https://github.com/google/honggfuzz

[18] W. Xu, S. Kashyap, C. Min, and T. Kim, "Designing new operating primitives to improve fuzzing performance," in *Proceedings of the 2017 ACM SIGSAC Conference on Computer and Communications Security*, ser. CCS '17. New York, NY, USA: Association for Computing Machinery, 2017, p. 2313–2328. [Online]. Available: https://doi.org/10.1145/3133956.3134046

[19] I. Yun, S. Lee, M. Xu, Y. Jang, and T. Kim, "QSYM : A practical concolic execution engine tailored for hybrid fuzzing," in *27th USENIX Security Symposium (USENIX Security 18)*. Baltimore, MD: USENIX Association, Aug. 2018, pp. 745–761. [Online]. Available: https://www.usenix.org/conference/usenixsecurity18/presentation/yun

[20] M. Zalewski. American Fuzzy Lop (AFL). [Online]. Available: http://lcamtuf.coredump.cx/afl/

[21] S. Österlund, K. Razavi, H. Bos, and C. Giuffrida, "ParmeSan: Sanitizer-guided Greybox Fuzzing," in *USENIX Security*, Aug. 2020. [Online]. Available: Paper=https://download.vusec.net/papers/parmesan_sec20.pdf Code=https://github.com/vusec/parmesan

Is Your Firmware Real or Re-Hosted?
A case study in re-hosting VxWorks control system firmware

Abraham A. Clements
Sandia National Laboratories
aacleme@sandia.gov

Logan Carpenter
Sandia National Laboratories
lcarpen@sandia.gov

William A. Moeglein
Sandia National Laboratories
wmoegle@sandia.gov

Christopher Wright
Purdue University
christopherwright@purdue.edu

Abstract—**Emulating firmware is increasingly popular for systems research, particularly vulnerability research. In this paper we describe how we extend HALucinator to work with real-world systems that use the popular VxWorks RTOS. We describe the Re-hosting Support Layer (its definition and implementation) with the functions necessary to get a Schneider Electric SCADAPack 350 remote terminal unit, a Schneider Electric Modicon 340 programmable logic controller, and Hughes 9201 BGAN inmarsat terminal up and re-hosted (at least partially). We share the process and our path of performing this work over the last year, and give a retrospective approach for re-hosting other RTOSes. We provide a case study with 3 real devices, and show that we can re-host portions of the firmware and perform analyses to show the success of our approach.**

I. Introduction

Firmware running on embedded systems is ubiquitous. Any modern system performing control or automation functionality likely contains an integrated micro-controller executing firmware. This firmware controls how the device behaves and interacts with the physical world. While we are dependent on these systems, analyzing firmware for security vulnerabilities is a challenging task because of its tight integration with hardware. This requires nearly all dynamic analysis of firmware to be performed executing the firmware on the hardware, which significantly limits the ability to inspect the its execution. Execution inspection capabilities are typically provided by a debugging port on hardware and are usually limited to a handful of breakpoints. Further, leaving the debugging port accessible is generally considered a poor security practice and thus is often not even an option for third parties trying to analyze firmware. Requiring hardware also increases the expense and decreases the scale at which automated analyses can be applied, e.g., programmable logic controllers can each cost several thousands of dollars. Automated vulnerability testing such as fuzzing requires running many instances of the device to enable effective discovery of vulnerabilities and the dollar cost of devices can significantly limit the scale at which testing can be performed.

Emulating embedded systems by re-hosting their firmware has been demonstrated as a technique to overcome the requirement of hardware in performing dynamic analysis of firmware [7], [10], [11], [27]. To do this, a firmware is run on a software emulator, which allows it be run on commodity desktops and servers. This also allows many instances of the system to be started – with the number of instances only limited by the availability of general purpose computing resources.

The primary challenge to re-hosting firmware is providing valid inputs for the hardware that is not implemented in the emulator. Emulators such as QEMU [6] provide the ability to emulate a variety of CPU architectures, but provide very limited support for the huge variety of peripherals (e.g., timers, UARTs, Ethernet controllers) used in commodity embedded systems. Many different approaches have been proposed to address these challenges. One approach is to implement the hardware at low-level memory mapped register interface as done in QEMU – a laborious task that does not scale well. Another approach is hardware-in-the-loop emulation [18], where accesses to peripherals are forwarded to physical hardware – which reduces its scalability. Machine learning [14] is an approach where interactions with peripherals are recorded on hardware and used to build models of peripherals. These models are then used during emulation. Another approach is to use a fuzzer [12] to provide inputs for the peripherals. Both machine learning and fuzzing peripherals limits control over the devices making them unsuitable for high fidelity emulation.

A promising approach is High Level Emulation (HLE) [8], [7], [10], [11] where common abstractions within the firmware are utilized to remove the need to provide low-level support for peripherals. Both Firmadyne [7] and Costin et al. [10], [11] utilize the Linux kernel abstractions to enable re-hosting Linux based firmware. HALucinator [8] uses hardware abstraction layers provided by micro-controller manufacturers, enabling re-hosting of simple bare-metal applications.

Our goal is to advance the art of re-hosting to enable answering questions about how low-level logic and vulnerabilities in Real-Time Operating Systems (RTOS) impact the larger systems in which they are a part. While we are not yet able to achieve this final end goal we report our current progress here. To achieve this goal we extend HALucinator to work with a commercial RTOS. For a more general review of re-hosting we refer the reader to [34]. RTOSes aim to make the process of writing firmware for embedded systems easier. These RTOSes provide the basic constructs for a real-time system and give the developer abstract mechanisms to define system behavior. These mechanisms are often organized as layers, which hide the working details of the system from higher layers. In addition, these operating systems define an interface–called a Board Support Package (BSP)–to enable portability across a large variety of hardware. These layers, and in particular the BSP, provide a natural place for HALucinator to decouple firmware from its hardware and enable re-hosting in an emulator.

Here we focus on VxWorks, a commercial RTOS

Workshop on Binary Analysis Research (BAR) 2021
21 February 2021, Virtual

https://dx.doi.org/10.14722/bar.2021.23006
www.ndss-symposium.org

commonly found in safety-critical industries such as aerospace, automotive, medical, and manufacturing [2], [15], [3]. It is used extensively by major companies including Siemens, Boeing, Bosch, Huawei, Northrop Grumman, and others. WindRiver, the maker of VxWorks, estimates there are on over 2 billion devices running VxWorks [25]. Probably the most publicized use of VxWorks was in the Mars Rover, where NASA Jet Propulsion Laboratory (JPL) used VxWorks in the Mars Exploration Rover [30]. VxWorks has also been demonstrated to have critical vulnerabilities [4], [26].

By leveraging and replacing some of the abstraction layers used for the development of VxWorks, we have found that we can enable HALucinator to re-host the firmware from these complex systems. We refer to our abstraction replacements as a re-hosting support layer (RSL) and currently we enable file system operations, execution of multiple asynchronous tasks, recording system logs, and interactive communication over both Ethernet and serial ports. We demonstrate our re-hosting support layer, performing a set of dynamic analyses on firmware from a Schneider Electric SCADAPack 350 remote terminal unit, a Schneider Electric Modicon 340 programmable logic controller, and Hughes 9201 BGAN inmarsat terminal. These devices were chosen because of the use in critical infrastructure, and underlying support for their processor's instruction set architecture in HALucinator. This enables us to focus on problems specific to re-hosting RTOS'es. We report our task analysis, initialization analysis, function/symbol analysis and execution statistics in section IV.

While the re-hosting support layer presented in this work is specific to VxWorks, we believe many of the concepts and lessons learned in its development may be applicable to other real-time operating systems. Thus, we also provide a retrospective approach for others to use in development of re-hosting support layers for additional RTOSes. In summary this work presents using HALucinator to provide a re-hosting support layer for VxWorks to enable emulation of 3 real-world devices, analysis, detailed explanation, and statistics recorded while re-hosting these devices, and a retrospective and advice on re-hosting embedded RTOS devices.

II. Background

Before describing our re-hosting support layer, we formally define some of the terminology used in this work. We then discuss the benefits of re-hosting and the scale we use for determining the utility of a re-hosted firmware. Next, since our work requires a functional knowledge of both HALucinator and VxWorks we provide a brief review of each.

A. Vocabulary

Firmware Re-hosting: The process of executing firmware on a platform other than its originally intended hardware.

Emulation vs Re-hosting: The terms emulating a firmware and re-hosting firmware are often used interchangeably. This is because the two ideas are so closely related. In this paper, we refer to emulating a system by re-hosting a firmware. That is, the goal is to emulate the system for a specific purpose and the means of doing it is re-hosting the firmware. We find using this terminology helps making decisions during re-hosting, because the right decision usually depends on what we are trying to emulate. For example, do we need to provide high fidelity for power management in our re-hosting? If we are emulating to test power management, then yes; otherwise, probably not.

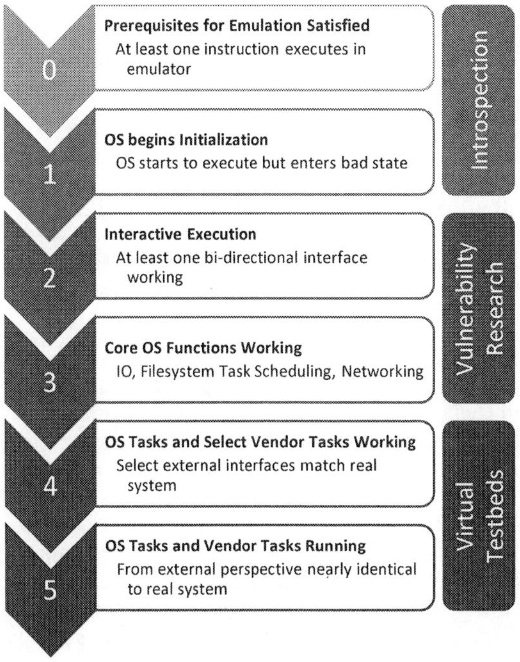

Fig. 1. Re-hosting Utility Scale

Re-hosting Support Layer (RSL): The functionality that is replaced during a firmware's execution to enable re-hosting. In the context of HALucinator and this paper, the re-hosting support layer is the set of handlers and models that enable HALucinator to re-host a firmware.

VxWorks vs Device Code: In developing a re-hosting support layer, it is often useful to distinguish the origin of the functionality being replaced. The origin of the code impacts how widely used the functionality is. Intercepting code that is part of VxWorks will be common across all systems using VxWorks and replacing it will enable wide application of the re-hosting support layer. On the other hand, device specific code will only be found on a device or a small family of devices. Replacing it limits applicability of the re-hosting support layer, but can increase fidelity of the emulated system. We will refer to code that is part of VxWorks as **VxWorks code** and all other code as **device code**.

B. Emulation Utility Scale

To aid in communicating the utility of an emulated system, we have created a scale to describe the capabilities a re-hosted firmware provides. The level of utility needed from an emulated system depends on the reason for emulating it. The scale is inspired by the levels of autonomous driving [1]. Our scale goes from zero to five, with zero having the least utility and five having the most.

As can be seen in the Figure 1, **Level 0**, means that at least one instruction executes in the emulator, implying that we have the ISA identified correctly and firmware loaded at the correct base address. At this point we can choose any address and start executing from it, but execution will likely not be meaningful. **Level 1** begins when execution starts at the correct entry point and the system starts to properly initialize.

At this point we likely have missing hardware requirements that will cause the firmware to not finish initialization. Levels 0 and 1 enable inspecting execution, but is not useful for much more than manual analysis of a few key points.

Level 2 begins when at least one bi-directional interface is working. Examples include reading/writing files, networking, serial ports, or an interactive shell. At **Level 3** all the core OS functions are working including file system, task scheduling, and networking. With a functional interface, levels 2 and 3 become useful for manual and automated vulnerability research like fuzzing.

After completing core OS functionality, device specific applications should be at least partially functional. **Level 4** begins when one or more of the device specific applications are working and it implies that select applications should behave similar to the physical system. **Level 5** is achieved when all OS and device specific applications are working. At this point, from an external – black box perspective – the emulated system should behave like the real system. It is important to note that Level 5 does not mean it is identical to the real system, as there are likely differences in timing and internal state from the real system. If you want perfectly fidelity you probably need to use the real system. The process of developing and adding our re-hosting layer follow the pattern of pushing the utility of the emulated system up this scale by focusing on the interfaces and software layers needed to move from one level to the next.

C. HALucinator

This work substantially extends HALucinator, and thus we review key parts of its architecture and design principals here. For a more thorough description we refer you to the original paper [8]. HALucinator provides a framework to perform High Level Emulation (HLE) for bare-metal firmware. It does this by identifying hardware abstraction functions in the firmware and replacing them. These functions abstract low-level hardware operations into high-level API's that simplify development.

HALucinator implements replacement functionality using three components in an attempt to maximize code reuse. These components are handlers, peripheral models, and external devices. The handlers interact directly with the emulator's state (i.e., registers and memory) to read/write relevant data to or from the emulated system's memory. Handlers are also the least portable between firmware, as they are implemented specifically per abstraction layer. The handlers often make calls to a peripheral model, where the model implements the behavior of an on-chip or external peripheral, such as a UART, or Ethernet controller in a generic way. This enables reuse of the models in re-hosting multiple firmwares, enabling the handler to be a thin translation layer, mapping the semantics of the firmware's API to a generic model of a peripheral.

To enable the peripheral models to receive input from and send output to a variety of devices, the peripheral models leverage HALucinator's IO Server. The IO Server publishes and receives tagged messages to and from external devices. The external devices are usually scripts that tie host system resources to the emulator. In this work we refer to the set of handlers and models needed to enable re-hosting a class of firmware as a re-hosting support layer (RSL).

The HALucinator paper showed that HLE can be used to re-host firmware in an interactive manner and it also enables automated vulnerability discovery for small bare-metal systems. In this work, we extend the HALucinator platform to enable re-hosting commercial firmware using the VxWork RTOS by developing a re-hosting support layer for VxWorks.

D. VxWorks

VxWorks started as a set of enhancements to VRTX [23]. In the late 1980's, Wind River developed its own kernel to replace VRTX within VxWorks. Over time, VxWorks went from support for 32-bit processors to becoming an RTOS with a networking stack and eventually 64-bit processing in the 2010's. VxWorks supports ARM, Intel and Power architectures, both 32-bit and 64-bit. One of the key features of VxWorks is that the OS kernel is separate from applications, board support packages, middleware, and other packages. This allows for updates of the OS and components, without having to change the applications. These same abstractions help facilitate re-hosting the firmware using HLE.

Our example firmware use VxWorks 5.5 and 6.4, so we focus on their details here. VxWorks 7 brings significant changes and we leave re-hosting it to future work. Figure 2 shows generalization of some key layers in VxWorks relevant to our re-hosting support layer. It starts from the top with applications and moves down through the software stack eventually reaching hardware. Conceptually, a re-hosting support layer needs to replace blocks such that every vertical column has a replacement before reaching hardware. Doing this will enable the re-hosted firmware to emulate the system it implements.

Starting at the top of Figure 2 we have a set of applications that are implemented as tasks in VxWorks. A number of these are provided with VxWorks and others are device specific. Not all the VxWorks applications will be present or executing on every system. Below the application layer, VxWorks provides a POSIX-like API through its IO Subsystem. It provides functions such as *open*, *close*, *read*, *write*, etc. This is a thin layer that looks up the driver that should handle the operation, and forwards the parameters to the appropriate driver functions. Drivers are registered with VxWorks by using calls to *iosDrvInstall* which registers the Create, Remove, Open, Close, Read, Write, and IOCTL functions for the driver and returns a driver. The driver is then passed to *iosDrvAdd* which associates it with a path. These two functions and the drivers associated with them are featured prominently in our re-hosting support layer.

VxWorks provides drivers for file systems (e.g., DosFs) tty devices (serial ports), and network devices. In addition to drivers provided by VxWorks, device specific drivers can also be added. The VxWorks drivers rely on device specific BSP implementations to perform their operations. VxWorks provides its own TCP/IP stack with the ability to register device specific protocols in the networking stack. Connection of these protocol stacks is done through VxWorks' Networking Mux interface. This provides an interface to register device specific drivers conforming to the MUX API. Implementing these functions enables data to be sent and received over the network. One of these types of interfaces is the Extended Network Device (END), which is used for Ethernet devices and is the most applicable to our re-hosting support layer.

III. VxWorks Re-Hosting Support Layer

With this overview of VxWorks we are now ready to describe our VxWorks re-hosting support layer. We start by

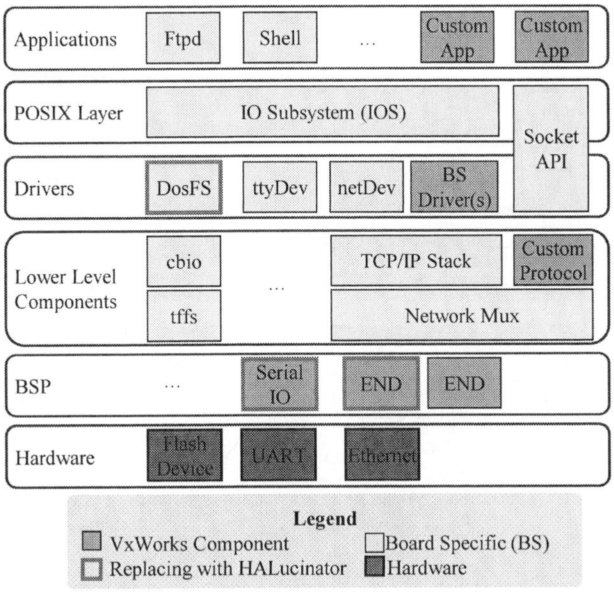

Fig. 2. VxWorks Layer Diagram. This is an example and is generic. Some of the boxes shown here may change, disappear and others may appear depending on the specific device.

laying out its pre-requisites and then proceed through each of the key components in the order that we recommend adding them. This order pushes the utility of the emulated system up the emulation utility scale. Our re-hosting support layer enables initializing VxWorks, executing multiple threads, triggering interrupts, serial communication, a DOS file system, and Ethernet communications.

A. Pre-requisites

Obtain Firmware. Before re-hosting firmware we need to obtain the firmware and determine how to load the firmware into HALucinator. The firmware used in this paper was all obtained by downloading it from their respective manufactures. In all cases, the firmware was a binary file in the downloaded package (i.e. the firmware was at most compressed, not encrypted or otherwise packed). In general, obtaining firmware can be a significant challenge [29], [35], [34]. As our goal is advancing the capabilities in re-hosting firmware, we chose devices for which obtaining the firmware was straight forward.

Determine Architecture. After obtaining the firmware we have to determine the processor architecture, load address for the firmware, memory map, and entry point to re-host the firmware. The processor architecture can be obtained by physical examination of the hardware on which the firmware runs, looking for strings in the firmware, or using tools such as binwalk [24] that use a heuristic based analysis to guess the processor architecture by examining the binary and looking for instructions. In our case, a combination of physical examination, strings, and heuristic approaches were used. All of our examples run on ARM micro-controllers that implement the ARM v5T instruction set [16].

Determine Load Address and Memory Map. Getting the correct load address for the firmware is essential for correct execution. If the processor chip is known and datasheets are available, much of the memory map can be obtained from there. Otherwise, we determined the correct loading addresses by loading into Ghidra [19] and examining the correctness of the disassembly after running Ghirda's default auto-analyses. We then used trial and error and examined the use of constant addresses to determine the correct load address. With the firmware loaded into Ghidra at the correct offset, we then use Ghidra to determine the rest of the memory map by looking for references to missing memory. We then add memory to satisfy these missing memories. For the purpose of re-hosting, over-provisioning memory does not impact the execution as it will just not be used. Thus, if it looks like a memory range may be accessed, we add a block of memory to enable the access whether or not it will actually occur. We also leverage dynamic analysis to identify additional regions of memory and iteratively add these as they are discovered.

Symbol Discovery and Function Naming. To effectively replace a layer in a firmware, we need to identify the addresses of the functions. The re-hosting support layer utilizes function names to identify functionality to replace. Labeling functions in firmware can be a challenging problem – LibMatch [8] and other solutions [37], [13], [22], [17] can be referenced for solving this problem. On VxWorks 5 and 6 these techniques are not needed, as they embed a partial symbol table in the binary. Tools such as Ghidra's "VxWorksSymTab_Finder.java" [20] and VxHunter [38] can extract function names from this table, and we leverage them to map symbol names to addresses in HALucinator. This enables us to refer to the functions by their symbolic names in configuration files for HALucinator. This increases both the readability of the configurations files and their portability between different firmware.

Determine Entry Point. Using the symbols, we look for the instruction that should execute first. We do this by looking for callers of the function *usrInit*. Tracing back up the call chain until we can go no further has led to the entry point where VxWorks starts execution. It is important to note that on the real system, a boot loader likely ran before this instruction, so it may be necessary to fix up some memory state for VxWorks to initialize properly. In addition, the firmware may have multiple ways of starting up (e.g., hard power ups, soft-reset, factory reset, etc). This can mean there are multiple ways that usrInit can get executed, each with a different set of assumed events that occurred previously. We generally try to boot into a hard power-up mode, performing a factory reset if possible. This setup will rely on the least amount of configuration being present at startup. How this is done is device specific, but the initialization process will generally indicate what state needs to be set and provide clues about expected values.

B. Logging

At this point the firmware should execute with a Level 1 utility (i.e., it will start initializing but likely fail quickly). One of the things we have found indispensable in pushing the utility to higher levels is to intercept and log error messages. This enables detecting when errors occur, their source, and often get a human readable message. Our re-hosting support layer provides the ability to capture *errnoSet*, and map it to a human readable string using values from [9]. We also capture calls to various device specific error and debug functions that were identified in the process of re-hosting. These are usually human passed readable strings providing clues about the nature of the error.

C. Initialization

VxWorks has a defined startup process that follows a set of steps to initialize memory and call additional bootstrapping code. The specific steps vary between systems, but generally include loading ROM code into memory and setting initial values at set addresses. One example of this data is the boot line, which allows certain parameters, such as network addresses and boot devices, to be set in a string. This string is loaded to a fixed memory address for the system that can be accessed later by bootstrapping code. If this startup code is not available, it is still necessary to initialize memory before jumping to bootstrapping code.

The system starts its kernel bootstrapping by calling a run-once root task, *usrRoot*, which is the first task executed by the kernel. This task is responsible for initializing hardware and spawning additional system tasks, such as serial communications and networking. Since the underlying hardware does not exist in the re-hosted system, we must replace functions which initialize hardware in order to prevent the system from hanging.

Both the memory initialization and kernel bootstrapping will be device specific. However, we have broken the VxWorks re-hosting support layer into generic components that can be reused depending on the system. For example, the SCADAPack initializes hardware components for serial communications, a DOS file system, and networking. This combination of devices is specific to the SCADAPack, but the initialization routines rely on drivers which can be replaced to provide generic hardware support.

While bringing up a system for the first time, it is often the case that each of these drivers will be added one at a time to ensure they are properly handled. In our case, each component can usually be disabled by simply skipping the initialization routines for that component. Any components that are not essential to the system or analysis can remain disabled. We apply an iterative process of enabling a component and trying to execute to the end of initialization (e.g., the end of *usrRoot*). If a new error is encountered or we get stuck somewhere, we examine the cause and address it by fixing up the offending device-specific code. In practice, this usually requires little more than skipping low-level hardware initialization functions that are waiting on hardware that is not present in the emulator.

For our sample firmwares, we do not execute the bootloader prior to starting VxWorks. Thus, it is necessary to set the bootline. We do this by intercepting the call to *bootStringToStruct* and writing our boot string to the address of the pointer in the first argument of the call. We then allow execution to continue as normal. In this way our bootline gets injected before it is used for initialization.

D. Interrupts

One of the primary reasons to use an RTOS is to enable a processor to perform asychronous tasks. The use of interrupts is essential for enabling this. VxWorks provides its own abstraction for managing interrupts and uses a method called *intConnect* to associate a callback function and priority with each interrupt. A generic interrupt handler is then called, which uses a BSP function to lookup the from the IRQ controller what interrupt occurred and map it to a VxWorks interrupt vector number. This method is usually called *xxxIntLevVecChk* where the xxx is a device specific identifier chosen by the developer. *xxxIntLevVecChk* is passed two parameters by reference; the first points to a level and the second points to the VxWorks vector number passed to *intConnect* for the interrupt that was triggered.

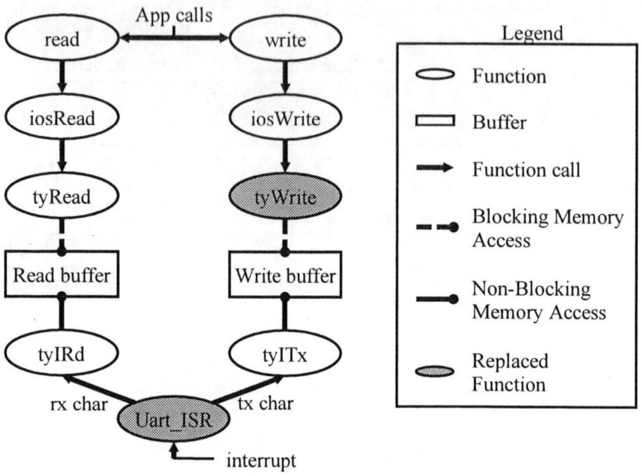

Fig. 3. Shows the read and write operations of serial devices implemented using the VxWorks ttyDev driver, and conceptual replacements made in our re-hosting support layer.

We implement interrupts by adding a simple interrupt controller to QEMU that has an array of memory mapped bytes, which if any are set, triggers an interrupt. We intercept the call *xxxIntLevVecChk* which will get executed to determine what interrupt occurs. We then lookup in our interrupt controller the interrupt source and return the value. VxWorks will then execute the handler for the desired interrupt.

E. Supporting Asynchronous Tasks

VxWorks has two modes for the scheduler to run in: synchronous and asynchronous. Our example firmwares utilizes the asynchronous scheduler that executes in a periodic manner. This is done by configuring a timer to trigger an interrupt at the period with its associated ISR executing the scheduler. We provide this functionality in our re-hosting support layer, by intercepting the execution of *sysClkEnable* and replacing it with a model that starts a timer. On expiration of the timer we trigger the interrupt associated with the system clock. We determine the interrupt used to trigger the clock by statically examining calls to *intConnect* and looking at those that are in the call tree of *sysClkInit*. We also intercept *sysClkDisable* with a handler that stops the timer to prevent the interrupt from occurring when it should not.

F. Serial Communications

Serial communication is used for talking to other devices and for debugging. VxWorks provides a tty driver [31] which provides terminal like behavior to a serial port and enables POSIX file API's to be used for serial port interaction. This driver registers the POSIX layer functions *creat*, *delete*, *open*, *close*, *read*, *write* and *ioctrl* with the IO subsystem. Applications can then open the serial ports like a file and use read/write and ioctl calls to configure and interact with them.

Figure 3 shows the events that occur when a call is made to read or write from an application. Consider a call to *read* on its execution it calls the IO subsystem's read function (*iosRead*).

iosRead looks up the driver that should handle the read and then calls the driver's read function. For *ttyDev* devices, this is *tyRead*, which attempts to take a semaphore before reading from a receive buffer. The semaphore will be given if there is data to be received or it will cause the task to be removed from execution until data is available and the task can be rescheduled. Writing works similarly, except a semaphore is used to ensure there is room in the write buffer before writing the data.

The ttyDev driver provides functions for the low-level device driver to use for reading (*tyIRd*) and writing (*tyITx*) serial data. The UART's ISR calls these functions to put data into the read buffer and get data from the write buffer. In this way, by defining a few low-level functions, different serial port hardware can easily be integrated into VxWorks.

To implement our re-hosting layer for serial, we replace *tyWrite* with a handler that reads out the data and sends it out HALucinator's IO server. This makes it so data is always sent immediately and removes the need for triggering an interrupt when data is sent. If devices directly use VxWork's ttyDev device, without customization, receiving serial data is done by triggering an interrupt when the data is received for the serial device from the IO server. Then, intercepting the device specific UART_ISR and calling *tyIRd* with the data. However, different receive models are possible and the SCADAPack uses a receive task to get the data from the serial port. In this case, its receive ISR releases a semaphore that the receive task blocks on. The receive task then reads the data in and calls *tyIRd* (actually called *utyIRd* on SCADAPack). To accommodate this, our serial ISR handler for the SCADAPack modifies the state to indicate to the original handler that data has been received and then allows it to execute. The receive task will then execute *tyIRd*, which we intercept to inject the received data prior to its execution; and then we allow it to execute.

In addition to the handlers supporting reading and writing, handlers are added to monitor ioctl calls. Inserting the serial port layer requires identifying the addresses of *tyWrite*, *tyIRd*, *tyIoctl* – which were in the symbol tables of our firmware samples – and the serial port ISR function. We find the serial port ISR by examining calls to *intConnect*.

We currently intercept the low-level driver functions for polling read/writes, but the same effect can be created by intercepting *tyRead* and waiting until data is received. Because we are using emulated hardware, we can use a virtually unlimited transmit buffer so there is no need to block on transmitting data and our interception *tyWrite* will occur before the low-level write function is called, enabling it to be used as if polling mode is configured.

G. File System

The file system of the SCADAPack, Modicon, and Hughes firmware all utilize the dosFS file system provided by VxWorks. Much like the *ttyDev*, VxWorks installs the file system as a driver using a call to *iosDrvInstall* — registering callback functions that provide read, write, create, delete, open, ioctl and close operations on files. We intercept calls to all these driver functions and map them to the host system in HALucinator. With the file system becoming a directory on the host system.

These functions are not named in the symbol tables in our firmware. For the sake of clarity we will refer to these as *dosFsXXX* where XXX is the operation the function performs (e.g, *dosFsRead*, *dosFsWrite*). In our re-hosting layer the functions *dosFsRead*, *dosFsWrite*, *dosFsClose* are mapped directly to their equivalent function on the host system using python's *os* library. The other functions require mapping VxWorks specific parameters to their equivalent on the host system. *dosFsOpen's* flags need to be mapped to their equivalent opening mode. In addition, VxWorks can create the directories when opening a file by setting a flag. We implement equivalent logic to create directories if this flag is given. Similarly, *dosFsDelete* is used for both files and directories and we handle both depending on the path specified.

The most complex of the functions is *dosFsIoctl*. *dosFsIoctl* takes as one of its parameters a pointer to the device (i.e., dosFS device), the file descriptor, a function code pointer and an untyped value. The function code determines what kind of operation is performed on the file. The 400plus project [21] identified 31 ioctl operations used in VxWorks. We implement the eight different operations we encountered in the SCADAPack firmware. Specifically, fioRead, fioSeek, fioWhere, fioRename, fioReadDir, fioTimeSet, and fioMove. We have also logged attempts to uses of other ioctl operations, enabling us to know if additional operations need to be implemented. Each of these ioctl operations use a different data structure for their value parameter. They follow POSIX defined formats, but offsets for various fields must be carefully determined for each firmware to ensure correct operation.

Adding the handlers for the re-hosting layer requires identifying the addresses of the *dosFsXXX* functions. None of these functions are named in the symbol tables of our firmware samples. However, they are easily identified by examining the call to *iosDrvInstall* in *dosFsLibInit*. Both these functions are in the symbol table of all our firmware samples. In addition, offsets for the data structures used for the ioctl functions may need to be updated. This can significantly increase effort and we are looking for ways to reduce it.

H. Ethernet

The re-hosting support layer supports Ethernet by intercepting the functions used by the VxWorks *muxLib* interface to talk to Extended Network Devices (ie. END in VxWorks documentation) [33]. Specifically, we intercept functions specified in the *END_OBJ* passed to *muxDevLoad* [32] Section 10.1. This structure defines the callback functions used to manage the Ethernet devices. It includes operations to send data, manage multi-cast addresses, load and unload the device, start and stop the device, and handle IOCTLs. We implement handlers for *xSend* which reads out the frame data and sends it using the IO Server. We also implement handlers for *xStart* and *xStop*, which enable and disable receiving of frames and triggering interrupts when frames are received at the IO Server. All other functions currently in the *END_OBJ* are stubbed out to enable monitoring their execution, but execute without modification. These stubs can be removed to improve re-hosting performance.

While the functions to send Ethernet frames are part of the *END_OBJ*, receive functions are not in the *END_OBJ*. VxWorks intends for developer defined code to receive the frame and call *muxReceive* after putting the frame in the appropriate network frame data structure. Further complicating receiving is that to minimize delaying other interrupts, *muxReceive* should not be called in the ISR. Thus, the ISR signals the *netTask* to do the actual reading of the frame and calling of *muxReceive*. Our re-hosting support layer intercepts the Ethernet ISR and makes a call to *netJobAdd* passing it the address of the function used to perform the receive outside the ISR. *netJobAdd* releases the semaphore in the *netTask* is waiting for, enabling it to be scheduled for execution. Upon execution, *netTask* calls the *ENDReceive* function. We intercept this function and replace its logic with functionality that: (1) reads the frame from the Ethernet model, (2) allocates the network data structure by making a call to *netTupleCreate*, (3) copies the Ethernet frame into the structure, and finally (4) calls *muxReceive* with the structure.

Locating the functions needed to add the Ethernet in the re-hosting support layer, requires manual reverse engineering as the functions intercepted are device specific. We locate the *END_OBJ* functions by statically and dynamically examining calls to *muxDevLoad. muxDevLoad* is a VxWorks function and was found in the symbol tables of all our sample firmware. The receive functions addresses were found by examining calls to *intConnect*. This gives the ISR for receiving the frames, and we then examine the ISR's for calls to *netJobAdd* to find the function used by the netTask to receive the frame. Using our Ethernet re-hosting layer we are currently able to send and receive an Ethernet frame and get a successful response to an ARP query. Work is ongoing to optimize the receiving of frames to enable more complex interaction.

IV. Firmware Analyses

To analyze the effectiveness of our re-hosting, we first examine the success of extracting the symbol table from our example firmware. We then demonstrate the utility of our re-hosted firmware by performing a series of analyses of interest to a firmware analyst. These include recovering the file systems, enumerating the tasks created, inspecting execution traces through custom tools we have built for Ghidra, and enabling the VxWorks shell when not initialized.

These analyses and our re-hosting capabilities are a work in progress. Thus, we focus primarily on the SCADAPack 350 as it is the firmware we have spent the most effort re-hosting. Typically, we develop for it and then port our solutions to the other devices. Currently, we are able to re-host the SCADAPack's firmware well enough to send and receive serial data and send and receive Ethernet frames. Porting to the Modicon and Hughes are a work in progress and we are still working to complete their initialization. We report our findings to date for all devices.

A. Symbol Recovery

Recovering of symbols is essential for the portability of our re-hosting support layer, as it enables the rapid adaptation of the layer to new firmware. Our firmware samples use VxWorks 5.5 and VxWorks 6.4 which embed a symbol table in the binary. We use Ghidra 9.2 [19] to load the binaries into memory using the offsets and memory layout determined manually. We then use the *VxWorksSymTab_Finder.java* script that ships with Ghidra to read the symbol table and populate it into a Ghidra project, after which Ghidra's default auto analyses are run to identify functions and other references. Table I shows the number of function names recovered, the total number of functions identified by Ghidra's analyses, the total number of symbols read, and the total number of symbols Ghidra reported. In the worst case, 53% of the functions identified by Ghidra have names in the symbol table. In the best case 86% of the functions are recovered.

TABLE I.
Symbols Recovered using Ghidra VxWorksSymTab_Finder

	Functions			Symbols		
Firmware	Recovered	Total	%	Recovered	Total	%
ScadaPack	4,904	6,440	76%	6,111	15,386	40%
Modicon	8,057	15,324	53%	16,914	23,004	74%
Hughes	19,164	22,221	86%	22,274	42,503	52%

TABLE II. Functions Intercepted During Initialization.

Grouping	**Handler**	**SP**	**Exe**	**Mod.**	**Exe**	**H.**	**Exe**
DosFS	dosFsCreate		2				
DosFS	dosFsDelete		3				
DosFS	dosFsIoctl		9				
DosFS	dosFsOpen		9				
DosFS	dosFsClose		11				
DosFS	dosFsRead		11				
DosFS	dosFsWrite		6				
DosFS	iosDevAdd	✓	6	✓	10	✓	8
Error	errnoSet	✓		✓	16	✓	170
Ethernet	eth_Ioctl		26				
Ethernet	eth_Send		1				
Ethernet	eth_Start		2				
H. Init	0xa0052280						1
H. Init	0xa042c1d8						192
H. Init	flPollTask	✓				✓	1
H. Init	FUN_a0010830						2
H. Init	FUN_a049242c						1
H. Init	FUN_a04ac780						1
H. Init	FUN_a04ac804						768
H. Init	inmFlashErase					✓	2
H. Init	sysSpin					✓	16
H. Init	usrMmuInit					✓	1
Init	bootStringToStruct	✓	1	✓		✓	1
Interrupts	xxxIntLvlVecChk	✓	57	✓		✓	203
Logging	intConnect	✓		✓	6	✓	40
Logging	intDisable	✓		✓	2	✓	6
Logging	intEnable	✓	22	✓	11	✓	13
Logging	intExit	✓	56	✓		✓	
Logging	taskSpawn	✓	24	✓	13	✓	13
Mod.	SendToDisplay			✓	1		
Mod. Init	CntSyst1MicroDeltaTime			✓			1
Mod. Init	FUN_2022bd5c				2		
Mod. Init	kl_NandFlashDrvInit			✓	1		
Mod. Init	taskDelay			✓	8		
Mod. Init	usrToolsInit			✓	1		
SP Init	FUN_020a6c10		1				
SP Init	at25Close	✓	2				
SP Init	at25Open	✓	2				
SP Init	at25ReadNBytes	✓	2				
SP Init	cbioDevVerify	✓	1				
SP Init	defaultSerialInit	✓	1				
SP Init	detectBootType	✓	1				
SP Init	eepromReadNBytes	✓	16				
SP Init	flCall	✓	3				
SP Init	getclock	✓	2				
SP Init	readBattery	✓	1				
SP Init	usbPhciInit	✓	1				
SP Init	writeSH3000Register	✓	5				
SysClk	sysClkEnable	✓	1	✓		✓	1
ttyDev	tyIoctl	✓	5	✓		✓	
ttyDev	tyRead	✓	1	✓		✓	382
ttyDev	tyWrite	✓		✓	33	✓	1017

*Check-mark means the symbol is recovered with default symbol finding script for the given device.

B. Re-hosting the firmware

We re-host the three firmware samples and let them execute as far as they can. Table II shows the functions we intercept and replace with our firmware re-hosting layer for each firmware. For symbols present in the symbol table a check mark is also given. Empty columns mean the handler did not execute on that device. Starting with the SCADAPack, you can see that it uses the Ethernet, DosFS, and ttyDev drivers. The majority (13) of it's handlers are to handle device specific initialization. Of these, all but *at25ReadNBytes*, *eepromReadNBytes*, and *detectBootType* skip the function or return a constant value. *at25ReadNBytes* and *eepromReadNBytes* are both device specific functions that execute the same handler. The handler returns values from a file that was created by reading the contents of the eeprom on the physical system. *detectBootType* writes a value to a global variable to indicate that the boot mode is a factory reset. The value was determined by examining callers to *detectBootType*. These handlers highlight some of the challenges with properly initializing the system that do not port well from device to device. Without access to the physical device, we would have had to manually reverse engineer callers to *at25ReadNBytes* and *eepromReadNBytes* to determine the valid values to return.

Of the three devices, the SCADAPack gets furthest through its execution. It completes execution of its initialization and is waiting to be configured. We boot it in a factory reset mode and so it has no control logic to execute. In addition, the device can speak a variety of control protocols over its serial ports. This means that in actual use they are likely connected to other devices and it is essential that non-protocol data–like debug strings and boot info–not be written to them. We can see this by the lack of calls to *tyWrite*. We are able to get it to receive and process both serial and Ethernet data, but this functionality was not exercised in the capture used to generate Table II.

The our re-hosting support layer for the Modicon 340 is the least mature of our samples. It currently gets stuck in the last function call of its *usrAppInit*–the last high level function of it's initialization. It is waiting on data from a SD Card that we have not yet implemented. From the handlers intercepted you can see that it is writing to a ttyDev. To get this firmware to the same point as the SCADAPack, we need to get the interrupt vector table to initialize and the start the system clock. At that point we can stop intercepting taskDelay–which we currently skip to prevent hanging forever. This allows us to get further in initialization to determine what resources the system uses, but prevents other tasks from being scheduled. We also need to determine how the system initializes its Ethernet interface as it does not appear to use the boot line for this purpose.

The Hughes 9201 BGAN completes its initialization, but does so with a large number of errors. It calls errnoSet 170 times and many of these are related to the creation of network devices and file systems. We are working to continue fixing up it's initialization so that these components will work. Even with these limitations we can learn some interesting things about the Hughes device. For example, it uses a ttyDev for printing out debugging information and runs the VxWorks shell. Figure 4 is a screen capture of the shell initialization. We can also see that number of symbols recovered is only one less than the firmware finds (e.g. 22,274 vs 22,275).

The current re-hosting capabilities are useful and we are working to expand them. One of the current limitations arise from changes to the initialization from our RSL improperly skipping parts of initialization that are needed but problematic (e.g., functions that polls on hardware preventing further

TABLE III. COMMON NAME TASKS CREATED

Task Name	Scadapack	Modicon	Hughes
tExcTask	✓		✓
tLogTask	✓	✓	✓
tNbioLog	✓	✓	
tTffsPTask	✓		✓
tNetTask	✓	✓	✓
tFtpdTask	✓		✓

TABLE IV. DEVICE SPECIFIC TASKS

Scadapack		Modicon	Hughes
t0	com1Tx	tJobTask	tEthSend
BULK_CLASS	masterReq	tErfTask	USB_RXTX
BULK_CLASS_IRP	mrTx1	tDhcpcStateTask	tTelnetd
tBulkClnt	com2Tx	tDhcpcReadTask	tBridgeAger
tRxTask0	mrTx2	tTftpd	tDhcpsTask
tRxTask1	com3Tx	tFtp6d	***tShell***
tRxTask2	mrTx3	tStartSnmpd	tPicDriver
fileWatch	mTcpServ	MidRangePPP_D_1	SYSLOG
com1Rest	mruServ	MidRangePPP_C_1	
com2Rest	mauServ	EnableUSB	
com3Rest	mastIpSta	tXbdService	
Startup	bkgrndIo	t920_PollTask	
udpConfig	softWatch		
ioCtrl	socketWatch		
ioRecv	HALThread		

execution, but also sets critical data structures). Another challenge is providing missing information. For example, the boot loader will pass VxWorks a boot string that configures things like networking and initial users. The general structure of this string is standardized, but values can be device specific. Some of the firmware contain a default string that can be used. Others have minimal strings that fail to initialize much of the desired hardware. Finally, differences in execution during re-hosting vs. physical execution also arise. For example, HALucinator's high overhead in triggering interrupts and executing its handlers make it run the system clock much slower than on the physical device. We suspect this at least contributes to the slow network processing, as it causes delays in switching between tasks that process the Ethernet traffic. We are evaluating adding the ability to inject code for handlers, instead of executing python code in a break point. This would greatly improve performance, at the cost of ease of development and potential portability of handlers. We are also considering integration of a generic system clock that runs within QEMU that uses the number of instructions executed instead of time to trigger. This would enable fine tuning the balance between time executing the clock's interrupt service routine and executing other code.

C. Task Analysis

Analyzing the tasks that firmware starts can tell an analyst a lot about what the system does and how it does it. To support this type of analysis we add a handler that logs the calls to the function used to create new tasks *taskSpawn*. We log all the parameters which gives us the task's: name, stack size, priority, entry point, flags, and parameters passed to the entry point. The common tasks created through their initialization process are shown in Table III and device specific tasks are shown in Table IV. From this you can see that all three run a logging task (*tLogTask*) and a networking task (*tNetTask*). The SCADAPack and Hughes device also both run VxWork's FTP server (*tFtpdTask*). The modicon device also appears to runs a FTP server *tFtp6d* and a Trivial FTP server *tTftpd* but these are specific the modicon device.

Looking at device specific tasks we can see that the SCADAPack starts a number of tasks for each serial port

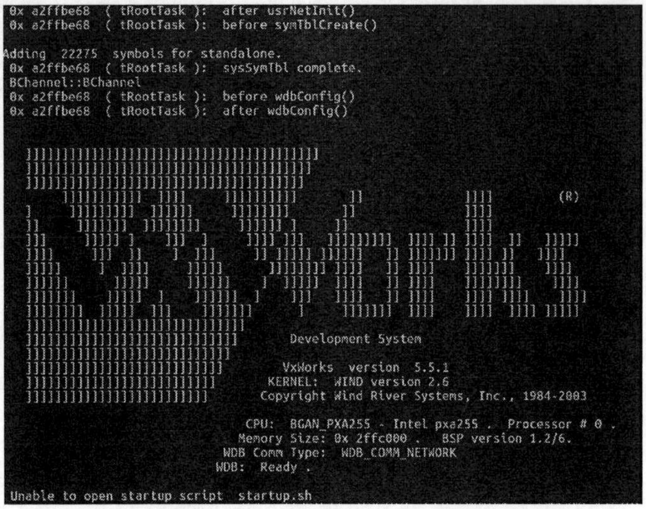

Fig. 4. Output from Hughes 9201 ttyDev during initialization

(tRxTaskN, comNRest, mrTxN, comNTx). The fact each serial port is managed by four tasks indicates complex and critical behavior occurring on the serial ports. This makes them of interest for further security analysis. Looking at the Modicon and Hughes device we also find a number of network facing services (e.g., DHCP, SNMP, Telnet) that could be of interest to security analysts.

As previously mentioned, the Hughes device executes a VxWorks shell over a serial port. We have been able to interact with the shell using re-hosting and use it to execute commands, inspect the system, and execute scripts. However, because of all the errors during initialization we cannot yet say whether this interface would be unprotected on physical systems. It is possible that later execution, or a missing part of initialization disables it or sets a password on it. In addition, it possible that physical protections like not routing the serial pins to pads on the PCB are used to protect the interface.

D. Discovering and Enabling the VxWorks Shell

VxWorks provides an interactive shell designed for interfacing with the operating system. The shell serves two purposes: as a command interpreter and for prototyping and debugging. The command interpreter is similar to a UNIX shell where commands are issued to exercise system functionality. The prototyping and debugging features allow for low-level introspection and control into tasks running on VxWorks. This allows the user to set breakpoints in code, call user routines, examine and modify memory, and catch errors on the system.

The shell must be included in the application by the developer. This is done by calling *shellInit* in the bootstrapping task, *usrRoot*. The shell would likely be included during system development since it is the primary mechanism for debugging applications. Each of the three devices we inspected contained the shell symbols, but not all started the shell task at startup. Since we control execution of the re-hosted firmware, we can enable the shell by inserting our own call to the *shellInit* function at startup.

Inspect Running Tasks. Going beyond the knowledge of what tasks have been started. The shell allows tasks to be listed and inspected dynamically. Showing what tasks are *running* at any given time. Additionally, the shell can show information about a task, such as the location of its stack, and spawn or suspend tasks. Comparing running tasks to started tasks can indicate where re-hosting fidelity needs to be improved.

Modify Filesystem. The shell can be used to traverse the device filesystem and modify files using a file editor. Modifying scripts on the re-hosted device filesystem can persistently modify behavior of the system. For example, some devices rely on scripts at startup for initialization.

Read/Write Memory. Memory can be read and written using shell commands. This can be used to leak information or modify the memory of a running process.

Run User Routines. The shell has a table of symbols which can be invoked from the command line. This mechanism can be used to run arbitrary user functions on the device.

E. Ghidra Integration

In many cases during the re-hosting process something goes wrong. Determining where this occurred and understanding it accelerates the re-hosting process. To support this we have developed a tool, called HQ-Tracer, which parses the execution log from HALucinator/QEMU and loads it into Ghidra. This tool colors all instructions executed in the trace and highlights the current instruction in the trace. It also enables interactively stepping through the traces in Ghidra using a command-like interface similar to GDB. These commands include stepping forward and backward X number of instructions (default of 1 at a time), continue until you exit the given function, and it allows to search for a specific address forward/backward. If you only have a single thread/task, there is a stack tracker that attempts to keep a call stack to quickly see the function call path to the current instruction, though this feature is disabled by default and can be toggled on. In addition, the trace enables executing python code as a command which enables performing customized filtering and stepping through the trace. During our debugging and discovery phases of re-hosting, we often would not understand why some things were not working. Loading the trace into Ghidra enabled us to quickly determine the location of the error and determine work arounds.

V. Approach For Re-hosting Other RTOSes

In re-hosting VxWorks we discovered multiple places where HALucinator needed extensions, and the approach used to re-host firmware in the original HALucinator paper needed refinement. Based on this experience we propose an approach to use as a starting point when re-hosting an RTOS. In this approach, we assume you can get the firmware loaded into HALucinator, identify the entry point and begin execution (i.e., you have reached Emulation Utility Level 1). We also assume that key functions of the RTOS have been identified. This can be done using symbols, function labeling techniques, or manually. If it needs to be done manually, then this approach can serve as a template to help identify what these function need to be identified. This process is primarily derived from the approach we took, but incorporates ideas and suggestions that we wish we had known starting out. We believe these ideas can shorten the process of building a re-hosting support layer for other operating systems.

(1) Instrument error handling and print statements. Once the execution in the HALucinator can begin, we recommend intercepting and logging calls to error handling functions first. This provides a high level way to track what the firmware is doing and determine where execution is going wrong. If these can be mapped back to human readable strings this is particularly useful, as it provides hints of how to fix the issue or even determine if the issue needs resolved. For example, if the error is for an interface you don't intend to use in the emulated system, then you may not need to fix it. In addition to error handling code instrumenting, print statements (e.g. *printf*, etc) provide indication of what is being executed and if things are going as expected.

(2) Understand and execute RTOS initialization to completion. With error handling and print statements instrumented, the next step is to get the OS initialization process to complete. This will require understanding the boot process for the OS and determining when initialization is complete, i.e., the system switches to its steady state operations. For VxWorks, this is generally the completion of execution of *usrRoot*. The initial goal is not to get everything to initialize correctly, but rather to get execution to reach the end of initialization. This lets you know what needs to be initialized and then to selectively work on individual components as needed.

We did this by stubbing out functions that prevented reaching the end of initialization. This includes hardware initialization functions that polled non-existent IO, task delay functions, clock reading functions, and anything else that prevents reaching the end of initialization. We replace these functions with stubs that indicate they executed successfully (e.g., returning zero) or just skipped their execution. For functions reading clock values we return an increasing value on each call.

The goal at this stage is to understand what needs to be initialized. To this end, we delay starting asynchronous context switching as long as possible. This simplifies debugging and execution tracing. If initialization is dependent on another task running and providing a resource, we often skip the execution of this function during the initial re-hosting stage. In this way, we can rapidly identify what needs to be initialized and determine where we will spend our effort in re-hosting.

(3) Identify tasks creation. With the system running through its initialization process you can now identify the tasks that it creates (or at least attempts to), their priorities and usually a human readable name. We do this by intercepting calls to *taskSpawn* and logging the tasks to a file, then allow execution to continue unmodified. We also instrument the task switching code to determine when a task starts execution.

(4) Identify interrupt handlers and driver registration. With the system running through its initialization process, you can now dynamically identify interrupt handlers, and driver registration. Replacement of these drivers will enable providing support for the hardware missing in the emulator. The drivers and their initialization functions are likely the source of most the errors encountered during initialization. We identify these functions by intercepting the driver registration functions *iosDrvInstall* and *iosDrvAdd*. Intercepting these functions will tell you what kind of devices the system is using and the functions used to interact with the system.

On VxWorks, a number of these drivers are software only components provided by VxWorks and they use another set of lower level callbacks to interact with the hardware. We found it much easier to intercept these lower level callbacks rather than the higher level set. For example, we intercept the utyLib functions (e.g., *tyWrite)* for the serial port. This allows the read and write functions provided by the tty driver to handle the semaphores and interprocess communication needed for multiple tasks to execute on the system in the firmware, rather than having to have our handlers manage these semaphores. Networking is much the same – a high level network driver is added that provides the POSIX file api, but VxWorks intends for network functionality to leverage the MUX interface.

Once you have identified the drivers, we suggest you work to bring them up one at a time, following the order the initialization function tries to initialize them, with one exception. We suggest delaying starting the scheduler for as long as possible, as debugging multiple tasks is significantly harder than a single task. However, we found at some point the initialization process starts other tasks and expects them to execute prior to its completion. In these cases, complete as much of the initialization as you can before starting the scheduler, then enable it. For each driver, work to understand their initialization process and how to determine that it is performed correctly. Then for each interface you care about, ensure that each driver initializes as completely as possible.

(5) Starting Non-cooperative Context Switching. When either initialization is completing without errors or initialization is dependent on having other tasks run, it is time to start non-cooperative context switching. This is done by starting a timer that triggers the system tick ISR periodically. We recommend to initially start slow, and then increase rate as needed for performance. At this point the operating systems should be running along with tasks that are not dependent on unsupported devices.

VI. Related Work

The first large scale academic works that enabled system-emulation and firmware re-hosting were Firmadyne [7] and work by Costin that is very similar [10], [11]. The ideas behind these works include extracting the file system from a Linux firmware, and re-hosting using their own Linux kernel using QEMU. Their tools work only for Linux firmware that can natively use chroot inside of QEMU. After re-hosting firmware, they perform static and dynamic analysis to report vulnerabilities.

The group that created Avatar [36] also created Avatar^2 [18], which was completely re-designed from the original Avatar implementation. Avatar^2 is a dynamic multi-target orchestration and instrumentation framework that allows various other tools (angr [28], QEMU [6], GDB, HALucinator [8], etc.) to integrate and communicate state between them during dynamic execution. It can also be used to perform hardware in the loop emulation of systems.

Using the drop-in fuzzer AFL [5], P^{2}IM [12] provides inputs to a modified QEMU emulator for any peripheral or hardware IO. Their approach is unique and different from existing emulation approaches, as it does not use hardware, traces, or detailed knowledge of the peripheral/hardware IO, rather they are relying on the fuzzer to provide all interactions. By using the drop-in fuzzer, it enables simple peripherals to be emulated, but its ability to enable complex data and stateful hardware is still either lacking or unknown. It also does not allow interactive system of system emulation as all IO is randomly generated. Leveraging machine learning, Pretender [14] records hardware interactions and all accesses to memory mapped input and output regions. These recordings are used to train a machine model that during re-hosting provides inputs for missing peripherals. Both of these approaches do not allow external inputs to peripherals making them unsuitable for system of system modeling or use cases beyond vulnerability analysis.

In "Challenges in Firmware Re-Hosting, Emulation, and Analysis", Wright et al. provide a comprehensive overview of the challenges faced during system emulation, firmware re-hosting, and analysis while providing classification and comparison techniques on five different axes [34]. Using the fidelity classification presented in that review, we note that HALucinator and Avatar^2 have higher fidelity than P^{2}IM and Pretender. We refer the reader to this paper for a more comprehensive review of the challenges faced during general system emulation and firmware re-hosting along with a wider evaluation of tools, as our focus is more in depth and focused on embedded devices that use VxWorks.

VII. Conclusion

With the re-hosting support layer we have implemented and deployed for a SCADAPack 350, Modicon 340 and Hughes 9201 BGAN, the time for porting the layer to another device using VxWorks can be significantly reduced. Re-hosting these devices can be used for vulnerability discovery or other general system analysis. We have thoroughly explained our re-hosting support layer, functions and tasks intercepted in VxWorks, and we have given a retrospective approach for re-hosting other RTOSes. We are continuing to expand our capabilities in this area with more devices in the works for re-hosting using our expanded HALucinator handlers and techniques.

Acknowledgment

Sandia National Laboratories is a multimission laboratory managed and operated by National Technology and Engineering Solutions of Sandia, LLC, a wholly owned subsidiary of Honeywell International Inc., for the U.S. Department of Energy's National Nuclear Security Administration under contract DE-NA0003525. This paper describes objective technical results and analysis. Any subjective views or opinions that might be expressed in the paper do not necessarily represent the views of the U.S. Department of Energy or the United States Government. SAND2021-2907 C

References

[1] "The 6 levels of vehicle autonomy explained." [Online]. Available: https://www.synopsys.com/automotive/autonomous-driving-levels.html

[2] "Command & data-handling systems." [Online]. Available: https://mars.nasa.gov/mro/mission/spacecraft/parts/command/

[3] "Customer success: Varian medical systems." [Online]. Available: https://www.windriver.com/customers/customer-success/medical/varian/

[4] "CVE-2019-12257." Available from MITRE, CVE-ID CVE-2019-12257., Dec. 2019. [Online]. Available: https://cve.mitre.org/cgi-bin/cvename.cgi?name=CVE-2019-12257

[5] AFL-Fuzz, "afl-fuzz." [Online]. Available: https://github.com/google/AFL

[6] F. Bellard, "Qemu, a fast and portable dynamic translator," in *Proceedings of the Annual Conference on USENIX Annual Technical Conference*. Berkeley, CA, USA: USENIX Association, 2005, pp. 41–41. [Online]. Available: http://dl.acm.org/citation.cfm?id=1247360.1247401

[7] D. D. Chen, M. Woo, D. Brumley, and M. Egele, "Towards automated dynamic analysis for linux-based embedded firmware," in *23rd Annual Network and Distributed System Security Symposium, 2016, San Diego, California, USA, February 21-24, 2016*, 2016. [Online]. Available: http://wp.internetsociety.org/ndss/wp-content/uploads/sites/25/2017/09/towards-automated-dynamic-analysis-linux-based-embedded-firmware.pdf

[8] A. A. Clements, E. Gustafson, T. Scharnowski, P. Grosen, D. Fritz, C. Kruegel, G. Vigna, S. Bagchi, and M. Payer, "Halucinator: Firmware re-hosting through abstraction layer emulation," in *29th USENIX Security Symposium (USENIX Security 20)*. USENIX Association, Aug. 2020, pp. 1201–1218. [Online]. Available: https://www.usenix.org/conference/usenixsecurity20/presentation/clements

[9] C. Co, "Vxworks error codes," Dec 2014. [Online]. Available: http://blog.lovecoco.net/168

[10] A. Costin, J. Zaddach, A. Francillon, and D. Balzarotti, "A large-scale analysis of the security of embedded firmwares," in *23rd USENIX Security Symposium*. San Diego, CA: USENIX Association, Aug 2014, pp. 95–110. [Online]. Available: https://www.usenix.org/conference/usenixsecurity14/technical-sessions/presentation/costin

[11] A. Costin, A. Zarras, and A. Francillon, "Automated dynamic firmware analysis at scale: A case study on embedded web interfaces," in *Proceedings of the 11th ACM on Asia Conference on Computer and Communications Security*. New York, NY, USA: ACM, 2016, pp. 437–448. [Online]. Available: http://doi.acm.org/10.1145/2897845.2897900

[12] B. Feng, A. Mera, and L. Lu, "P2im: Scalable and hardware-independent firmware testing via automatic peripheral interface modeling (extended version)," *ArXiv*, vol. abs/1909.06472, 2019.

[13] firminsight, "firminsight." [Online]. Available: https://github.com/ilovepp/firminsight

[14] E. Gustafson, M. Muench, C. Spensky, N. Redini, A. Machiry, Y. Fratantonio, D. Balzarotti, A. Francillon, Y. R. Choe, C. Kruegel *et al.*, "Toward the analysis of embedded firmware through automated re-hosting," in *22nd International Symposium on Research in Attacks, Intrusions and Defenses*, 2020.

[15] J. Laukkonen, "Will bmw's infotainment solution idrive you up the wall?" Feb 2020. [Online]. Available: https://www.lifewire.com/examining-the-bmw-idrive-interface-534742

[16] A. Limited, *ARM Architecture Reference Manual*, ARM. [Online]. Available: https://developer.arm.com/documentation/ddi0100/latest/

[17] H. Mohanan, P. Bendapudi, A. Kumarasubramanian, R. Jalan, and R. Venkatesan, "Function matching in binaries," Apr 2012, uS Patent 8,166,466.

[18] M. Muench, D. Nisi, A. Francillon, and D. Balzarotti, "Avatar^2: A multi-target orchestration platform," in *Workshop on Binary Analysis Research, colocated with Network and Distributed Systems Security Symposium, San Diego, USA*, San Diego, UNITED STATES, Feb 2018. [Online]. Available: http://www.eurecom.fr/publication/5437

[19] NSA, "Ghidra." [Online]. Available: https://ghidra-sre.org/

[20] NSA, "Vxworkssymtab_finder.java." [Online]. Available: https://github.com/NationalSecurityAgency/ghidra/blob/fe8d863c47f79d904c10c2c49d16ea4c1b674020/Ghidra/Features/GnuDemangler/ghidra_scripts/VxWorksSymTab_Finder.java

[21] E. Perez, "400plus/iolib.h." [Online]. Available: https://github.com/400plus/400plus/blob/master/vxworks/ioLib.h

[22] R. Qiao and R. Sekar, "Function interface analysis: A principled approach for function recognition in cots binaries," in *47th Annual IEEE/IFIP International Conference on Dependable Systems and Networks*. IEEE, 2017, pp. 201–212.

[23] J. F. Ready, "Vrtx: A real-time operating system for embedded microprocessor applications," *IEEE Micro*, vol. 6, no. 4, pp. 8–17, 1986.

[24] ReFirm Labs, "binwalk." [Online]. Available: https://github.com/ReFirmLabs/binwalk

[25] W. River, "Functional safety." [Online]. Available: https://www.windriver.com/functionalsafety

[26] ——, "Security vulnerability response information: Tcp/ip network stack (ipnet, urgent/11)." [Online]. Available: https://www.windriver.com/security/announcements/tcp-ip-network-stack-ipnet-urgent11/

[27] S. Shah, "The arm-x firmware emulation framework." [Online]. Available: https://github.com/therealsaumil/armx

[28] Y. Shoshitaishvili, R. Wang, C. Salls, N. Stephens, M. Polino, A. Dutcher, J. Grosen, S. Feng, C. Hauser, C. Kruegel, and G. Vigna, "SoK: (State of) The Art of War: Offensive Techniques in Binary Analysis," in *IEEE Symposium on Security and Privacy*, 2016.

[29] S. Vasile, D. Oswald, and T. Chothia, "Breaking all the things—a systematic survey of firmware extraction techniques for iot devices," in *Smart Card Research and Advanced Applications*, B. Bilgin and J.-B. Fischer, Eds. Cham: Springer International Publishing, 2019, pp. 171–185.

[30] A. Volosincu, "Vxworks: Past and future," Jul 2018. [Online]. Available: https://blogs.windriver.com/wind_river_blog/2018/07/vxworks-past-and-future/

[31] VxWorks, "Vxworks reference manual : Libraries." [Online]. Available: https://www.ee.ryerson.ca/~courses/ee8205/Data-Sheets/Tornado-VxWorks/vxworks/ref/libIndex.html

[32] *VxWorks Network Programmer's Guide 5.5*, Wind River, 500 Wind River Way, Alameda, CA, 94501, 8 2002. [Online]. Available: http://www.ing.iac.es/~docs/external/vxworks.old/Network-Guide-5.5.pdf

[33] *VxWorks Network Protocol Toolkit User's Guide*, Wind River, 500 Wind River Way, Alameda, CA, 94501, 8 2002.

[34] C. Wright, W. A. Moeglein, S. Bagchi, M. Kulkarni, and A. A. Clements, "Challenges in firmware re-hosting, emulation, and analysis," *ACM Computer Surveys*, vol. 54, no. 1, Jan. 2021. [Online]. Available: https://doi.org/10.1145/3423167

[35] S. J. Yang, J. H. Choi, K. B. Kim, and T. Chang, "New acquisition method based on firmware update protocols for android smartphones," *Digital Investigation*, vol. Volume 14, pp. S68 – S76, 2015, the Proceedings of the Fifteenth Annual DFRWS Conference. [Online]. Available: http://www.sciencedirect.com/science/article/pii/S1742287615000535

[36] J. Zaddach, L. Bruno, A. Francillon, and D. Balzarotti, "Avatar: A framework to support dynamic security analysis of embedded systems' firmwares," in *Network and Distributed Systems Security Symposium*, Feb 2014.

[37] R. Zhu, Y.-a. Tan, Q. Zhang, Y. Li, and J. Zheng, "Determining image base of firmware for arm devices by matching literal pools," *Digital Investigation*, vol. Volume 16, pp. 19 – 28, 2016. [Online]. Available: http://www.sciencedirect.com/science/article/pii/S1742287616000037

[38] W. Zhu, R. Liu, J. Wang, and Y. Zhou, "Vxhunter: A tool set for vxworks based embedded device analyses," in *black hat ASIA 2019 Workshop*. blackhat.com, March 2019. [Online]. Available: https://www.blackhat.com/asia-19/arsenal/schedule/index.html#vxhunter-a-tool-set-for-vxworks-based-embedded-device-analyses-14165

Dinosaur Resurrection: PowerPC Binary Patching for Base Station Analysis

Uwe Müller, Eicke Hauck, Timm Welz, Jiska Classen, Matthias Hollick
Secure Mobile Networking Lab, TU Darmstadt
{umueller,ehauck,twelz,jclassen,mhollick}@seemoo.de

Abstract—**Even though PowerPC mostly disappeared from the consumer device market, its architectural properties continue being popular for highly specialized systems. This particularly includes embedded systems with real-time requirements that are deeply integrated into critical infrastructures as well as aeronautics, transportation, control systems in power plants, etc. One example is Terrestrial Trunked Radio (TETRA), a digital radio system used in the public safety domain and deployed in more than 120 countries worldwide: base stations of at least one of the main vendors are based on PowerPC. Despite the criticality of the aforementioned systems, many follow a security by obscurity approach and there are no openly available analysis tools. While analyzing a TETRA base station, we design and develop a set of analysis tools centered around a PowerPC binary patcher. We further create various dynamic tooling on top, including a fast memory dumper, function tracer, flexible patching capabilities at runtime, and a fuzzer. We describe the genesis of these tools and detail the binary patcher, which is general in nature and not limited to our base station under test.**

I. Introduction

The TETRA specification dates back to 1995 and serves a similar purpose as Global System for Mobile Communications (GSM)—wireless voice and data transmission but for emergency services [5]. While both specifications stem from the same era, TETRA was designed with safety and security applications in mind. More than 120 countries over the world deployed it [31]. It is the predominating technology used by the police, fire departments, and ambulances across Europe. As a governmental project with many dependencies, the roll-out took longer than expected. Thus, despite being rather old from a technological perspective, it is very new from an organizational standpoint—there are no plans to transition to a more recent technology. As of today, the older analog communication it was meant to replace still exists as fallback. While GSM, known as 2G cellular network, got multiple major revisions and is updated to 5G now, TETRA remains on 2G-like transmission quality. 3G and onwards have more modern extensions for emergency communication systems, but TETRA sufficiently serves the purpose of voice and text message transmission. TETRA uses completely independent infrastructure, which ensures that it is available during mobile carrier outages, which is likely the reason to stick to this technology.

Being an interesting target for security research, we acquired a TETRA base station for testing purposes, manufactured by one of the top five vendors. Surprisingly, this base station is running on a customized PowerPC platform. PowerPC is a RISC architecture originating from the same era as the TETRA specification. Despite mostly disappearing from the consumer device market, PowerPC has interesting properties for Industrial Control Systems (ICSs) and network equipment. Popular real-time operating systems, which form the base of such devices, continue having PowerPC support [14], [20].

The TETRA specification is publicly available except for its export-restricted encryption modes [5], [6]. The only open-source Software-Defined Radio (SDR) implementation lacks features like sending data to a base station [36]. Thus, TETRA base stations cannot be tested over-the-air with existing tools. Moreover, over-the-air testing is very limited when it comes to crash analysis. Instead, we create a PowerPC binary patcher and testing toolsuite with the following features:

- A generic PowerPC binary patcher capable of inserting custom hooks written in C into Executable and Linking Format (ELF) files.
- A thread-aware function call tracer compatible to the *Callgrind* format.
- Extension of the underlying *Enea* Operating System Embedded (OSE) commands to dynamically execute arbitrary firmware functions on the system.
- A fuzzer that observes the base station's state and panic messages.

In this paper, we focus on the PowerPC binary patcher, function call tracer, and dynamic function caller. Parts of this work are publicly available on GitHub [33]. Since TETRA is critical infrastructure, this paper does not cover any vulnerability research or reverse-engineering of security-critical functions.

Our base station setup and why we decided against emulation-based approaches are described in Sec. II. In Sec. III, we start with reverse-engineering the firmware that we aim to patch. The actual PowerPC binary patcher is designed and implemented in Sec. IV. Implementations of various dynamic debugging capabilities including a function tracer are provided in Sec. V. The fuzzing framework is described in Sec. VI. We conclude our work in Sec. VII.

Workshop on Binary Analysis Research (BAR) 2021
21 February 2021, Virtual

https://dx.doi.org/10.14722/bar.2021.23009
www.ndss-symposium.org

II. BACKGROUND

In this following, we document how we set up the base station to enable custom firmware injection. Then, we discuss advantages and disadvantages of emulation-based approaches compared to running on physical hardware.

A. Base Station Setup

The TETRA Base Station (BS) analyzed in this paper consists of a Base Radio (BR) and a Site Controller (SC). The site controller serves firmware and configuration files to the base radio via Trivial File Transfer Protocol (TFTP). To this end, they are connected via an Ethernet cable. Since 10BASE-T and 100BASE-TX only require two pairs of pins to operate and this data rate is sufficient, the remaining two pairs are used for a proprietary CP2 clock signal operating at 20 MHz. In our setup, we split this cable to connect the base radio to the proprietary site controller CP2 clock signal but control firmware and configuration files via a Raspberry Pi. Even though this setup requires physical access, it is still valuable for firmware analysis. The overall setup is depicted in Fig. 1.

Moreover, the base radio has an authenticated serial interface that can issue selected commands. These commands include an *AirTracer*, which shows all TETRA air interface traffic. Except from that, the debugging capabilities are limited.

For safety reasons, we configured the base station to an invalid frequency, attach a dummy load instead of an antenna, and place it into an Electromagnetic Field (EMF) shielded room.

B. Binary Analysis Options

The firmware sent via TFTP comes as ELF file. The ELF file is not stripped, meaning that it does not only contain basic information about the target, but even includes function names. However, the target architecture is PowerPC and the precise CPU variant is undocumented. The ELF file can be analyzed statically and dynamically. Especially dynamic analysis methods vary a lot, such as full-system emulation, emulation of single functions or simply running on the base radio with special hooks. We considered the following methods:

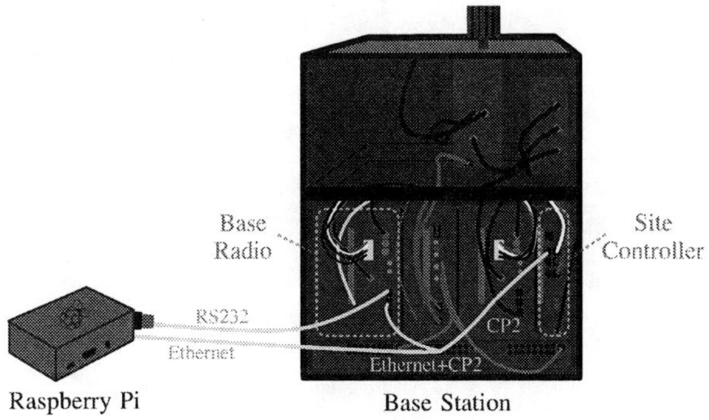

Fig. 1: TETRA base station setup with firmware injection.

1) Firmware Emulation: Quick Emulator (QEMU) can emulate PowerPC and attach a debugger to it to step through the code [26]. Loading the ELF file into QEMU and booting it fails at code related to hardware detection. This error can be bypassed by hooking the hardware detection function and returning a valid hardware model. Then, the firmware tries to configure and enable a timer that does not exist in QEMU for this machine. This timer is likely for the CPU scheduling routine and, thus, the operating system cannot run without it. It might be possible to fix these issues, however, they also show how hardware-dependent the firmware is.

Another option would be to only partially execute selected parts of the firmware for security analysis. *Unicorn* [32], which is based on QEMU, recently got experimental PowerPC support in a fork [30]. However, PowerPC support did not exist when we started this project. Moreover, while executing a packet handler and passing a single input to it is simple to achieve with *Unicorn*, more advanced utilization comes with similar issues as booting the whole firmware in QEMU due to its hardware dependencies. Even worse, *Unicorn* lacks peripheral support included in QEMU.

In general, this can be solved with a lot of engineering work to implement interrupts, timers, and even thread switches. For example, *Avatar* solves hardware dependencies [37], [22], and *Frankenstein* goes as far as emulating a Bluetooth firmware with a virtual modem and task switches [27]. Recently, not only single parsers of a *Mediatek* baseband were fuzzed [19], but even the *Shannon* baseband firmware was emulated including hardware components [15]. However, implementing this for a TETRA base station requires a lot of work, even with the progress in the field of PowerPC emulation. Thus, despite this would bring better introspection capabilities, we stick to the concept of physically running modified firmware.

2) Physically Running Modified Firmware: A different option is to inject modified code into the base radio. This eliminates challenges like hardware dependencies. However, this approach comes with other difficulties, such as creating a valid firmware image, being limited to the base radio's speed, non-determinism due to uncontrollable side-effects, as well as limited interaction with the target.

Nonetheless, we choose the second option. It allows us to modify packets before they are sent over-the-air, trace execution on the physical hardware for complex operations, and more. While there are some basic PowerPC binary patchers [18], [29], ours is able to patch the firmware using C and reconstruct a valid, bootable firmware image for the base station.

III. STATIC FIRMWARE ANALYSIS

As a first step, we perform a static analysis of the firmware binary running on the base radio.

A. Firmware Version and Operating System

Despite acquiring the TETRA base station in 2017, its firmware build dates indicate that it was last updated in 2007. Since it was a test device, this is reasonable. For the mere purpose of designing a PowerPC binary patcher this does not make any difference. It is unlikely that the vendor fully re-implemented the firmware since then. The TETRA specification only got minor updates over the recent years.

The bootloader, which is stored separately in a ROM on the base radio, is called *"Enea POLO Bootloader"*. This stands for Portable OSE Boot Loader [1, p. 8]. The version string *"061201"* indicates a build date in 2006. Without any modifications, the bootloader accepts unsigned firmware images over Ethernet via TFTP. Given the base station setup, where the base radio directly connects to the site controller, this still does not allow any attacks from an outside network. If the bootloader fails to load a firmware binary via TFTP, it launches a built-in shell. Otherwise, it continues executing the `_START` symbol in the firmware.

The firmware contains the string *"(C) Copyright 2003 Enea Embedded Technology"*, and the boot log hints to OSE as operating system in version 4.5.2. OSE 5 was announced in 2004 [2]. The string *"built by 'awr012' at Jan 19 2007 17:00:53"* suggests a more recent build date, meaning that the underlying OSE might have received a few more recent patches. OSE supports build options that compile both the operating system and applications into one binary [1]. Thus, the build date for the TETRA functionality is likely the same.

As of today, OSE is still maintained and sold by *Enea AB*, a Swedish company [3]. According to the operating system description, it is well-suited for TETRA, since it is optimized for high-performance communication systems with hard real-time characteristics. Its deployment areas include telecom networking systems and wireless devices.

Basic functionality extracted from the OSE manuals was documented publicly in 2005 [1]. Moreover, an old OSE kernel reference manual from 1998 was leaked [4]. The original manuals are not publicly available.

B. Firmware Format

The firmware is packed as a `gzip`-compressed ELF file. This is a common format that can be analyzed with tools like `readelf`.

The header shows that the base radio runs on a 32 bit PowerPC processor, which is a well-documented processor family [9]. Moreover, the string *"m8xxIOMemMap"* inside the firmware hints to the more specific *MPC8xx* family by *Motorola* [10], which has been acquired by *Freescale Semiconductor*. Dissecting the base radio reveals an *MPC8260ADS* System on Chip (SoC), which contains a modified version of the *MPC603e* big-endian PowerPC CPU [8]. We estimate that it has 48 MB RAM. When calling the command `board` in the bootloader, the following additional information is printed:

```
Motorola MPC8260ADS board
Bus clock 66MHz, core clock 264MHz, CPM clock 165MHz, BRG
     clock 83MHz
```

Ghidra supports this architecture [23], allowing static reverse-engineering.

The ELF file is non-stripped—it exports many symbols. In total, the firmware exports 7007 function and further 10 512 non-function names. Hence, even though the firmware is rather complex, it can be analyzed without source code and a fair reverse-engineering effort.

C. Interrupt Vectors

Based on the generic PowerPC documentation [9], we start by analyzing the interrupt handlers. These are located at offset `0x100` in the binary with the reset vector that calls `zzexception`. Most interrupt handlers are either not set, throw an exception via `SysAccessExcept`, or call an interrupt service routine using `GenIsr`.

D. Libraries and Function Prefixes

We can infer which public libraries are used along with proprietary libraries that start with common prefixes from the non-stripped ELF file. A list of the most interesting functions that we are able to assign a purpose to are listed in Tab. I.

The network stack contained in libraries like `ipcom` was developed by the Swedish company *Interpeak AB*, which was acquired by *Wind River Systems* in March 2006 [21]. The base radio's Command-Line Interface (CLI) has a `version` command that prints all information about the network stack:

```
(#) IPCOM   $Name: ipcom-ose-r5_12_3
(#) IPLITE  $Name:
(#) IPTCP   $Name: iptcp-any-r1_6_2
(#) IPTFTPS $Name: ipappl-any-r1_12_2
```

Understanding the network stack is vital to exchange data with the base radio over Ethernet instead of the existing serial interface. In the following, we will create new network services and fuzz existing ones.

The CLI that is accessible via the serial interface is contained in the `shell` and `cmd` functions. We will use these later on to add custom commands, such as calling arbitrary firmware functions with chosen parameters out of context during runtime.

TABLE I: Function groups in the ELF and their purpose.

#	Prefix	Purpose
40	—	`zlib`, symbol names match library [11].
140	—	`libc`, symbol names match library [12].
70	`efs_`	High-level file system functionality.
41	`clfs_`	Low-level file system functionality.
429	`ipcom_`	IP communication.
147	`iplite_`	IP communication.
75	`iptcp_`	Transmission Control Protocol (TCP).
17	`iptftp_`	Trivial File Transfer Protocol (TFTP).
11	`tftp_`	Trivial File Transfer Protocol (TFTP).
48	`snmp_`	Probably Net-SNMP library.
38	`scomm_`	Site communication with UDP socket abstraction.
11	`pthread_`	OSE POSIX-compliant thread wrapper.
26	`ose_`	Generic OSE functions.
116	`afm_`	OSE Atomic File Manager (AFM).
18	`fam_`	OSE Flash Access Manager (FAM).
18	`shell_`	OSE Command Line Shell.
79	`cmd_`	Shell commands like `ls` or `cat`.
25	`rtc_`	OSE Real Time Clock (RTC).
85	`pmd_`	OSE Post Mortem Dump (PMD).
133	`bs_`	Probably basic system process and timer management.
171	`core_`	Core functionality.
35	`sysconf_`	Configuration access.
177	`zz`	Functions that force the syscall interface.
21	`xx`	Kernel-side implementation of functions like `xxmutex_lock`.

IV. PowerPC Binary Patcher

Enea OSE comes with a debugging toolsuite called *Illuminator* [2]. However, *Illuminator* is closed-source and only available for *Enea*'s customers. From the few things that are publicly documented, it seems to integrate into the OSE development platform and likely requires source code of the target [1]. Since we neither have access to the base radio source code nor to *Enea*-internal tools, we implement a binary patcher that can extend the firmware ELF file. This binary patcher is the foundation to building debug tools like dumping memory during runtime or tracing function execution.

A. Hooking PowerPC Functions

The binary patcher aims to allow functions to be extended in the beginning (`PRECALL`), end (`POSTCALL`), or to be overwritten (`REPLACE`). Adding instructions prior to or after a function is very useful for analysis and does not require to understand the code of the target function. Many binary analysis frameworks support these types of hooks, such as FЯIDA [24].

NexMon, a binary patching framework for ARM, inserts a new function at a free memory location and then overwrites selected branch instructions [28]. This is *NexMon*'s default hooking approach and significantly reduces the instruction overhead spent in the hook itself. However, this means that the patcher needs to know all references to a function, i.e., replace each `bl memcpy` instruction with `bl memcpy_patch`. Additionally, functions may also be referenced by function tables instead of branch instructions, which also need to be replaced. Since disassemblers tend to make a lot of mistakes during static analysis [25], there is a high chance to miss function references.

A more reliable solution is to modify the target function. A typical function prologue and epilogue in PowerPC assembler are shown in Listing 1. Interestingly, all functions in our target firmware start with the `stwu` and `mflr r0` instructions in any order. Both instructions are position-independent and can be moved to any other position in the address space without side effects. Thus, we can replace the first instruction of the original function and transparently jump to a `PRECALL` or `REPLACE` hook. A `PRECALL` hook needs to take care of executing the replaced first instruction of the original function before returning to the second instruction of the original function.

```
stwu r1, -0x10(r1) ; r1 is the stack pointer, make room
     ; Replace this with branch to hook
mflr r0            ; Move contents of link register to r0
stw  r0, 0x10(r1)  ; Push r0 onto stack
; Function code
lwz  r0, 0x10(r1)  ; Load r0 from stack
mtlr r0            ; Move contents of r0 to link register
addi r1, r1, 0x10  ; Restore old stack pointer
blr                ; Branch link return
```

Listing 1: Common function entry and exit.

B. Trampoline Code

In theory, replacing the first instruction would already be sufficient for patching functions assuming that the original code and the patch are using the same Application Binary Interface (ABI). However, using this simple approach we could not carry any additional metadata in hooks, such as a function's runtime or the current thread. Additionally, this triggered a `gcc` cross-compiler bug in our first implementation attempt. Thus, we introduce a special trampoline code, which is individual for each hooked function. It saves the context of the call to the stack, adds metadata like the original function name and address, which in turn allows to return to the original code path.

Another reason for the trampoline code are the PowerPC calling conventions. In contrast to architectures like x86, which push the return address to the stack when calling a function, PowerPC does not have a native stack. Instead, the stack is a software construct, and PowerPC requires special registers to store information like the return address. Access to the link register is only possible with the `mflr` (move from link register) and `mtlr` (move to link register) instructions, as they are used in Listing 1. Yet, these instructions are not mandatory—a function that does not call subsequent functions does not save the link register.

Moreover, the first eight function parameters and return values are passed as registers. Thus, if a function signature that defines all these parameters is unknown, the purpose of each register cannot always be determined.

The trampoline code saves the context including all up to eight possible function arguments, link register, function name and call stub address into a Call Information Frame (CIF). We store the CIF pointer to the register `r14`, which is non-volatile by convention, meaning that follow-up functions must preserve its contents [17]. The CIF allows calling the original function in exactly the same context as it was called originally, which is required by `PRECALL` and `POSTCALL` hooks.

C. Trampoline Performance

A patched function contains additional trampoline code consisting of three components to keep it flexible.

1) *Individual Code per Hook*
Hook-specific code prepares the trampoline CIF for the hook, such as the call stub address or the function name as string, which requires 17 instructions.

2) *Saving the Context*
Moreover, there is generic code that can be reused for all hooks to save volatile registers in the trampoline call information frame. This requires 15 instructions.

3) *Restoring the Context*
Finally, to restore volatile registers from the trampoline CIF, there is additional generic code, which requires 12 instructions.

In total, each trampoline code introduces an overhead of 44 instructions, in addition to the implementation of the actual functionality that is added using the hook. For example, a void function, if not optimized, could be represented with a single `blr` instruction, while more complex functions require an arbitrary amount of instructions.

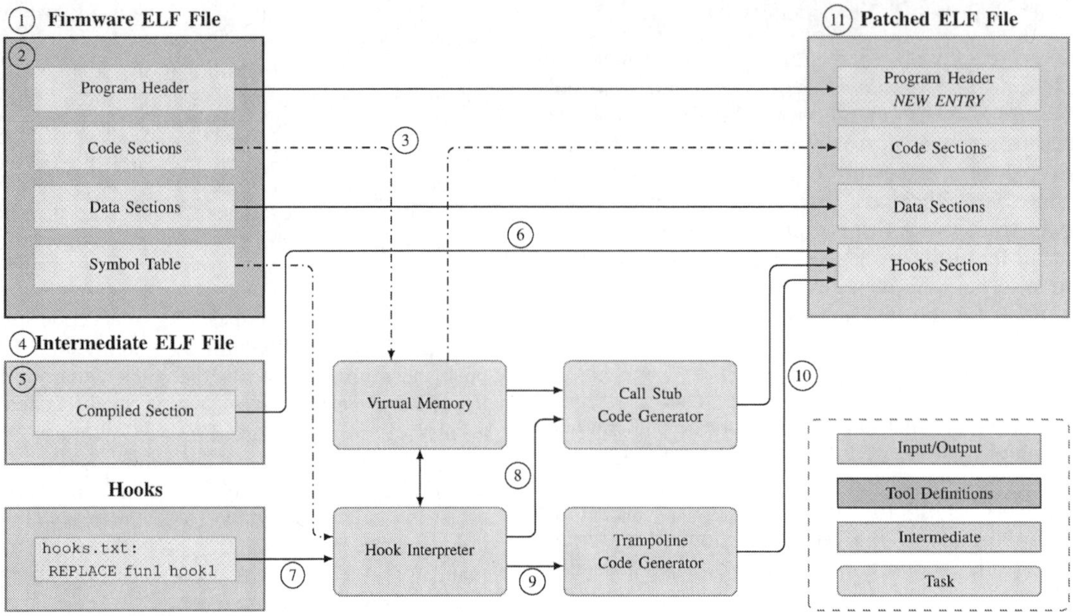

Fig. 2: Applying custom hooks to the original firmware ELF.

D. Applying Patches to the Firmware ELF

The base radio has two unused memory regions: One 252 kB region in the beginning directly after the interrupt vectors, and another one of 15.6 MB after the ELF `.bss` section. While the second region would be optimal in terms of space, it cannot be reached using a single instruction jump from the two program code sections. A PowerPC branch instruction can be absolute or relative. The branch instruction itself is encoded into 6 bit, leaving 24 bit for the absolute or relative address [16]. The remaining 2 bit of the 32 bit instruction encode if the branch is relative or absolute and if it includes the link register or not. However, the empty 15.6 MB section starts at the address `0x2098d68`, which requires a 26 bit representation. This cannot be represented with an absolute branch, and a relative branch from the highest code address at `0x27f7db` would still require 25 bit. Thus, the only solution to address this space would be using function pointers by loading the address into a register, which adds further overhead to the hooks. Instead, we leave some distance to the interrupt vector definitions, which is required for stability, and end up with the hook region `0x2500–0x3ffff`, which is 246.75 kB. While this has been sufficient for our experiments, the binary patcher could be extended to use the second memory region when accepting the additional overhead of a function pointer table.

We load our code into a new section at offset `0x2500` into the ELF file. This extends the program header table and moves the remaining parts of the ELF file. Thus, we use `libelf` [13] to add new program headers and keep track of file offsets in section headers. We still need to fix the program header size manually with our toolchain afterward.

The overall patching process is depicted in Fig. 2. More precisely, the steps to patch the ELF are as follows:

1) *Load Original ELF*
This is achieved using `libelf`.
2) *Read ELF Headers and Symbol Table*
These values are stored into internal variables.
3) *Map Memory*
The ELF data is mapped into a virtual memory according to the section header, such that it can be accessed by the virtual address.
4) *Load Compiled Intermediate ELF*
Using `libelf`, the intermediate ELF is loaded.
5) *Read Intermediate ELF Headers and Symbol Table*
We use the same approach as for the original ELF.
6) *Copy Compiled Hooks*
The `.compiled` section of the intermediate ELF is copied into a local buffer, which contains all code and data of the cross-compilation. The same local buffer is used to add the trampoline code, so this buffer must be 32 bit-aligned by adding zeros if necessary.
7) *Load Hook Configuration*
Load and read the hook configuration file `hooks.txt` including function name wildcards.
8) *Generate Call Stub*
If the original function starts with a `stwu` or `mflr` instruction, as supported by our binary patcher, this instruction is used to generate a call stub. Otherwise, the hooking process aborts with an error message. The generated code is added to the code buffer, which also holds the code of the intermediate ELF.
9) *Generate Trampoline Code*
Then, the hook-specific trampoline code is generated according to the configuration file, and added to the same code buffer.

10) *Hooking*
Using the mapped memory, the code at the virtual address of the original function entry is overwritten with a branch instruction to the virtual address of the newly generated trampoline code.

11) *Add Changes to Original ELF*
The new and modified data including headers is written into the new ELF.

The generated ELF can now be loaded into the site controller or the Raspberry Pi's TFTP server, such that the base radio bootloader can launch the customized firmware.

V. Dynamic Firmware Analysis Tools

Now that we are able to modify the original firmware, we can continue to add debug and analysis capabilities. Most importantly, we built tools for fast data exchange other than the serial RS232 interface, a function tracer, and a dynamic patcher.

A. Memory Dumps and Data Exchange

The site controller has a serial RS232 and an Ethernet interface. While the CLI is based on the serial interface, the Ethernet interface is faster and better suited to exchange larger amounts of data.

We add an Ethernet-based UDP service using the `scomm` library. This library uses the `br_service_table` to register services that can send and receive UDP packets on a service-defined port using the structure shown in Listing 2. Once we extend this service table, our custom UDP service is active.

Each `scomm_service` defines three callbacks. The `socket_cb` is only a wrapper, which can change the parameter order before calling the `scomm_recv_callback`. Every time the `scomm_recv_callback` receives a packet, it calls the `rx_cb` and passes an `scomm_packet` containing the data. The `tx_cb` is called by `scomm_packet_transmit` after packet transmission.

Using a custom UDP service, we add various memory observation commands to the OSE CLI. These are triggered via the slow serial interface, but the memory contents are exchanged using the Ethernet connection. The CLI can dump specific memory regions, the whole memory, watch a memory region, and search the memory for strings and hexadecimal data.

```
struct scomm_service {
  uint32_t port;
  uint32_t unknown1;
  uint32_t unknown2;
  socket_rx_cb rx_cb;
  socket_rx_cb tx_cb;
  socket_sock_cb socket_cb;
  uint32_t status;
};
```

Listing 2: `scomm_service` struct defining a UDP service.

B. Function Call Tracer

Static code analysis can be challenging: Which functions are actively executed by the firmware? What is contained in the function parameters? Even simple information like function references is not always correctly determined by disassemblers.

Enea OSE is a multithreaded operating system. For individual observation of each process, the process identifier and every function enter and leave can be logged resulting in a call tree. If two functions are entered subsequently, this adds a new level to the call tree. While the call tree calculation can take place outside of the patched firmware binary to optimize performance, the logging itself needs to be added to the binary. In addition to function enter and leave interactions, we log the CPU cycle counter to estimate the time spent in each function.

The code that implements this functionality is shown in Listing 3. The process identifier is only available after OSE is booted and undefined otherwise. The `calltrace` functionality can be added as a hook to every function. The hook definition allows wildcards, meaning that a hook to `dlai_*` would log every function call in the air interface downlink. The trace is transmitted using a Telnet service over Ethernet.

We test the function tracer on a large set of wildcards covering the most important aspects of the firmware, as shown in Tab. II. In some function groups, the trace hook leads to a firmware crash. This happens despite the generated code is valid. The station's watchdog is set to larger intervals than the additional hook instructions take to execute. Thus, we assume that this is due to some real-time requirements in functions

TABLE II: Function groups and associated hook crashes.

#	Prefix	Crash
95	`aie_`	—
45	`aiea_`	—
50	`aiei_`	—
12	`mac_pdu_`	—
289	`tx_`	Crash after a few seconds.
49	`rx_`	Crash immediately after boot.
74	`sm_`	—
174	`dlai_`	—
28	`ulai_`	—
42	`cca_`	`OSE_EPROCESS_ENDED`
40	`ccai_`	—
10	`lapd_`	—

```
uint32_t calltrace() {
  uint32_t pid = 0;
  if (ose_ready) {
    pid = current_process();
  }
  calltrace_log_enter(pid);
  // Get cycle count from CPU registers for time measurement
  uint64_t begin = cpu_cycle_count();
  // Call original function w/o knowing anything about it
  uint32_t ret   = orig_call();
  // Get cycle count again for duration
  uint64_t end   = cpu_cycle_count();
  calltrace_log_leave(end - begin);
  return ret;
}
```

Listing 3: Gather calltrace information.

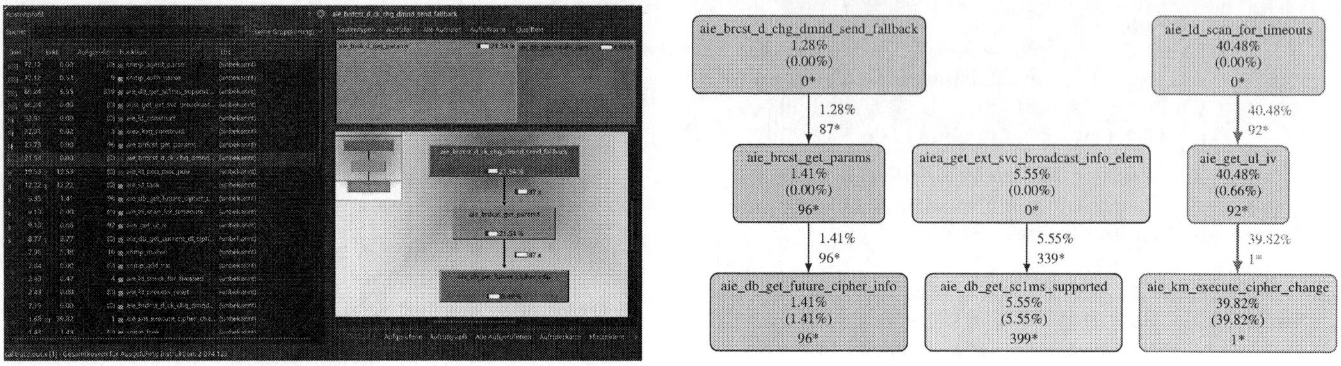

(a) *KCachegrind* interpretation.

(b) `gprof2dot` interpretation.

Fig. 3: Function trace converted to *Callgrind* for further interpretation.

involved into sending and receiving packets, as the prefixes `tx_` and `rx_` indicate. This assumption is affirmed by the fact that OSE interrupt processes, which are close to hardware, have special restrictions: on PowerPC, they are not allowed to execute floating point or vector operations and cannot access the heap [1, p. 14]. While the basic hook mechanism does not contain such operations, the `calltrace` function does. As a solution, interrupt processes can be excluded from function tracing.

The `calltrace` output is still not that intuitive for interpretation. Using a custom `tbrc2callgrind.py` script, we convert the log output into the *Callgrind* format [34]. Originally, *Callgrind* output is meant to show how much time is spent in which function to allow programmers profiling and improving performance. While we do not aim at improving the base radio's performance, the output still provides us with insights about which functions are called by a thread and how they depend on each other. The *Callgrind* format is supported by various tools that provide a human-readable representation. These include the *KCachegrind* [35] tool shown in Fig. 3a as well as the `gprof2dot` [7] script that converts the the graph into the a format for plotting as shown in Fig. 3b.

C. Patching During Runtime

In the setup described in Sec. II-A, the base radio loads a patched firmware ELF file from the site controller or the Raspberry Pi. This requires a reboot of the base radio, which takes a while. This is not ideal for debugging purposes. Thus, we extend the patching toolchain to support partial firmware modification during runtime.

The overall process relies on the previously described ELF patcher. When comparing two generated ELFs files, they only differ in the following information: the hooks section, which contains the actual patches, and single 4 B-instructions with jumps to these hooks. A patched ELF file always contains the same new entry in the program header, thus, the code and hook section do not move.

Assuming that the ELF of the firmware version running on the base radio is known, it is very simple to diff it against a version that modifies these patches. For debugging purposes, two versions can be disassembled with `objdump` and diffed, making the patches human-readable. For example, the difference added by the `PREHOOK printf calltrace` looks as follows:

```
405360c405360
< 1cd5c4: 94 21 ff 18  stwu r1,-232(r1) ; orig. instruction
---
> 1cd5c4: 48 02 dc 2e  ba   2dc2c        ; jump to trampoline
586913a586914,586934
>  2dc1c: 94 21 ff 18  stwu r1,-232(r1) ; new hook code
>  2dc20: 48 1c d5 ca  ba   1cd5c8 <printf+0x4>
> ; further instructions that are added...
```

We parse the diffing results block-wise, meaning that we separate it into continuous blocks of assembler code. A function for memory modification is already contained in the patched standard firmware and the code section is not protected against writes during runtime. Thus, we can apply these changes to the base station while it is running. The blocks are applied in ascending order, meaning that the patches are written before the hook jumps are applied. This prevents the original firmware from jumping into invalid patches.

Since this process requires cross-compilation, it is not executed on the base radio directly. Instead, the base radio is attached to a Raspberry Pi or a laptop that generates and pushes the firmware patches.

D. Dynamically Calling Functions with Arguments

The ELF-based patching approach requires firmware recompilation and pushing the resulting diff into the base radio's memory. Often, debugging does not require complex patches but simple functionality like calling a single function with parameters out of context. For example, a function without arguments and return value located at `addr` could be executed as follows. Note that the `void` usually is not written explicitly:

```
void (*addr)(void)
```

However, passing arguments can get complicated due to the PowerPC calling conventions. The CIF-based approach introduced in Sec. IV solves this and even saves additional metadata. When calling a single function that returns, we can let the cross-compiler take care of passing arguments. For simplicity, we only differentiate between functions without parameters and functions with the maximum number of arguments, since we can leave arguments empty, and define the following generic function call wrapper that is always added to the firmware:

```
void* execute_address(int argc, void* addr, void** args) {
  if (argc == 0) {
      return ((void* (*)(void))addr)();
  } else {
      return ((void* (*)(void*, ...))addr)(args[0],
          args[1], args[2], args[3], args[4],
          args[5], args[6], args[7]);
  }
}
```

This wrapper can be called directly from the base radio CLI without an additional compilation step. For example, we could now execute the `printf` function as follows:

```
printf("Hello %s %d", "World", 42);
```

The CLI can pass these three arguments to `printf`, which is located at address `0x1cd5c4`. Since we do not implement the same syntax as C, we still need to tell it the number of arguments and the argument types:

```
CSS: exaddr 0x1cd5c4 -p 3 %s "Hello %s %d" %s "World" %d 42
Hello World 42
```

The return type is interpreted to print it to the CLI. In principle, a function returning a `void` pointer could point to anything. We implement three options to handle the results depending on the expected result. If we expect the result to be a scalar, we print it directly to the console. Alternatively, we handle the result as address and print a given number of bytes from its destination. As a third special case we assume that the result is a null-terminated string and print it.

VI. Fuzzing with Hyphuzz

A method to evaluate firmware security is fuzzing. Randomized inputs are generated and sent to interesting parsers to locate bugs. In the case of a TETRA base radio, we can send such inputs to protocol handlers. We pick the UDP-based `scomm` stack for an initial evaluation of our fuzzer.

A. *Hyphuzz* Overview

Hyphuzz, the TETRA base radio fuzzer, runs on two devices. While the harness code runs on the base radio itself, the controller runs on a Raspberry Pi. This separation is necessary to be able to observe if the base radio crashed, and, in the worst case, even power cycle it using a USB-controlled power switch. However, for performance reasons, payloads are generated and injected on the base radio. A high-level overview showing this separation is depicted in Fig. 4. It consists of five components described in the following.

1) Worker: The worker is the *Hyphuzz* core component running on the base radio. It initializes a Pseudo-Random Number Generator (PRNG) using the `seed` parameter and based on this generates mutated packets injected into the target handler. We implement several test cases that randomize different parts of the packet, which can be specified using the `testCase` parameter. The `skip` parameter can be used to produce packets with the same `seed` again but discard N packets, which is useful for crash reproduction. Once started, *Hyphuzz* runs autonomously until it is stopped or the base radio reboots. It regularly reports its state to the controller using a UDP connection.

2) Command Server: The worker receives commands from the command server, which also runs on the base radio. The command server listens on UDP and waits for fuzzing parameters or the instruction to stop the fuzzer. Moreover, the command server can be used to determine if the base radio is still alive or crashed.

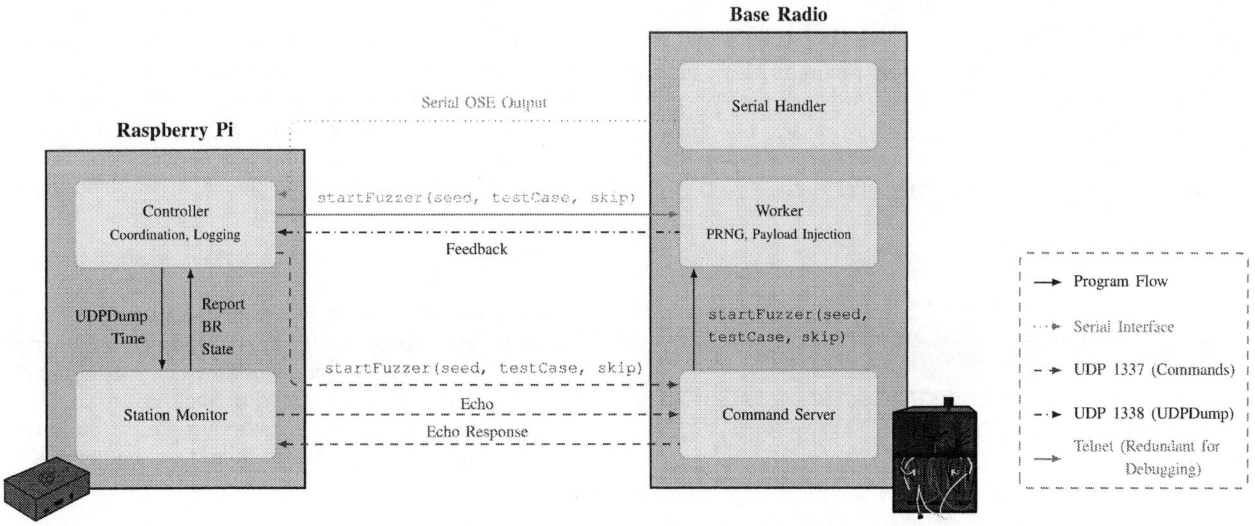

Fig. 4: Overview of the *Hyphuzz* components.

3) Controller: The controller runs on the Raspberry Pi and coordinates the overall fuzzing process. It sends fuzz cases to the worker and logs the worker's fuzzing feedback into a file. Once the base radio hangs up or reboots, the controller logs the latest statistics and serial debug output before starting the next fuzzing round.

4) Station Monitor: The station monitor oversees the base radio's current status. If the base radio stopped sending feedback for a specific amount of time, it has likely crashed or hang up. Typically, the base radio restarts itself automatically and becomes responsive again. However, sometimes, it just freezes. In this case a hard reset is automatically enforced via the power switch. Interestingly, we also have some cold boot side effects when the base radio restarts itself. Thus, we additionally enforce a hard reset even after automatic reboots and after each fuzzing round to enforce a clean state.

5) Serial Handler: The serial handler is not contained in the base radio's firmware ELF file. Instead, it seems to be a separate component integrated into the ROM similar to the bootloader. As such, we cannot modify it. However, we use it for feedback. Some crashes produce OSE error messages printed to the serial interface prior to a base radio reboot when the remaining system is already stuck.

B. Target Handler Selection and Harnessing

In the following, we select a suitable protocol parser for fuzzing and harness it to accept randomized inputs.

1) Security Considerations: The `scomm` stack can only be reached using a wired Ethernet connection.

First of all, an attacker would need physical access to the base station to attach cables—and with this capability, it is already possible to inject arbitrary firmware. Thus, research on this interface cannot uncover any critical findings on this sensitive target. The `scomm` stack is exclusively used for trusted backbone services. While this is the opposite of what a security researcher would aim at under normal conditions, keep in mind that the target is critical infrastructure and we do not want to uncover anything dangerous in the scope of this paper. Note that this is no technical limitation of *Hyphuzz*, it could be adjusted to also fuzz the TETRA air interface.

Second, the fuzzer's findings can be confirmed using an Ethernet connection. An `scomm` Proof of Concept (PoC) is as simple as sending Ethernet frames, which ensures reproducibility. In contrast, over-the-air PoCs could have severe impact if accidentally launched without EMF shielding.

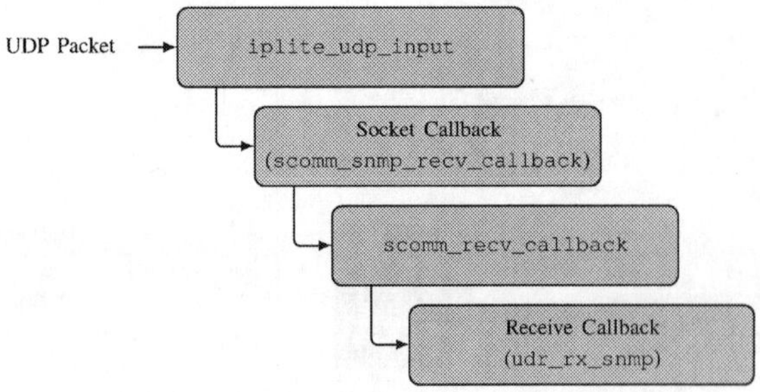

Fig. 5: UDP packet reception process.

2) Harnessing: In order to harness the `scomm` UDP protocol stack, we target the function `scomm_recv_callback` that handles incoming packets. All UDP traffic on the Ethernet interface gets processed by this function. Every time a packet is received, `scomm_recv_callback` looks up the corresponding service by using the port number defined in the packet. Each service has a callback function, which continues parsing the packet for this service. The full call graph for handling a UDP packet is shown in Fig. 5. Note that the functions calling `scomm_recv_callback` are simply wrappers that take care of calling it with the correct parameters. While this seems unnecessary from a reverse-engineering perspective, this might have looked slightly different before being optimized by a compiler. For example, the wrapper for the Simple Network Management Protocol (SNMP) callback looks as follows:

```
void scomm_snmp_recv_callback(uint32_t *rxSocketHandlePtr,
     struct NetPacketInfo *netPacketInfo, int
     packetStatus) {
        scomm_recv_callback(netPacketInfo, packetStatus,
             161, *rxSocketHandlePtr);
return;
}
```

The target function `scomm_recv_callback` takes four parameters. `netPacketInfo` is the most relevant for fuzzing. It contains a data structure with the full UDP packet and additional metadata. Our fuzzer randomly replaces bytes in this structure to generate new inputs. The `packetStatus` flag is always `1` for incoming packets. Successful packet processing is indicated by changing it to `2`. An unexpectedly closed socket leads to a status of `4`. While there are also other values for the status, these are not relevant for the purpose of our fuzzer. `161` is the port number for SNMP, passed as fixed value. `rxSocketHandlePtr` is slightly redundant and contains a pointer to an integer used as handle to reference the receive socket.

C. Crashes and Error Handlers

In the following, we describe the OSE kernel crash report format and provide insights into crash statistics during fuzzing.

1) OSE Kernel Error Messages: Depending on the crash caused by the fuzzer, the serial interface sometimes reports an OSE error message. These messages are generated by the function `krn_err_hndlr`. They were already useful during development of the fuzzer itself. Listing 4 shows an example for a stack overflow triggered due to our own programming error during fuzzer development. The general crash information contain the thread's name and the registers hint to the location of the issue.

2) Crash Statistics: Out of 453 crashes produced and logged during our fuzzing campaign, 206 (45 %) contain a kernel error message. These error messages can be used for initial triage and root cause analysis. Since an error message means that the kernel successfully detected a failure state and the base radio reboots afterward, such errors are potentially safe except from the base radio's availability. Note that silent crashes and hangs are more interesting but even harder to debug.

On this fuzzing campaign, the execution time until the fuzzer caused a crash was between 17 s and 31 min:14 s. 12 % of the test cases crashed within the first 27 s. Interestingly,

```
[ERROR HANDLER INVOKED]  fatal:YES  error:
                         OSE_ESUPERV_STACK_OVERFLOW(0x0102)
                         caller:<UNKNOWN>(0x00)
        [ERROR DETAILS]  user:NO  code:0x080000102
                         subcode:0x0aebd60
[PROCESS CONTROL BLOCK]  name:fuzzer_thread type:OS_BG_PROC
                         (64) status:<UNKNOWN>(0) priority:0
                [STACK]  top:0x0aec55f limit:0x0aebd60
         [CALLING CODE]  n/a:0
            [REGISTERS]  R0=3718B74E R1=00AEBD38 R2=002877CC
                         ...
               [ACTION]  Writing post mortem debuger info
               [ACTION]  Resetting BR
```

Listing 4: Stack overflow triggered during fuzzer development.

TABLE III: Crash types and their frequency.

#	Error Type	Caller
158	OSE_EILLEGAL_PROCESS_ID	OSE_SEND_W_S
33	OSE_ENOT_SIG_OWNER	OSE_SEND
8	OSE_ENOT_SIG_OWNER	OSE_SIGSIZE
4	OSE_EPROCESS_ENDED	<UNKNOWN>
3	OSE_EILLEGAL_SYSTEMCALL	OSE_WAIT_SEM

22 % of the crashes happen in the upper time range, between 30 min and 31 min:14 s. While we do not know the precise root cause of the crashes in the upper time range, they might be associated to a special base radio or OSE property that triggers after half an hour or memory buffer being exceeded after that time span. The remaining 66 % of the crashes are equally distributed over time.

3) Crash Types: In the following, we briefly describe the most common error messages. Tab. III summarizes these crashes and their frequency. The comparably outdated kernel reference manual still contains useful information about the error types [4], which allows further insights.

`OSE_EILLEGAL_PROCESS_ID`: If the kernel observes an illegal block or process identifier, it raises this error. The `subcode` is the corresponding invalid identifier. The caller, which causes this error, always happened to be the function `send_w_s`. Its purpose is to send a signal from one process to another. However, this function is also used within the fuzzer's UDP dumper. Thus, we modify the fuzzer to send the debug information via the serial interface. Since this crash persists, we can exclude that it is a false positive due to the fuzzer's UDP-based design.

`OSE_ENOT_SIG_OWNER`: This error is triggered when a process invokes a system call requesting a signal buffer that it does not own. The `subcode` is the address of the corresponding signal buffer. During our fuzzing campaign, we observe two different values for the signal buffer. One is owned by the process `DLA1`, and the other is owned by `iplited`.

`OSE_EPROCESS_ENDED`: When a prioritized or background process ended, this error occurs. The `subcode` contains the process identifier. In our case, the terminated process is `ose_shell`, which serves the CLI.

`OSE_EILLEGAL_SYSTEMCALL`: This error is provoked when an interrupt process executes a system call that is only allowed for non-interrupt processes. We observe this in the two interrupt processes named `VEC03` and `VEC62`. The illegal system call in both cases is `wait_sem`. As the name suggests, this system call waits until the specified semaphore is acquired—however, interrupt processes should terminate as quick as possible. We were not able to reproduce this specific type of issue by replaying packets, even though it occurred a few times during the fuzzing campaign. Thus, it seems to be very timing and state dependent.

D. Performance

The *Hyphuzz* controller spends most of the time waiting for the worker. Its main optimization is to timely detect hangs and reboots and respond with a hard reset.

The worker's overhead is quantified by additional measurement code reported to the controller, which calculates the corresponding average and writes it to the log file. We use CPU cycles for runtime comparison. We measure four components:

1) the generation of the call target's input parameters,
2) the process of sending feedback to the controller via UDP,
3) the actual time spent in the target function, and
4) the cleanup performed after this call.

We execute the worker five times with different fuzz cases that call the target function 20 000 times per case. The average times of this experiment are listed in Tab. IV. The fuzz case generation requires the largest overhead with 9.5 % of the time. Overall, the worker introduces 11.7 % overhead.

TABLE IV: Average overhead introduced by the individual parts of the worker compared to the actual target call.

Activity	CPU Cycles	Overhead
Target Call	117 207	—
Input Generation	11 084	9.5 %
Feedback	1318	1.1 %
Cleanup	1278	1.1 %
Total Overhead	13 680	11.7 %

VII. Conclusion

In this paper, we developed a powerful PowerPC binary patching and dynamic instrumentation framework. Using a TETRA base station, we demonstrated that our implementation works in practice. The patched binaries run stable on this complex system even during fuzzing, and the framework assisted us in internal follow-up security analysis.

Features like the ELF patcher and function tracer are very generic and can be useful for similar projects, such as other outdated but still in use critical infrastructure or retro computing projects. Moreover, the insights gained into OSE and its possible error states can be helpful for other security researchers that encounter this closed-source operating system.

Acknowledgment

We thank Jannik Jürgens and Sven Neubauer for the initial setup of the base station environment as well as Patrick Dworski for the analysis of existing functionality and protocols like the *AirTracer*. Moreover, we thank Dominik Maier and A. Birkl for proofreading this paper.

This work has been funded by the LOEWE initiative (Hessen State Ministry for Higher Education, Research and the Arts, Germany) within the emergenCITY centre.

Disclaimer

No dinosaurs were harmed and no new dinosaurs were bred during our experiments.

Availability

The PowerPC binary patcher and generic tools are publicly available on GitHub [33]. Due to its security and public safety critical nature, we will neither release the TETRA firmware extracted from the base station nor the fuzzer.

References

[1] Sebastian Aland, Markus Happe, Nico Loose, and Florian Schoppmann. Seminarausarbeitung OSE. http://homepages.uni-paderborn.de/fschopp/hauptstudium/docs/rtos.pdf, June 2005.

[2] Embedded Staff. Enea Embedded Technology announces new version of OSE RTOS. https://www.embedded.com/enea-embedded-technology-announces-new-version-of-ose-rtos/, April 2004.

[3] Enea OSE Sysems AB. Real-time Operating System Enea OSE. https://www.enea.com/products-services/operating-systems/enea-ose, January 2021.

[4] Enea OSE Systems AB. OSE Kernel Reference Manual, 420e/OSE93-1 R1.0.4. https://docplayer.net/55608737-Ose-kernel-reference-manual-kernel-enea-ose-systems-ab.html, 1998.

[5] ETSI. ETSI EN 300 392-1 V1.6.1 (2020-04): Terrestrial Trunked Radio (TETRA); Voice plus Data (V+D); Part 1: General network design. https://www.etsi.org/deliver/etsi_en/300300_300399/30039201/01.06.01_60/en_30039201v010601p.pdf.

[6] ETSI. ETSI EN 300 392-7 V3.5.1 (2019-07): Terrestrial Trunked Radio (TETRA); Voice plus Data (V+D); Part 7: Security. https://www.etsi.org/deliver/etsi_en/300300_300399/30039207/03.05.01_60/en_30039207v030501p.pdf.

[7] José Fonseca. `gprof2dot`. https://github.com/jrfonseca/gprof2dot, January 2021.

[8] Freescale Semiconductor Inc. MPC8260 PowerQUICC™II Family Reference Manual, Rev. 2. https://www.nxp.com/docs/en/reference-manual/MPC8260UM.pdf, December 2005.

[9] Freescale Semiconductor Inc. Programming Environments Manual for 32-Bit Implementations of the PowerPC Architecture, Rev. 3. https://www.nxp.com/files-static/product/doc/MPCFPE32B.pdf, September 2005.

[10] Freescale Semiconductor Inc. PowerQUICC™I and PowerQUICC II Families. https://www.nxp.com/docs/en/fact-sheet/PWRQUCROADMPFS.pdf, January 2021.

[11] Jean-loup Gailly and Mark Adler. `zlib` - A Massively Spiffy Yet Delicately Unobtrusive Compression Library. https://www.zlib.net/, January 2021.

[12] GNU C Library Contributors. The GNU C Library (`glibc`). https://www.gnu.org/software/libc/, January 2021.

[13] gnutools. `elfutils`. https://sourceware.org/elfutils/, January 2021.

[14] Green Hills Software. INTEGRITY RTOS - The most reliable and secure operating system. https://www.ghs.com/products/rtos/integrity.html, March 2021.

[15] Grant Hernandez and Marius Muench. Emulating Samsung's Baseband for Security Testing. *BlackHat USA 2020*, August 2020.

[16] IBM Knowledge Center. PowerPC Branch Instruction. https://www.ibm.com/support/knowledgecenter/en/ssw_aix_71/assembler/idalangref_bbranchinst.html, January 2021.

[17] IBM Knowledge Center. PowerPC Register Usage and Conventions. https://www.ibm.com/support/knowledgecenter/en/ssw_aix_72/assembler/idalangref_reg_use_conv.html, January 2021.

[18] JasperRLZ, Jdaster64, PistonMiner, and Zephiles. Tools for Paper Mario: The Thousand Year Door. https://github.com/PistonMiner/ttyd-tools, 2021.

[19] Dominik Maier, Lukas Seidel, and Shinjo Park. BaseSAFE: Baseband SAnitized Fuzzing through Emulation. *The 13th ACM Conference on Security and Privacy in Wireless and Mobile Networks (WiSec '20)*, July 2020.

[20] Microsoft. Overview of Azure RTOS ThreadX. https://docs.microsoft.com/en-us/azure/rtos/threadx/overview-threadx, March 2021.

[21] Jessica Miller. Wind River to Acquire Interpeak. https://www.windriver.com/news/press/pr.html?ID=3002, March 2006.

[22] Marius Muench, Dario Nisi, Aurélien Francillon, and Davide Balzarotti. Avatar 2: A Multi-target Orchestration Platform. In *Proc. Workshop Binary Anal. Res.(Colocated NDSS Symp.)*, volume 18, pages 1–11, 2018.

[23] National Security Agency. Ghidra. https://ghidra-sre.org/, 2021.

[24] Ole André V. Ravnås. FЯIDA JavaScript API: Instrumentation. https://frida.re/docs/javascript-api/#instrumentation, January 2021.

[25] Chengbin Pang, Ruotong Yu, Yaohui Chen, Eric Koskinen, Georgios Portokalidis, Bing Mao, and Jun Xu. SoK: All You Ever Wanted to Know About x86/x64 Binary Disassembly but Were Afraid to Ask. In *2021 2021 IEEE Symposium on Security and Privacy (S&P)*, pages 194–212, Los Alamitos, CA, USA, May 2021. IEEE Computer Society.

[26] QEMU. Quick Emulator. https://www.qemu.org/, 2021.

[27] Jan Ruge, Jiska Classen, Francesco Gringoli, and Matthias Hollick. Frankenstein: Advanced Wireless Fuzzing to Exploit New Bluetooth Escalation Targets. In *29th USENIX Security Symposium (USENIX Security 20)*, pages 19–36. USENIX Association, August 2020.

[28] Matthias Schulz, Daniel Wegemer, and Matthias Hollick. Nexmon: The C-based Firmware Patching Framework. https://nexmon.org, 2017.

[29] Shellphish. Patcherex. Shellphish's automated patching engine, originally created for the Cyber Grand Challenge. https://github.com/angr/patcherex/, 2021.

[30] simigo79. Unicorn Engine PowerPC Fork. https://github.com/simigo79/unicorn-ppc, 2020.

[31] TETRA Industry Group. TETRA Around the World. https://web.archive.org/web/20120313035919/http://www.tetrahealth.info/worldCountries.htm, 2011.

[32] Unicorn. The Ultimate CPU Emulator. http://www.unicorn-engine.org/, 2021.

[33] Timm Welz Uwe Müller, Eicke Hauck. PowerPC Binary Patcher. https://github.com/jrfonseca/gprof2dot, February 2021.

[34] Valgrind Developers. Valgrind Technical Documentation: Callgrind Format Specification. http://valgrind.org/docs/manual/cl-format.html, January 2021.

[35] Josef Weidendorfer. KCachegrind. https://kcachegrind.github.io, January 2021.

[36] Harald Welte. The Osmocom TETRA project. https://osmocom.org/projects/tetra/wiki/OsmocomTETRA, 2016.

[37] Jonas Zaddach, Luca Bruno, Aurelien Francillon, Davide Balzarotti, et al. AVATAR: A Framework to Support Dynamic Security Analysis of Embedded Systems' Firmwares. 2014.

Polypyus – The Firmware Historian

Jan Friebertshäuser, Florian Kosterhon, Jiska Classen, Matthias Hollick
Secure Mobile Networking Lab, TU Darmstadt
{jfriebertshaeuser,flokosterhon,jclassen,mhollick}@seemoo.de

***Abstract*—Embedded systems, IoT devices, and systems on a chip such as wireless network cards often run raw firmware binaries. Raw binaries miss metadata such as the target architecture and an entry point. Thus, their analysis is challenging. Nonetheless, chip firmware analysis is vital to the security of modern devices. We find that state-of-the-art disassemblers fail to identify function starts and signatures in raw binaries. In our case, these issues originate from the dense, variable-length ARM *Thumb2* instruction set. Binary differs such as *BinDiff* and *Diaphora* perform poor on raw ARM binaries, since they depend on correctly identified functions. Moreover, binary patchers like *NexMon* require function signatures to pass arguments. As a solution for fast diffing and function identification, we design and implement *Polypyus*. This firmware historian learns from binaries with known functions, generalizes this knowledge, and applies it to raw binaries. *Polypyus* is independent from architecture and disassembler. However, the results can be imported as disassembler entry points, thereby improving function identification and follow-up results by other binary differs. Additionally, we partially reconstruct function signatures and custom types from *Eclipse* PDOM files. Each *Eclipse* project contains a PDOM file, which caches selected project information for compiler optimization. We showcase the capabilities of *Polypyus* on a set of 20 firmware binaries.**

I. Introduction

Security of modern devices does not only depend on the operating system but also the hardware and firmware they run on. Systems on a chip run their own embedded Real-Time Operating System (RTOS) that is an additional target for attackers. Due to resource constraints, both the chip and the RTOS miss modern security mechanisms, and, thus, become an entry point into the operating system [3], [4], [6], [25], [30], [31], [35]. The firmware running on those chips is difficult to extract. Once extracted, analysis of raw binaries comes with many challenges. Even though most parts of raw binaries are not obfuscated to preserve performance, they often miss strings and other helpful indicators for reverse-engineering. Moreover, they lack memory region and function start annotations, in contrast to Executable and Linking Format (ELF) or Portable Executable (PE) binaries. Note that even on ELF and PE binaries, modern recursive disassemblers fail to identify 25 % of function starts on average if they are stripped [33, p. 9].

Especially within wireless baseband research, it is typical to encounter raw firmware binaries that have similarities, as they originate from the same family of wireless chips. In this paper's case study, we use a set of Bluetooth binaries that cover a history of approximately one decade of firmware development. For a subset of these, partially leaked or manually reverse-engineered symbols are available. However, to enable binary patching, security analysis, and further experimentation with Bluetooth and Wi-Fi firmware on popular devices, these symbols need to be ported to all firmware versions [31], [36].

Binary diffing compares binaries without source code. Currently, the state-of-the-art tools for this are *BinDiff* [43] and *Diaphora* [29]. They identify similar functions in a binary even if names are stripped. To this end, they can compare disassembler and decompiler output and consider call graph statistics. While *BinDiff* and *Diaphora* work well on most binaries, this is not the case for raw firmware. Both depend on functions being identified correctly. However, disassemblers like *IDA Pro* and *Ghidra*, which support these binary diffing tools, fail at function identification on the Advanced RISC Machine (ARM) *Thumb2* instruction set. Yet, fixing disassembler issues with the ARM *Thumb2* instruction set is rather complex and comes with different properties per compiler setting [28]. Surprisingly, due to avoiding false positives, the most recent version of *IDA Pro* fails to identify significantly more functions in firmware binaries than older versions.

Binaries within a firmware family are very similar. They are typically compiled for the same architecture—*ARM7*, *Cortex M3* and *M4* in our case—as well as with the same compiler options. Thus, matching functions look almost the same in binary format, except from relative branches and memory references. *Polypyus* takes advantage of these binary similarities to identify matches within seconds that state-of-the-art binary diffing tools cannot find. Our contributions are as follows:

- A benchmark of recent ARM *Thumb2* disassemblers and decompilers, including how their results impede *BinDiff* and *Diaphora* performance.
- Design and implementation of *Polypyus*, a binary-only firmware historian that works disassembler-independent.
- Evaluation of *Polypyus* on a decade of *Broadcom* and *Cypress* Bluetooth firmware history.
- Reconstruction of function signatures and types from *Eclipse* Persistent Document Object Model (PDOM) files for various *Cypress* wireless chips.

The *Polypyus* binary differ is available on *GitHub* [38]. While the evaluation in this paper focuses on Bluetooth firmware, we also successfully used the binary differ on *Broadcom* Wi-Fi firmware. Since it does not require any disassembler, it is not limited to ARM. However, its parameters might need to be adjusted for optimal results.

Workshop on Binary Analysis Research (BAR) 2021
21 February 2021, Virtual
https://dx.doi.org/10.14722/bar.2021.23004
www.ndss-symposium.org

This paper is structured as follows. Sec. II evaluates the function identification performance of various disassemblers and shows how failures lead to low-quality diffing results. Thus, we propose the *Polypyus* binary-only differ and describe its implementation in Sec. III. We evaluate binary-only diffing on 20 different Bluetooth firmware versions in Sec. IV. Moreover, we reconstruct function signatures and type information from 19 different PDOMs of *Cypress* Bluetooth, Wi-Fi and Zigbee firmware in Sec. V. We discuss related work in Sec. VI and conclude our findings in Sec. VII.

II. Function Start Identification Issues

This section shows that various disassemblers make severe mistakes on raw ARM *Thumb2* binaries and how these lead to subsequent errors within binary differs. Sec. II-A explains why already identifying instructions is a complex problem for disassemblers. This is confirmed by the benchmark results of *IDA Pro*, *Ghidra*, *Binary Ninja*, and *radare2* in Sec. II-B [27], [32], [42], [34], and Sec. II-C cherry picks common disassembler mistakes. Sec. II-D discusses the impact of these mistakes on binary differs. Our results agree with another recent study that compares disassemblers on stripped PE and ELF files [33].

A. Disassembling Instructions

Most functions start with pushing registers or loading a global variable. Thus, a disassembler can linearly inspect a binary, search for `push` instructions, and end functions on `pop` instructions. However, a function might have various branches that end at different `pop` instructions. Moreover, there are exceptions like branching to the Link Register (LR) or contents of a function pointer table. Thus, instead of aggressively scanning for `push` instructions, some disassemblers implement a recursive approach meaning that they only consider an initial function and follow its subsequent calls.

The underlying problem of identifying functions is the high instruction density. Considering 2 B random input and then running this with the *Capstone* disassembler [8], configured for ARM *Thumb2* little endian, random input is a valid 2 B instruction with 89 % probability or the start of a valid 4 B instruction with 9 % probability. Any mistake in identifying an instruction's start, which could be at a 2 B or a 4 B offset, leads to misinterpreted instructions.

B. Disassembler Benchmark

In practice, we observed many disassembler mistakes during manual firmware analysis. We design and run a disassembler benchmark with the most popular tools to quantify this observation in Sec. II-B1. The disassembler performance highly depends on their setup, thus, we also explain the initial configuration in detail. The results in Sec. II-B2 show significant differences in disassemblers.

```
0x000: 00 04 20 00        dcd bootcheck
0x004: bd 03 00 00        dcd __reset+1
0x008: 6d 01 00 00        dcd __tx_NMIHandler+1
0x00c: a1 01 00 00        dcd HardFaultInt+1
 ...
                      __tx_NMIHandler
0x16c: 00 bf              nop
0x16e: 00 bf              nop
0x170: 22 e0              b    WDogInt
```

Listing 1: *CYW20735* ROM starting with interrupt vectors.

1) Benchmark Considerations: A benchmark requires verifiable results—yet, known symbols for raw, stripped firmware binaries are rare. Hence, we only benchmark one specific example throughout this paper. However, we observed similar behavior on disassemblers within ARM-based Wi-Fi and fitness tracker firmware.

Partial symbols for the benchmarked Bluetooth firmware leaked as part of *WICED Studio* `patch.elf` files [14]. They include function names, function starts, and global variable names for the *BCM20703*, *CYW20719*, *CYW20735*, and *CYW20819* chips listed in Tab. I. Note that these symbols lack function ends. The start of a new function is not necessarily the end of the previous function, since compilers put variables after the end of functions. Such variables do not always belong to that specific function but sometimes are part of a library. Thus, we can only benchmark function starts.

It is required to know the ROM and RAM region of a Bluetooth firmware to dump it. Within the Bluetooth firmware the ROM starts at `0x0` and the RAM at `0x200000`.[1] ROM can be read and executed, while RAM can also be written. There is no execution prevention. The ROM of each firmware starts as shown in Listing 1. The `reset` vector is always located at offset `0x4`. It starts the firmware by initializing hardware components and booting the underlying *ThreadX* operating system. Even though this knowledge about a firmware binary has to be reverse-engineered in the first place, it is substantial for disassembler performance. Thus, we provide the disassemblers with the ROM and RAM position as well as the `reset` vector, if possible.

In the following, we use the *CYW20735* firmware for a benchmark. It has 10 791 functions. 10 584 of these functions are located in ROM. However, 207 functions are located in in RAM, instrumented by the so-called *Patchram* [31]. The ROM is changed with up to 256 breakpoints that point to RAM. Patched functions in RAM might be different from the leaked symbols, which can lead to a few mistakes. Thus, we ignore functions located in the RAM regions for our statistics.

IDA Pro: *IDA Pro 6.8* linearly sweeps over the whole firmware to identify instructions when possible and additionally approaches recursive descent. By default, *IDA Pro 7.x* only disassembles functions if a proper starting point is provided and continues with recursive descent.

For comparability, we disable the automatic analysis in *IDA Pro 6.8*. Then, for all *IDA* versions, we perform the following setup. We select ARM little endian as architecture and select *ARMv7-M* in the options. After binary import with default settings, we create ROM and RAM program sections and mark the first address in ROM as *Thumb* via `Alt+g`. For comparability, we mark the `reset` vector as offset and create a new function at its location as first step of the analysis. While *IDA Pro 7.x* starts analysis once provided with the `reset` vector, we manually re-enable automatic analysis after this step in *IDA Pro 6.8*.

[1] Note that on firmware prior to 2012, which is based on the *ARM7TDMI-S* core, the RAM starts at `0x80000`.

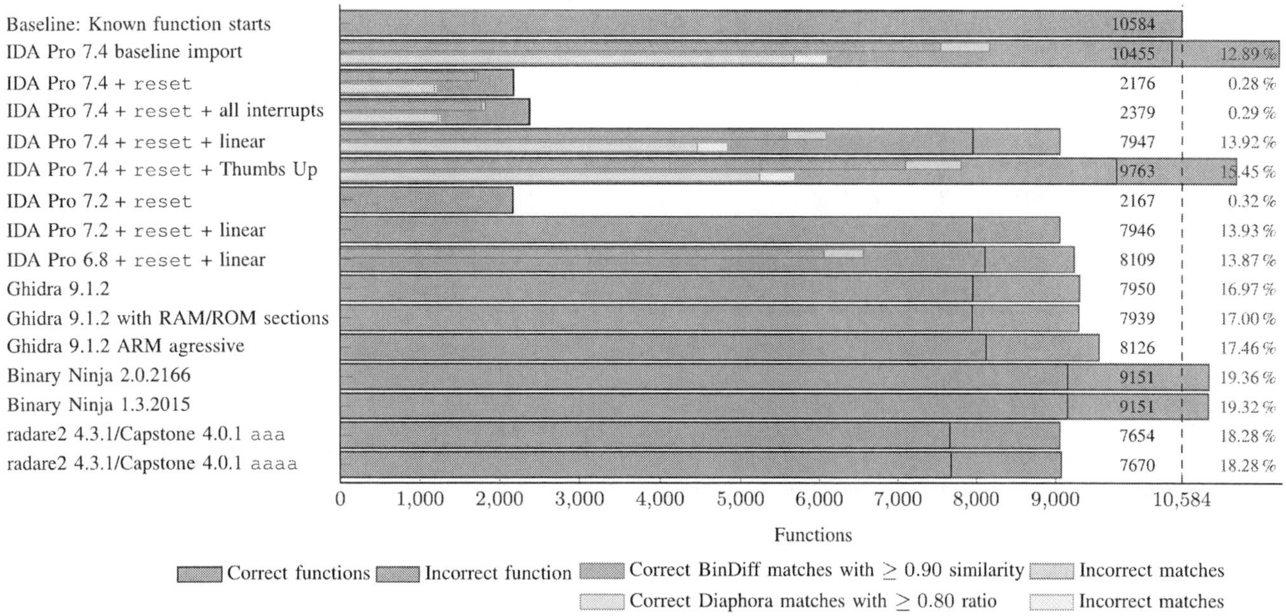

Fig. 1: Disassembler performance for function start identification on the *CYW20735* firmware.

IDA Pro 7.x can be forced to perform a linear analysis to create instructions where possible similar to the *IDA Pro 6.8* default mode of operation. The area for this analysis can be defined with the following command, which we use within the ROM section:

```
idc.plan_and_wait(start, end)
```

Another tool to recognize function starts in ARM binaries is the *Thumbs Up* plugin for *IDA Pro* [28]. Initially, it performs a linear analysis on ROM sections utilizing the same command as above, and then makes heuristics on the already identified functions to apply them to the remaining ROM.

Ghidra: We import the binary as ARM *v7* little endian, with default compiler and analysis options. Then, we run the same analysis again with the experimental aggressive instruction finder. For comparison, we also create a fresh import and initially run the aggressive instruction finder, which leads to the same result as running these steps separately.

Binary Ninja: We set analysis and triage to `full`. Moreover, we configure the base address and the entry point. *Binary Ninja* automatically detects the correct architecture options.

radare2: For *radare2* we use the *Capstone* disassembler by setting the architecture to `arm` and 16 bit length. First, we run the basic auto analysis with `aaa`, and then we run the extended analysis using `aaaa`.

2) Benchmark Results: Fig. 1 shows an overview of the disassembler performance. *Binary Ninja* identified the most functions, while the recursive approach in *IDA Pro 7.x* has the lowest false positive rate.

IDA Pro: On *IDA Pro 7.x*, just starting at the `reset` vector is insufficient to find subsequent functions via branches. This only slightly increases when considering the full interrupt vector table. Too many function calls in the *CYW20735* firmware are implemented as offsets in function tables and other constructions the disassemblers fail to identify. Yet, this approach resulted in only 7 false positives.

The forced linear sweep identifies 7947 functions but also recognizes many false positives. Surprisingly, the automatic linear sweep without any options in *IDA Pro 6.8* provides better results with 8109 functions.

For the disassembler quality, there is almost no difference between *IDA Pro 7.2* and *IDA Pro 7.4*. In contrast, the *Thumbs Up* [28] scripts significantly improve the *IDA Pro 7.4* disassembler but do not solve all issues.

The subsequent analysis based on correctly provided functions still leads to false positives in *IDA Pro 7.4*. This even leads to some functions that cannot be marked as such as they are already located within other functions. Note that automatic analysis was still enabled during function import.

Ghidra: *Ghidra 9.1.2* identifies 7950 correct functions. The experimental aggressive instruction finder identifies 176 additional correct functions. At the same time, it also identifies 70 false positives.

Adding memory segments and marking the ROM as non-writable also does not significantly change the results, even though it improves readability of the decompiler output. In our setup, the number of false positives is identical, while the correct functions decrease by 11 when adding sections. This is the opposite of the expected impact.

Binary Ninja: Both *Binary Ninja* versions perform very similar. With 9151 correctly identified functions, they find the most true positives. In the newer version, the correct functions stay the same but the false positives increase by 4, which might just be some non-determinism within the disassembler.

radare2: *radare2*'s `aaa` analysis identifies 7654 correct functions. The *radare2* extended analysis adds 16 correct functions but 3 false positives. Overall, running the extended analysis is not much improvement but takes several minutes. Despite taking very long, *radare2* identifies the fewest functions.

C. Common Disassembler Mistakes

Many disassembler mistakes are easy to spot as a human, yet hard to solve programmatically. In the following, we provide an intuition on these mistakes. Even though it is not the purpose of this paper to improve the disassembler per se, *Polypyus* is able to provide the disassembler with some hints.

a) Invalid Function Length: A very common mistake is ending functions too early, e.g., on the first return instruction when there are multiple function returns. Also the opposite is possible, e.g., *IDA Pro 7.2* considers the `reset` vector function on the *BCM4335C0* to be 14 736 B, which is a major part of this firmware. Also *Ghidra 9.1.2* has issues with function lengths, e.g., it often identifies a function start with a `push` instruction correctly but ends before a return instruction.

b) Correct Instructions but no Function: Even when the *IDA Pro* disassembler does not make any mistakes with the instruction offsets, it often does not recognize function starts within the instructions. This happens if there are no references to the function [28], however, firmware often has indirect function offset tables, meaning that no correctly identified reference does not necessarily indicate dead code.

c) Data Marked as Code: The symbol import of all correct function starts still produces false positives in *IDA Pro*. Often, data is misinterpreted as code. Even the reset vector table is interpreted as function at offset `0x0`.

D. Impact on Binary Diffing

Disassembler issues lead to subsequent binary diffing problems. Sophisticated statistics based on call graphs fail if a few functions within such a graph are missing. Moreover, binary diffing is also applied to false positives. Yet, *BinDiff* and *Diaphora* both require function starts, and thus, some false positives do less harm than not identifying most functions. Our observations on binary diffing performance agree with a previous comparison [41], however, that test case was a more narrow patch analysis and used a symbolized binary.

BinDiff: We show the impact of function recognition on binary diffing by running *BinDiff 6* on *IDA Pro 7.4* with the *CYW20735* and *CYW20819* firmware for the following settings: *(1)* all function starts but no names imported from the known symbols, *(2)* `reset` vector with forced linear analysis in the ROM section, and *(3)* recursive only function detection via `reset` vector. *BinDiff* provides a similarity score and we consider all results with a score ≥ 0.90. Functions below this threshold might still be correct, however, they contain also many false positives. In practice, such false positives impede further reverse-engineering.

Setting *(1)* returns 7539 correct matches, setting *(2)* decreases to 5590 matches, and *(3)* further decreases to 1692 matches. In contrast, setting *(1)* has a false positive ratio of 0.084, setting *(2)* is almost the same with a ratio of 0.089, but setting *(3)* lowers this to 0.018. These numbers show that *BinDiff* results depend on the function starts identified by the disassembler. However, false positives within function start identification significantly increase false positives.

Moreover, we run *BinDiff 4.2* on *IDA Pro 6.8*. As *IDA Pro 6.8* sightly outperforms *IDA Pro 7.x* during database initialization of both firmware versions, *CYW20735* and *CYW20819*, this effect duplicates within the *BinDiff 4.2* results, and identifies 6059 functions correctly in a setup comparable to *(2)*, at a similar false positive ratio of 0.083 Thus, surprisingly, the outdated setup works better.

Thumbs Up looks very promising when considering disassembler results. However, the false positives it identifies impede binary diffing as well.

Diaphora: We take the same statistics as with *BinDiff*. We run *Diaphora* including slow heuristics for all settings and consider the best matches as well as all partial matches with a ratio ≥ 0.80. In contrast to *BinDiff*, *Diaphora* considers decompiler output. As a first baseline, we run *Diaphora* on the database with `reset` and linear sweep. Without decompiler and slow heuristics, it finds 3320 matches. The decompiler increases this to 4409 matches without slow heuristics and 4838 matches including slow heuristics.

Using these thresholds, *Diaphora* provides a similar false positive rate as *BinDiff* but with fewer matches. However, as it is an open-source project, it would be possible to add more heuristics in the future.

radiff2: When running *radiff2* on the binaries, we encounter two issues. First, raw binaries are not supported [40]. Then, after adding all analysis options to the `-G` parameter, *radiff2* only identifies 42 matches within a few seconds and prints *"Exceeded anal threshold while diffing fcn.cafe and fcn.babe"* multiple times.

Ghidra Versioning: The *Ghidra* versioning works best if provided with correct function signatures. It sometimes identifies similar functions correctly without them but performs significantly worse than *BinDiff*, even on non-raw binaries. Moreover, enabling all analysis options typically leads to crashes, preventing us from making a fair comparison.

III. Raw Binary Diffing Approach

As shown in the previous section, faults within the disassembler lead to subsequent issues with binary diffing. Yet, firmware compiled with similar options is often byte-identical except from relative references. Based on this observation, we build the *Python*-based tool *Polypyus*, following the Greek historian Polybius. *Polypyus* learns byte similarities from a firmware history and applies these to new firmware binaries.

A. Polypyus Workflow and Tool Integration

The history can be collected from firmware with reverse-engineered or leaked symbols. *Polypyus* supports the `.symdefs` format generated by common ARM compilers and a proprietary `patch.elf` format provided by *WICED Studio*. Moreover, it can read and write function definitions as `.csv`.

Function import and export scripts allow integration into existing disassemblers, however, *Polypyus* does not depend on them. It runs standalone. When importing *Polypyus* results into

```
                    mm_freeACLBuffer
0x17b4c: 00 28               cmp  r0, #0
0x17b4e: 02 d0               beq  locret_17b56
0x17b50: 08 38               subs r0, #8
0x17b52: f2 f7 43 b8         b.w  dynamic_memory_Release
                    locret_17b56
0x17b56: 70 47               bx   lr
```

Listing 2: `mm_freeACLBuffer` within *CYW20735.*

```
                    mm_freeACLBuffer
0x0d0dc: 00 28               cmp  r0, #0
0x0d0de: 02 d0               beq  locret_d0e6
0x0d0e0: 08 38               subs r0, #8
0x0d0e2: f4 f7 f7 bf         b.w  dynamic_memory_Release
                    locret_d0e6
0x0d0e6: 70 47               bx   lr
```

Listing 3: `mm_freeACLBuffer` within *CYW20819.*

a projects, this does not only add matched functions but indirectly improves disassembler quality, because the disassembler is provided with correct function starts and disassembles subsequent functions. After importing *Polypyus* matches to the disassembler, it is still possible to run binary diffing tools. They find more matches than *Polypyus* and profits from improved assembly quality in general, as previously shown in Fig. 1.

B. Binary Matchers

Listing 2 and 3 show the same function within the memory manager for two different firmware versions. Except from a relative branch instruction they are byte-identical. *Polypyus* combines these functions as follows:

```
mm_freeACLBuffer: 00 28 02 d0 08 38 ** f7 ** ** 70 47
```

We call this representation a matcher. The more input files provided to *Polypyus*, the more matchers are created.

During the learning phase, *Polypyus* applies fuzzyness to equally long functions with the same name. Bytes that differ, as in branch instructions, are masked. Even non-fuzzy functions can be byte-identical, such as mathematical operations.

Creating a new matcher requires a function's length. If the length is not determined by the input format, it is required to determine the function length. Functions do not necessarily end where the next function starts, as the compiler tends to put variables at the end of functions, which are not always part of the same function. Thus, we recommend using an external disassembler and importing the length determined by the disassembler into *Polypyus*, instead of simply assuming function starts being equal to function ends.

A matcher with a high fuzziness comes at the risk of false positive matches. The most common example for this is a function that only contains a 2 B or 4 B branch instruction to another function. This would create the following matcher:

```
jump_function: ** ** ** **
```

```
bb_setBdAddress
    push   {r4, lr}
    bl     bcs_pmuWaitForBtClock
    ldr    r1, =bb_localAccessCode
    ldr    r0, =rm_deviceBDAddr
    bl     bb_computeAC
    ldr    r1, =bb_localAccessCode
    ldr    r0, =rm_deviceBDAddr
    bl     bb_progMasterPiconetInfo
    pop.w  {r4, lr}
    b.w    bcs_pmuReleaseBtClock
```

Listing 4: `bb_setBdAddress` on *CYW20735 & CYW20819.*

However, there can be more complex and still very fuzzy matchers. For example, the function `bb_setBdAddress`, which sets the Bluetooth device MAC address, reads identical with symbols, as shown in Listing 4. Due to the relative addresses, it generalizes to the following matcher:

```
bb_setBdAddress: 10 b5 ** f0 ** ** ** 49 ** 48 ff f7 b2 ff
    ** 49 ** 48 ff f7 e9 ff bd e8 10 40 ** ** ** **
```

As the branch to `bb_computeAC` happens to be at the same offset within the baseband library, it still creates four matching bytes despite being a location-dependent operation.

C. Minimum Length and Cost Function

Polypyus prevents false positives by considering a minimum function length and a fuzziness cost function that is relative to the function length. While the parameters presented in this paper are tuned to work well with the Bluetooth firmware set, binaries of different architectures might benefit from adapting these parameters.

Minimum Length: A minimum function length prevents short fuzzy matchers causing false positives. In the Bluetooth firmware set, thresholds between 10 B and 24 B are reasonable. For all functions in our symbolicated firmware subset, we consider a prefix of length k. Then, we search for other functions with the same prefix, as depicted in Fig. 2.

Each function contains at least one 2 B instruction. Thus, at $k = 2$, each function at least matches itself, meaning that the amount of total matches is the same as the total number of functions. With increasing k, the total matches slightly decrease, as some functions are smaller than the prefix length and, thus, are not considered as equal. To determine a

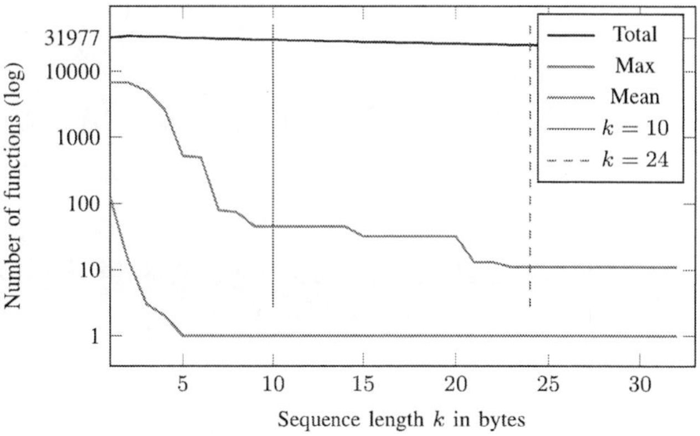

Fig. 2: Relation between the prefix length to the number of functions in the symbol data with the same prefix.

threshold for the minimum length, we consider the mean and the maximum matches depending on k. The mean represents the average number of functions per prefix, and the maximum the highest number of functions with the same prefix.

The numbers in Fig. 2 indicate that there exist a few short functions that can be found several times in all firmware versions. Hence, *Polypyus* favors longer functions in case there are multiple matching matchers. This solves the issue caused by one matcher being the prefix of another matcher.

Furthermore, we want to limit the problem that a small function matches all function prologues of unknown functions. The maximum number of functions per prefix drops significantly before the prefix length of $k = 10$ and again at $k = 24$, after which it stays almost constant. This drop shows that additional bytes in the prefix help to distinguish between functions. Based on this observation, the *Polypyus* default configuration for the minimum function length is 24 B.

Cost Function: Without a cost function, *Polypyus* would simply create fully fuzzy matchers for each byte length and ignore the bytecode. Intuitively, a cost-based approach restricts the creation of matchers. More fuzziness means higher costs. Dense clusters of fuzziness are more expensive than sparsely distributed fuzzy bytes. A function's allowance is based on its length and configurable thresholds. We define the following requirements for a matcher's fuzziness cost function:

(1) Fuzziness should not be allowed in short functions.

(2) The maximal fuzziness should only be allowed if it is sparsely distributed through the function.

(3) The cost attributed to a long succession of fuzziness should be higher than the sum of multiple shorter succession of the same total length.

(4) The cost function should be adjusted to the high ARM *Thumb2* code density.

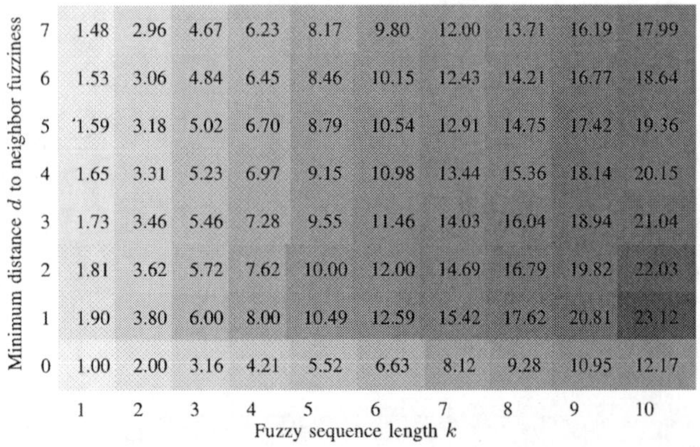

Fig. 3: The cost of a fuzzy-marked sequence of bytes based on the sequence length and its minimal distance to another fuzzy-marked sequence in the same function.

Polypyus applies the cost of a matcher as follows:

$$\text{matcher-cost}(m) = \sum_{(k,d)\in F_m} \text{sequence-cost}(k,d) \quad \text{(A)}$$

$$\text{matcher-cost}(m) \leq (|m| - \mu)\cdot\phi \quad \text{(B)}$$

$$\text{sequence-cost}(k,d) = \frac{k}{p(\lceil k/2 \rceil)}\cdot(1 + \text{proximity-penalty}(d)) \quad \text{(C)}$$

$$\text{proximity-penalty}(d) = \begin{cases} 0 & ,d = 0 \\ 0.9^d & ,\text{ otherwise} \end{cases} \quad \text{(D)}$$

where m is the matcher, μ is the minimal function size defined above, d and ϕ are the minimal and the maximal relative distance to the next fuzzy byte in the matcher, and $p(k)$ is the likelihood of a uniformly sampled half-word sequence to be code without assumptions on the first half-word in ARM *Thumb2*. Fig. 3 presents the costs of individual fuzzy sequences for combinations of the byte distance d and the sequence length k.

We validate weather the cost function satisfies the requirements *(1)–(4)*.

(1) Disallow Short Functions: The cost function does not allow fuzziness in short functions. According to Equation A, a fuzzy sequence of length k always costs at least k. Equation B limits the allowed maximal matcher cost to a term that is negative for functions shorter than the minimal function length. Matchers that are smaller than the minimal function length plus $1/\phi$ involve no costs. Then, costs grow linearly with a gradient of ϕ, which disallows short functions. Considering a fixed matcher size, the equation underrates the maximal fuzziness to be smaller than ϕ by a relative factor that is proportional to the function size, and descends with a growing matcher size.

(2) Require Sparse Fuzziness: Equation D defines a penalty factor that exponentially falls with an increasing minimal distance to the next fuzzy byte sequence and converges to zero. Meanwhile, the term $\frac{k}{p(\lceil k/2 \rceil)}$ in Equation C exponentially increases with the sequence length k. This way, short clusters of fuzzy bytes and long successions of fuzzy bytes are costly.

(3) Penalty for Long Successions: The function $p(k)$ that represents the probability of a byte to be valid code can be approximated by 0.977^k (see Sec. II-A). We ensure that the penalty for clustering decreases slower than the cost for long fuzzy sequences rises. If this is the case and if the third requirement given above is not violated by any of the initial values, then no combination of the byte distance d or sequence length k can violate the requirement. Therefore, the proximity penalty is an exponentially decreasing function with 0.9^k that falls slower than $\frac{k}{0.977^k}$ grows, with respect to the approximation error. As shown in Fig. 3, the initial values do not violate this requirement.

(4) ARM Thumb2 Code Density: The cost of a fuzzy sequence is proportional to the likelihood that it will not match just code. This is a reasonable metric for our scenario.

The Equations A–D describe the requirements to create a common function class in *Polypyus*. If a function class is not meeting the requirements, we test, with a greedy algorithm, whether subsets of the functions meet them, in which case these subsets form a common function class. All functions that are not part of common function class form standalone, non-fuzzy matchers to find exact matches of these functions.

D. Function Prologue Matchers

Function-based matchers substitute the need for binary diffing with other tools. However, as described in the typical workflow in Sec. III-A, *Polypyus* is meant to support existing disassemblers and state-of-the-art binary diffing tools. Thus, also identifying functions without assigning their correct name helps in the overall process.

In addition to the normal matchers, *Polypyus* has the option to also learn function prologues. This feature must be explicitly enabled. Within the Bluetooth firmware history, many functions start with common instructions, such as pushing and initializing the same registers. *Polypyus* learns the most common prologues from the history and applies these to the target binary to create unnamed functions. The default setting in the user interface is 8 B prologue length, and *Polypyus* only considers frequent prologues.

E. Fast Matching Algorithm

When provided with the four symbolized firmware binaries and one target binary, *Polypyus* creates matchers and finds matches based on those within a few seconds on a recent consumer-grade laptop, e.g., 8.5 s to create matchers from three binaries in a history and 9.5 s to find matches in a target binary. This performance is achieved by several optimizations:

- A matcher prefix tree deduplicates the matchers.
- Match finding is a depth first search in the prefix tree.
- Bins in the tree reduce the number of visited matcher fragments.
- Search is restricted to partitions of the binary that potentially contain code.

IV. Raw Binary Diffing Evaluation

In the following, we analyze the quality of matches on a history collected from 20 chips with build dates ranging over a decade. An overview of these is shown in Tab. I.

A. Known Firmware Changes and History

Over this decade, the underlying ARM core changed. The oldest available datasheet of the *BCM20702A1* chip from 2010 states that it uses an *ARM7TDMI-S*-based microprocessor with integrated RAM and ROM [12]. The slightly newer *BCM4335C0* firmware from 2012 is already based on a *Cortex M3* [11]. In 2016, the core changed again to a *Cortex M4* [13]. Even though datasheets are not available for all chips, the *Cortex M4* introduces additional instructions, which can be determined with a disassembler. Not all *Cortex M* versions introduce new instructions, meaning that the newest chip series could also be based on a different core.

In 2016, *Broadcom* sold their wireless IoT division to *Cypress* [10]. However, *Broadcom* kept customers like *Apple* and *Samsung*. Since then, firmware was developed independently.

In the *Samsung Galaxy S10* firmware, stack canaries were introduced. These change function prologues and harm performance on matchers created without stack canaries.

The *iPhone 11* firmware introduced a few debug strings with function names. These could be annotated and used to train *Polypyus*. However, some of the function names

TABLE I: Bluetooth firmware history for disassembler and *Polypyus* benchmarks.

Chip	Device	Build Date	Symbols	Known Functions	ROM Size	ARM Core	Full Matches	+ Starts
BCM2046A2	iMac Late 2009	2007	—	—	0x31c00	ARM7TDMI-S (?)	0	10
BCM2070B0	MacBook 2011, Thinkpad T420	Jul 9 2008	—	—	0x57800	ARM7TDMI-S (?)	0	9
BCM20702A1	Asus USB Dongle	Feb (?) 2010	—	—	0x5fc00	ARM7TDMI-S	0	33
BCM4335C0	Google Nexus 5	Dec 11 2012	—	—	0x8f000	Cortex M3	266	2392
BCM4345B0	iPhone 6	Jul 15 2013	—	—	0xb3000	Cortex M3	371	2989
BCM20703A1	MacBook Pro early 2015	Dec 23 2013	—	—	0xc7000	Cortex M3	708	4350
BCM43430A1	Raspberry Pi 3/Zero W	Jun 2 2014	—	—	0x8f400	Cortex M3	209	1859
BCM4345C0	Raspberry Pi 3+/4	Aug 19 2014	—	—	0xc1c00	Cortex M3	307	2546
BCM4358A3	Samsung Galaxy S6, Nexus 6P	Oct 23 2014	—	—	0x8f000	Cortex M3	275	1978
BCM4345C1	iPhone SE	Jan 27 2015	—	—	0xb7000	Cortex M3	295	2477
BCM4364B0	MacBook/iMac 2017–2019	Aug 21 2015	—	—	0xd4000	Cortex M3	340	2804
BCM4355C0	iPhone 7	Sep 14 2015	—	—	0x90000	Cortex M3	231	1838
BCM20703A2	MacBook/iMac 2016–2017	Oct 22 2015	✓	8603	0xc7000	Cortex M3	101	1583
BCM4347B0	Samsung Galaxy S8	Jun 3 2016	—	—	0xf4800	Cortex M4	414	2720
BCM4347B1	iPhone 8/X/XR	Oct 11 2016	—	—	0xfc000	Cortex M3	695	3599
CYW20719B1	Evaluation board	Jan 17 2017	✓	15 036	0x1d2000	Cortex M4	1519	6214
CYW20735B1	Evaluation board	Jan 18 2018	✓	10 791	0x14f000	Cortex M4	2241	7129
CYW20819A1	Evaluation board	May 22 2018	✓	10 276	0xf6800	Cortex M4	1543	5772
BCM4375B1	Samsung Galaxy S10/S20	Apr 13 2018	—	Canaries	0x130000	Cortex M4 (?)	14	362
BCM4378B1	iPhone 11/SE2	Oct 25 2018	Strings	Canaries	0x132800	Cortex M4 (?)	15	380

Polypyus is provided with inputs from four symbolicated firmwares. Matching results are for function identification and starts with *Polypyus* defaults: 24 B minimum length for function identification and optional 8 B prologues for function starts.

TABLE II: Firmware similarity by function names.

Firmware A	Firmware B	Unique Symbols	Common Symbols
BCM20703A2	CYW20719B1	12 161	5655
BCM20703A2	CYW20735B1	8402	5496
BCM20703A2	CYW20819A1	8215	5332
CYW20719B1	CYW20735B1	4790	10 435
CYW20719B1	CYW20819A1	6115	9515
CYW20735B1	CYW20819A1	1927	9570

indicate that *Broadcom* did a lot of refactoring and firmware improvements on this latest firmware. Moreover, the additional debug print statements change the binary structure.

Overall, refactoring is a significant factor within the Bluetooth firmware history. As shown in Tab. II, when considering common function names, the *BCM20703A2* firmware from 2015 significantly differs from those of the *Cypress* evaluation boards. However, the evaluation board firmware from 2017 and 2018 is very similar, except from some additional libraries depending on the board version that appear as unique symbols.

Additionally, firmware versions have different feature sets. For example, the oldest evaluation board within the Bluetooth firmware set has the most functions. Moreover, chips in laptops tend to have larger ROMs than those in smartphones.

B. *Polypyus Binary Diffing Results*

We run *Polypyus* on the full firmware set listed in Tab. I. For the history, all firmware versions with symbols are considered. If the target is a firmware with symbols, we exclude the target itself from the history. Matches found by the function matchers configured to the 24 B default are listed separately to the matches found with 8 B prologues.

a) History Observations: First of all, the matches in Tab. I are very platform-dependent. *Polypyus* does not find any matches in the older *ARM7TDMI-S* core, as this is using a different binary format. Moreover, for the *BCM20703* firmware, which is still a *Cortex M3*, the evaluation boards that run on the *Cortex M4* do not provide high-quality input. However, the *BCM20703* symbols help identifying functions in other *Cortex M3* based firmware.

Even though we do not have datasheets for the newest *BCM4375B1* and *BCM4378B1* firmware, we assume that they are still based on a *Cortex M4* due to their instruction set. The stack canaries are compiled into most functions, and this impedes *Polypyus* performance. However, if *Polypyus* would be trained with a new classifier that specifically searches for stack canaries, these could as well have a positive impact on function start identification.

The test set of the three evaluation boards performs the best. The *CYW20735* evaluation board, which was built after the *CYW20719* but before the *CYW20819*, profits a lot from the known symbols of the other firmware.

b) Match Quality: For the firmware with symbols, we evaluate the match quality as shown in Fig. 4. The quality of the identified functions is very high. The prologues have more false positives, which can be improved by increasing the prologue size—however, this would also reduce the total number of prologue matches.

Approximately 1/3 of the incorrect functions in Fig. 4 is actually correct when we analyze these by hand. The symbol names do not match because these functions were obviously renamed. Renaming includes obvious typos, such as `md4` to `md5`, or consistency of names within libraries. However, we did not remove them from the experiments, as we do not know this for every function.

The false positives that remain can be further eliminated by increasing the minimum function length to a value like 30 B. However, we found that also matches at a minimum function length of 8 B are still more accurate than *BinDiff* on a flawed *IDA Pro* database. In the *CYW20735* firmware, the default of 24 B identifies 2184 correct functions at a false positive rate of 2.88 %. A minimum function length of 30 B reduces this to 1804 functions at a false positive rate of 2.66 %. However, a 8 B minimum function length increases the correct functions to 3521 with a false positive rate only of 3.95 %. This shows how effective the *Polypyus* cost function is.

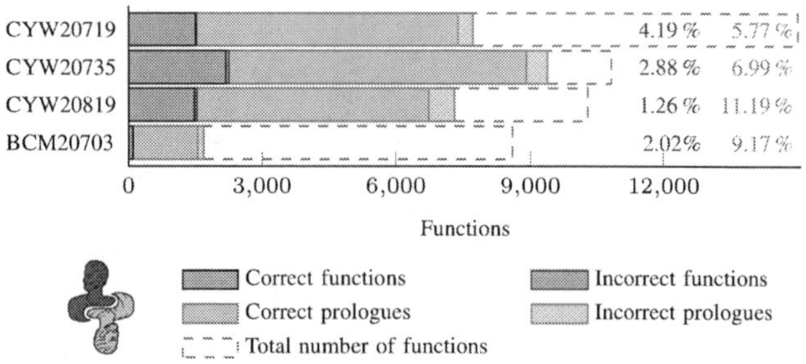

Fig. 4: *Polypyus* matches within the symbolized firmware, incorrect matches due to function name changes not removed.

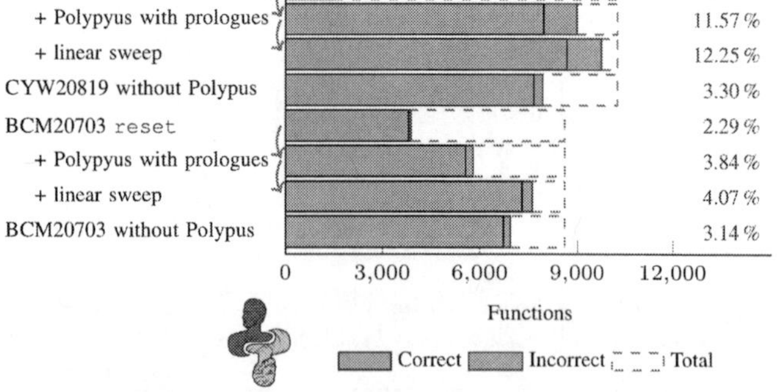

Fig. 5: Effectiveness of *Polypyus* import in *IDA Pro 7.4* including prologues, incremental steps marked with ⟶.

C. Disassembler Improvement

Since *Polypyus* is meant to integrate into existing workflows with other disassemblers, we evaluate its impact when working with *IDA Pro 7.4*. We evaluate all firmware versions with symbols. First, we start with the `reset` vector, then we add function names and prologues identified by *Polypyus* (market with + *Polypyus*), and finally, we run a linear sweep over the ROM (marked with + *linear sweep*). For comparison, we run the same experiment without *Polypyus* and just mark the `reset` vector and run a linear sweep.

The results shown in Fig. 5 indicate that *Polypyus* indeed helps with identifying functions in all firmware versions. With one exception, it also reduces the false positive ratio. This might either be the case because *Polypyus* identified more false function prologues in the *CYW20819* firmware compared to the others or because of *IDA Pro 7.4* dynamics after the import that identify false functions, as it was already the case for the fully correct function import in Fig. 1.

Another interesting observation that can be seen in Fig. 4 is that function detection works better on the *BCM20703* firmware with a *Cortex M3* than on the remaining *Cortex M4* firmware. This might be due to the more complex instruction set or different compiler settings.

V. Function Signature and Type Reconstruction

In addition to function starts, binary patching with C-based frameworks requires correct function signatures to pass arguments. *NexMon* is such a binary patcher supporting ARM [37]. Initially developed for *Broadcom* Wi-Fi chips, it has been ported to fitness trackers, vacuum cleaners, and more [9], [24]. As of now, each *NexMon* port has a `wrapper.c` file that defines selected functions required for supported patches. The wrapper is hand-written and based on manual reverse engineering. Thus, adding a new firmware version is a huge effort that we aim to automate in the following.

WICED Studio [14] contains Persistent Document Object Model (PDOM) files for Bluetooth, Wi-Fi and Zigbee chips. Not all of them are for sale and we do not have their raw firmware, however, we can still use the PDOM information to restore function signatures and custom types.

A. Eclipse and PDOM Purpose

The PDOM architecture consists of a client, an indexer and a database [16]. PDOM clients are *Eclipse* features like the C/C++ search page, searching for declarations and reference actions, content assist, and more. This information is stored in the PDOM database for fast access. In case it is not available, a slower direct access via the Document Object Model (DOM) is possible. Depending on the project size, a full indexer could index a project within seconds or hours. Thus, for large projects, a faster indexer that stores less information into the database is a common setting. All PDOMs analyzed in the following only contain partial information.

B. Utilizing PDOM in Reverse

The PDOM database contains valuable information about a project that exceeds the raw binary. Function signature and type information can be restored by using the database in the reverse direction. Since this is not the intended use case, we need to reverse-engineer the PDOM format. While it is sparsely documented with a few notes from 2006 [15], it is still maintained and open-sourced within the *Eclipse* project. Based on the *Eclipse* implementation, we create a custom PDOM database extractor that stores all information into a *SQLite* database. Even though the database extraction is slow, the *SQLite*-based import into *IDA Pro* is fast.

The database is structured by indexes. The file header contains offsets to the indexes, e.g., linkages, a file index, or an index of defective files [19]. In our case, only the linkage indexer is relevant. Each linkage is a top-level node of stored bindings. Two types of linkages differentiate between C and C++ nodes [21]. There are around 80 different bindings, but we only require a small subset to identify functions, parameters, and return types.

A linkage node is structured as follows [21]:

PDOMNode	PDOMNamedNode	PDOMLinkage
8 B	4 B	16 B

In the following, we analyze the function `btsnd_hcic_ble_remove_from_white_list` of the *CYW20735B1* PDOM file to provide an example for the data structure. Since it is a C++ function, it is based on the `PDOMCPPFunction` record [17]. This function is stored at offset `0xfa4b12` with its binary values shown in Fig. 6. We can follow its pointers to obtain further information by executing the PDOM library function `getRecPtr` [20]. For the function name pointer `0x1f496b`, `getRecPtr` returns the file offset `0xfa4b5a`, which contains the function name length and its name as string.

The number of parameters is directly encoded as `0x2`. Then, to retrieve the function parameter names, we follow the `first_param` pointer `0x1f4979` and apply the `PDOMCPPParameter` definition [18]. Since only the first parameter pointer is defined in a `PDOMCPPFunction`, each

PDOMNode	PDOMNamedNode	PDOMBinding	PDOMCPPFunction
00 01 short factory_ID	00 1f ptr name	00 1f 49 7e ptr first_decl	00 00 00 02 int num_params
00 07 short node_typ	49 6b	00 00 00 00 ptr first_def	00 1f 49 79 ptr first_param
00 11 ptr parent		00 00 00 00 ptr first_ref	1f 00 1f 49 71 00 type function_type
9d 98		00 00 00 00 ptr local_to_file	99 3e 7a f1 int signature_hash
		00 00 00 00 ptr first_extref	00 00 00 00 ptr exception_spec
			00 42 short annotation
			00 02 short required_arg_count
			00 00 00 00 00 00 execution function_body
			00 00 00 00 00 00 type declared_type

Fig. 6: `PDOMCPPFunction` node for `btsnd_hcic_ble_remove_from_white_list` C++ function definition.

TABLE III: PDOM history with function signature similarity benchmark.

Eclipse PDOM Input		CYW20735B1		CYW20719B1		CYW20706A2	
Chip	Build Date	Same Names	Signature Similarity	Same Names	Signature Similarity	Same Names	Signature Similarity
CYW20706A2	May 2 2016	2236	74.20 %	2377	72.44 %	1817	88.51 %
CYW20706A2	Aug 24 2016	1334	91.95 %	998	87.46 %	446	100 %
CYW20719B0	Aug 4 2016	2345	94.90 %	2595	93.94 %	1819	69.97 %
CYW20719B0	Aug 24 2016	767	95.56 %	820	95.79 %	382	70.53 %
CYW20719B0	Jun 28 2017	1138	98.42 %	863	97.58 %	410	76.55 %
CYW20719B1	Jun 7 2017	1271	97.75 %	994	100 %	431	80.35 %
CYW20721B1	May 30 2018	1040	97.94 %	788	99.19 %	235	95.03 %
CYW20729B0	Aug 23 2016	3476	81.24 %	5749	79.43 %	2603	69.49 %
CYW20735B0	May 2 2016	2255	80.31 %	2500	78.58 %	1805	68.73 %
CYW20735B0	Aug 24 2016	2132	97.34 %	2030	95.16 %	1211	76.78 %
CYW20735B1	May 30 2018	1249	100 %	991	97.35 %	417	78.66 %
CYW20739B0	May 2 2016	2294	80.21 %	2542	78.62 %	1811	68.81 %
20729B0 Zigbee	Aug 24 2016	79	93.16 %	263	90.81 %	43	93.65 %
20729B1 Zigbee	Jun 19 2017	171	93.28 %	376	92.71 %	50	94.56 %
20739B1 Zigbee	Jun 7 2017	1547	93.17 %	1007	95.33 %	439	72.75 %
43xxx Wi-Fi	5pm, Aug 31 2016	673	88.22 %	1153	88.46 %	281	89.55 %
43xxx Wi-Fi	8pm, Aug 31 2016	398	92.49 %	687	92.24 %	94	71.48 %
43xxx Wi-Fi	Jun 7 2017	1714	84.10 %	2354	87.32 %	1008	85.38 %
43012C0 Wi-Fi	Aug 9 2017	1011	96.06 %	707	93.00 %	311	91.55 %
		4594/11 810	91.07 %	6364/14 725	90.28 %	2833/8603	81.18 %
Combined Same Name/Total Functions		**38.90 %**		**43.22 %**		**32.93 %**	

Persistent Document Object Model (PDOM) files extracted from *Cypress WICED Studio 6.2* and *6.4*. Not all chips listed here are publicly available as evaluation kit, thus, some binaries are missing in the function identification analysis. Projects that were built multiple times contain partially redundant PDOM files.

parameter contains a pointer to the next parameter. By following these pointers and applying names, we can extend the function signature as follows:

```
btsnd_hcic_ble_remove_from_white_list(addr_type, bda)
```

However, extracting a type requires further actions. A type can be direct, indirect, storable, or null [21]. In our case, the 6 B `function_type` definition starts with `0x1f`, which means that it is an indirect type. Indirect types are stored in an additional record, in our case stored at `0x1f4971`. The type is unpacked using the `unmarshalType` and `unmarshal` functions [23], [22]. Note that unpacking types can get rather complex. In our case, the function type is `BOOL32`. Furthermore, the function type record is directly followed by records containing information about the first and second parameter type. Applying all types results in the following final function signature:

```
BOOL32 btsnd_hcic_ble_remove_from_white_list(UINT8
    addr_type, UINT8* bda)
```

C. Function Signature Reconstruction Results

Tab. III shows that the PDOMs contained in *WICED Studio* can restore approximately 40 % of the function signatures of the previously extracted Bluetooth firmware. On the left-hand side, all PDOM databases and their project creation times are listed. For some chips, multiple projects exist with different amounts of indexed information.

If a function with the same name exists in both databases, we calculate their signature similarity based on the return value as well as parameter count, types, and names. Undefined types are skipped in the comparison. Otherwise, each non-matching property marks a function signature as non-similar. For example, some functions exist in multiple firmware versions but got additional parameters over time and are not similar.

Even the Wi-Fi and Zigbee firmware contain useful inputs for the Bluetooth firmware because they partially share the same code base and vendor-specific library functions.

VI. Related Work

Polypyus is not the first tool leveraging binary similarity for diffing and function start recognition. Since it works disassembler-independent and finds matches in a large firmware history within seconds, it is nonetheless a useful tool for the reverse-engineering community. Moreover, the PDOM reconstruction provides closed-source function signatures.

Interestingly, even though there is plenty of related work about finding function starts [2], [5], [7], [39], a recent disassembler benchmark confirms our results that 25 % of function starts are missed [33]. *Polypyus* learns from two or more input binaries instead of huge pre-compiled known inputs, and still provides decent results on function starts and diffing.

Recent work shows very promising results reaching more than 98 % of correctly identified functions including function ends [1]. However, this work focussed on *x86* binaries, both 32 bit and 64 bit. The *x86* instruction set is less dense than ARM *Thumb2*, thus, these results cannot be compared, and the existing tools cannot be applied to our firmware binaries.

IDA Pro implements *F.L.I.R.T.* signatures to recognize library functions [26]. However, these are limited to *IDA Pro*, meaning that they can only be used with a valid license. The user uploads the function signatures of one binary to a server and then imports them into another binary. This limits user control over the diffing process. While the implementation is closed-source, the documentation states that it considers 30 B signatures and is limited to a fixed set of architectures. Since *F.L.I.R.T.* signatures are imported from a single binary instead of a firmware history, the signature generation likely depends on the disassembler to recognize and filter position-dependent instructions. Thus, not all architectures are supported.

Polypyus is more generic and way more independent. When using it on both Bluetooth and Wi-Fi firmware, it finds a lot of firmware-specific functions that are common across the binaries, which are not only part of libraries and especially not part of any open-sourced library.

VII. Conclusion

With *Polypyus*, we created a fast binary-only differ that integrates into the existing workflow with other binary analysis tools. History generation and function matching run within a few seconds, making it a suitable tool for projects with a large firmware set. Even though we did not evaluate *Polypyus* for other architectures than ARM *Thumb2*, matchers are binary-only. This means that it can be used for any architecture, including proprietary instruction sets, as long as there is some notation of functions that *Polypyus* can learn from.

The *Polypyus* function identification and diffing combined with the reconstruction of function signatures and types from *Eclipse* PDOM files will be helpful for C-based binary patching, such as *NexMon* for Bluetooth and Wi-Fi firmware.

Acknowledgment

We thank Christian Blichmann and Joxean Koret, the core developers of *BinDiff* and *Diaphora*, for their feedback. Moreover, we thank Jordan Wiens for the help with *Binary Ninja* and Eyal Itkin for the *Thumbs Up* support. We thank Ralf-Philipp Weinmann for feedback on this paper, Jakob Link for testing *Polypyus* with *Broadcom* Wi-Fi firmware, and Anna Stichling for creating the *Polypyus* logo.

This work has been funded by the German Federal Ministry of Education and Research and the Hessen State Ministry for Higher Education, Research and the Arts within their joint support of the National Research Center for Applied Cybersecurity ATHENE.

Availability

Polypyus is publicly available on *GitHub* [38]. The binary differ works without disassembler. As of now, the diffing results can be imported by accompanying *IDA Pro* and *Binary Ninja* scripts.

The repository comes with a large firmware set of binaries, including all binaries with symbols as well as selected binaries without symbols, such as the *iPhone 11* and *Samsung Galaxy S10/S20* symbols.

Moreover, the repository contains the generic PDOM to *SQLite* extractor as well as an PDOM importer for *IDA Pro*.

References

[1] Jim Alves-Foss and Jia Song. Function Boundary Detection in Stripped Binaries. In *Proceedings of the 35th Annual Computer Security Applications Conference*, ACSAC '19, page 84–96, New York, NY, USA, 2019. Association for Computing Machinery.

[2] Dennis Andriesse, Asia Slowinska, and Herbert Bos. Compiler-Agnostic Function Detection in Binaries. In *2017 IEEE European Symposium on Security and Privacy (EuroS&P)*, pages 177–189. IEEE, 2017.

[3] Hugues Anguelkov. Reverse-engineering Broadcom Wireless Chipsets. https://blog.quarkslab.com/reverse-engineering-broadcom-wireless-chipsets.html, Apr 2019.

[4] Nitay Artenstein. Broadpwn: Remotely Compromising Android and iOS via a Bug in Broadcom's Wi-Fi Chipsets. https://blog.exodusintel.com/2017/07/26/broadpwn/, 2017.

[5] Tiffany Bao, Jonathan Burket, Maverick Woo, Rafael Turner, and David Brumley. BYTEWEIGHT: Learning to Recognize Functions in Binary Code. In *23rd USENIX Security Symposium (USENIX Security 14)*, pages 845–860, San Diego, CA, August 2014. USENIX Association.

[6] Gal Beniamini. Over The Air: Exploiting Broadcom's Wi-Fi Stack (Part 1). https://googleprojectzero.blogspot.com/2017/04/over-air-exploiting-broadcoms-wi-fi_4.html, 2017.

[7] Andrew R. Bernat and Barton P. Miller. Anywhere, Any-Time Binary Instrumentation. In *Proceedings of the 10th ACM SIGPLAN-SIGSOFT Workshop on Program Analysis for Software Tools*, PASTE '11, page 9–16, New York, NY, USA, 2011. Association for Computing Machinery.

[8] Capstone. The Ultimate Disassembler. https://www.capstone-engine.org/, 2020.

[9] Jiska Classen and Daniel Wegemer. Fitbit Firmware Modifications. https://github.com/seemoo-lab/fitness-firmware, 2019.

[10] Cypress Semiconductor Corporation. Cypress to Acquire Broadcom's Wireless Internet of Things Business. https://www.cypress.com/news/cypress-acquire-broadcom-s-wireless-internet-things-business-0, June 2016.

[11] Cypress Semiconductor Corporation. *BCM4339: Single-Chip 5G WiFi IEEE 802.11ac MAC/Baseband/Radio with Integrated Bluetooth 4.1 and FM Receiver*, March 2017. Rev. *H.

[12] Cypress Semiconductor Corporation. *CYW20702: Single-Chip Bluetooth Transceiver and Baseband Processor*, November 2017. Rev. *M.

[13] Cypress Semiconductor Corporation. Bluetooth (BR + EDR + BLE) Connectivity Solution Families. https://www.cypress.com/products/ble-bluetooth, 2020.

[14] Cypress Semiconductor Corporation. WICED Software. https://www.cypress.com/products/wiced-software, 2020.

[15] Eclipse Foundation. PDOM & Indexing. https://wiki.eclipse.org/CDT/designs/PDOM, 2006.

[16] Eclipse Foundation. PDOM Overview. https://wiki.eclipse.org/CDT/designs/PDOM/Overview, 2008.

[17] Eclipse Foundation. PDOM CPP Function. https://git.eclipse.org/c/cdt/org.eclipse.cdt.git/tree/core/org.eclipse.cdt.core/parser/org/eclipse/cdt/internal/core/pdom/dom/cpp/PDOMCPPFunction.java, Jan 2021.

[18] Eclipse Foundation. PDOM CPP Paramter. https://git.eclipse.org/c/cdt/org.eclipse.cdt.git/tree/core/org.eclipse.cdt.core/parser/org/eclipse/cdt/internal/core/pdom/dom/cpp/PDOMCPPParameter.java, Jan 2021.

[19] Eclipse Foundation. PDOM Database Offset. https://git.eclipse.org/c/cdt/org.eclipse.cdt.git/tree/core/org.eclipse.cdt.core/parser/org/eclipse/cdt/internal/core/pdom/PDOM.java, Jan 2021.

[20] Eclipse Foundation. PDOM getRecPtr. https://git.eclipse.org/c/cdt/org.eclipse.cdt.git/tree/core/org.eclipse.cdt.core/parser/org/eclipse/cdt/internal/core/pdom/db/Chunk.java, Jan 2021.

[21] Eclipse Foundation. PDOM Linkage. https://git.eclipse.org/c/cdt/org.eclipse.cdt.git/tree/core/org.eclipse.cdt.core/parser/org/eclipse/cdt/internal/core/pdom/dom/PDOMLinkage.java, Jan 2021.

[22] Eclipse Foundation. PDOM unmarshal. https://git.eclipse.org/c/cdt/org.eclipse.cdt.git/tree/core/org.eclipse.cdt.core/parser/org/eclipse/cdt/internal/core/dom/parser/cpp/CPPFunction.java, Jan 2021.

[23] Eclipse Foundation. PDOM unmarshalType. https://git.eclipse.org/c/cdt/org.eclipse.cdt.git/tree/core/org.eclipse.cdt.core/parser/org/eclipse/cdt/internal/core/pdom/dom/cpp/PDOMCPPLinkage.java, Jan 2021.

[24] Dennis Giese. Not all IoT Devices are Created Equal: Reverse Engineering of Xiaomi's IoT Ecosystem. In *beVX*, 2018.

[25] Grant Hernandez and Marius Muench. Emulating Samsung's Baseband for Security Testing. *BlackHat USA 2020*, August 2020.

[26] Hex-Rays. IDA F.L.I.R.T. Technology: In-Depth. https://www.hex-rays.com/products/ida/tech/flirt/in_depth/, 2020.

[27] Hex-Rays. IDA Pro. https://www.hex-rays.com/products/ida/, 2020.

[28] Eyal Itkin. Thumbs Up: Using Machine Learning to Improve IDA's Analysis. https://research.checkpoint.com/2019/thumbs-up-using-machine-learning-to-improve-idas-analysis/, 2019.

[29] Joxean Koret. Diaphora. http://diaphora.re/, 2020.

[30] Dominik Maier, Lukas Seidel, and Shinjo Park. BaseSAFE: Baseband SAnitized Fuzzing through Emulation. *The 13th ACM Conference on Security and Privacy in Wireless and Mobile Networks (WiSec '20)*, July 2020.

[31] Dennis Mantz, Jiska Classen, Matthias Schulz, and Matthias Hollick. InternalBlue - Bluetooth Binary Patching and Experimentation Framework. In *The 17th Annual International Conference on Mobile Systems, Applications, and Services (MobiSys '19)*, Jun 2019.

[32] National Security Agency. Ghidra. https://ghidra-sre.org/, 2020.

[33] Chengbin Pang, Ruotong Yu, Yaohui Chen, Eric Koskinen, Georgios Portokalidis, Bing Mao, and Jun Xu. SoK: All You Ever Wanted to Know About x86/x64 Binary Disassembly but Were Afraid to Ask. In *2021 2021 IEEE Symposium on Security and Privacy (S&P)*, pages 194–212, Los Alamitos, CA, USA, May 2021. IEEE Computer Society.

[34] radare. radare2. https://rada.re/n/radare2.html, 2020.

[35] Jan Ruge, Jiska Classen, Francesco Gringoli, and Matthias Hollick. Frankenstein: Advanced Wireless Fuzzing to Exploit New Bluetooth Escalation Targets. In *29th USENIX Security Symposium (USENIX Security 20)*, pages 19–36. USENIX Association, August 2020.

[36] Matthias Schulz. *Teaching Your Wireless Card New Tricks: Smartphone Performance and Security Enhancements Through Wi-Fi Firmware Modifications*. PhD thesis, Technische Universität, 2018.

[37] Matthias Schulz, Daniel Wegemer, and Matthias Hollick. Nexmon: The C-based Firmware Patching Framework. https://nexmon.org, 2017.

[38] Secure Mobile Networking Lab. Polypyus on GitHub. https://github.com/seemoo-lab/polypyus, 2020.

[39] Eui Chul Richard Shin, Dawn Song, and Reza Moazzezi. Recognizing Functions in Binaries with Neural Networks. In *24th USENIX Security Symposium (USENIX Security 15)*, pages 611–626, Washington, D.C., August 2015. USENIX Association.

[40] Siguza. radiff2 -A doesn't work on raw binaries #13541. https://github.com/radareorg/radare2/issues/13541, 2019.

[41] Maddie Stone. What's Up with WhatsApp. https://github.com/maddiestone/ConPresentations/blob/master/Jailbreak2019.WhatsUpWithWhatsApp.pdf, 2019.

[42] Vector 35 Inc. Binary Ninja. https://binary.ninja/, 2020.

[43] zynamics. BinDiff. https://www.zynamics.com/bindiff.html, 2020.